GW01315880

Bast and Sekhmet

Previous titles by Storm Constantine

Fiction:
The Enchantments of Flesh and Spirit
The Bewitchments of Love and Hate
The Fulfilments of Fate and Desire
The Monstrous Regiment
Aleph
Hermetech
Burying the Shadow
Sign for the Sacred
Calenture
Stalking Tender Prey
Scenting Hallowed Blood
Stealing Sacred Fire
Thin Air
Sea Dragon Heir
The Thorn Boy

Short Story Collection:
The Oracle Lips

Non-Fiction:
The Inward Revolution (with Deborah Benstead)

BAST AND SEKHMET

Eyes of Ra

STORM CONSTANTINE
&
ELOISE COQUIO

ROBERT HALE · LONDON

© *Storm Constantine & Eloise Coquio*
First Published in Great Britain 1999

ISBN 0 7090 6418 7

Robert Hale Limited
Clerkenwell House
Clerkenwell Green
London EC1R 0HT

2 4 6 8 10 9 7 5 3 1

Typeset in 10/12pt Souvenir by
Derek Doyle & Associates, Liverpool.
Printed in Great Britain by
St Edmundsbury Press Limited, Bury St Edmunds,
and bound by
WBC Book Manufacturers Ltd, Bridgend

Contents

This book is dedicated to the memory of our first feline companions Star (Pusskin) and Runty, who gave us love and friendship in life and will be forever remembered. They were our inspiration and led us to the path.

Our thanks go to Bast and Sekhmet for all the gifts they have given us, not least the companionship of their children who share our lives and rule our households at the moment, Banshee, Cassiel, Cleo Midnight, Grommit, Ishtahar, Lilith, Maya, Osiris, Pashti, Spooky Mulder and Tubbsy.

Acknowledgements

Many people were invaluable in helping us research and write this book. We would like to thank primarily those who helped the project take shape: Caroline Wise of Atlantis Bookshop, whose encouragement and support helped us secure a contract for the book; E.A. St George, whose work was such an inspiration, truly a gift from the goddesses; Tamara Siuda for her advice and expertise where ours was lacking; Christina Paul and Stephanie Cass for their knowledge of the goddesses; Andy Collins for showing us a different way; Judith Page for her knowledge and gifts; Robert Kirby, our agent, for finding the book a home and our editor, John Hale, for having faith in us.

Next, we would like to thank all those whom we love because they have always been there for us. Jim Hibbert, Storm's partner, for his humour, his light, his cooking skills and his patience; Eloise's husband, Paul Kesterton for being loving and supportive in times of complete madness, and a great friend against all the odds!; all our parents, Albert and Wendy Coquio for not being fazed by the strangeness, and Norma and John Bristow for their continuing support; Chris and John Kesterton for being Eloise's surrogate family while her mother and father are sojourning in foreign climes; Robin and Naomi, Eloise's adoptive brother and sister, for sharing good times; Steve Chilton for being one of the girls; his girlfriend, Claire Cartwright, for appreciating this; Mark Hewkin for his continuing friendship and help with desktop publishing; Yvan Cartwright for computer therapy; Simon Beal for doing the web site and joining in with our work; Vikki Lee France and Steve Jeffery for their friendship and ongoing work for Inception, the information service; Jamie Summers for Eloise's initial introduction and inspiration into the world of wyrd; Kirsten Rose for good chats and encouragement; Freda Warrington and Ruby for their interest, friendship and participation – thanks also to Ruby for her beautiful artwork, the book would have looked very different without her; and Tigger Nelson-Gennard, who was there at the beginning.

Other people have helped us and contributed towards this book, and we would like to thank them too: Kirsty Wood, Yuri Leitch and Helen Wilson for their artwork; Sean Russell Friend for bizarre stories, artwork and interesting times; Graham Stewart for the photographs; Karl Duncan and Matthew Goulding at Atlantis Bookshop for their support; Steve Wilson, double Leo, fellow traveller; and all those who contributed to the last chapter and whom we have not already mentioned – Paul Weston, Chandira, Lynn Hall, Lorye Keats Hopper, Karen Deeley, Julia Phillips and Trisha West.

Finally, our love and thanks to the wyrdest of our wyrd sisters: Deb Howlett, Deb Benstead, Karen Townsend and Paula Wakefield. Without their friendship, magic and vision, the book would not have been possible.

Prologue

Journey to the Temple
of Bast

A Visualization Recorded by Eloise Coquio

I walk across the hot, red sands at the edge of the vast eastern desert. The sun burns above me in a cloudless sky the deep blue of lapis stone. I breathe in the clean air of a different time and hold out my arms to the sunlight. I feel feline and sensual here, at home inside my skin.

Ahead of me, I see the golden sandstone pylons of a mighty temple rearing up to meet the sun. My feet carry me towards it. I seem to float above the ground, carried by a force outside myself. The feeling is alien but peaceful, as if all is as it should be.

The gentle breeze carries sounds of faint music to my ears and the sound draws me on, like driftwood on a tide. As I get closer I can make out the airy music of flutes, the earthy, deep throb of drums and the strange chattering sounds of sacred rattles. The rhythm is familiar. It is the song that has called to me on moonlit nights in another time. Its haunting notes resonate within me. I feel it in my blood, my bones, my sinews.

I walk past the entrance to a wadi, where there is a cool

watering hole sheltered by tall trees. Here a pride of lions lie resting, seeking sanctuary from the fierce heat of the sun. They raise their heads to me in welcome and appraise me through slitted eyes. The lionesses sit together, mothers, sisters and daughters, their amber eyes full of wisdom and secrets. I wish I could sit with them, but my feet draw me onwards. I bow my head to them as I pass by.

As I approach the mighty pylon of the temple, I can see for the first time that its surface is covered in painted reliefs. Amongst the symbols, there are cat-headed figures and tall seated cats. This is the temple of Bast.

As I pass beneath the pylon, I feel myself begin to change. My clothes are replaced by a long white dress of fine linen. My hair no longer hangs free but is braided and shines with rich oils.

A multitude of cats shelter from the sunlight in the shade of the pylon and watch me lazily, without interest. The air around me throbs with their purrs and the sound merges with the strange music drifting on the warm breeze from within the cool blackness of the temple.

The temple itself stands tall above the land like a wondrous palace in a child's story. At the top of the steps I turn for a moment and see the shining waters of the Nile beneath me. The river reflects the sunlight like a mirror as it curves, snakelike, through the Delta. I have to shield my eyes to look on it; it is glaring in its splendour.

Inside the great gateway, two obelisks of shining black granite stretch up towards the sky. I try to see their tapered pinnacles but the sun is so blazingly fierce, the obelisks are merely black shadows against its radiance. The obelisks are covered with ancient carvings and it seems as if they are silent messengers, carrying the secrets hidden within these sacred symbols up into the realm of the Sun God.

I take one tentative step through the gateway, into the outer court of the temple. The air around me changes. It is cooler here. The sunlight is no longer fierce and scorching but gentle as it filters down through the leaves of many tall temple trees. Around me, I can see priests and women of the temple dressed in crisp robes of white and turquoise. They wear heavy golden jewellery at their ears and throats and, as they walk, I can smell the rich scent of their sacred perfume on the air.

I feel that I am expected here. There is recognition on some of the faces around me. Some of the women shout greetings in an ancient tongue that is alien to me, but which I can still understand completely. I have found in this place a sense of belonging, a sense of returning to a home for which I have searched throughout many lifetimes.

10

Prologue

In the centre of this oasis of calm I can see a round pool of crystal clear water. A woman sits beside it and stares into its cool depths. Her long fingers trail across the surface of the water, making pictures for her to interpret. I know that this scrying pool is sacred. Its placement ensures that it reflects the fire of the sun by day and the cool silver of the moon by night. I know that in this place of perfection nothing happens by chance.

I feel the pull of the inner chambers and begin to walk on towards the great doorway cut into the back wall of the courtyard. The doorway is huge and the light within is dim. It is flanked on either side by carvings of regal cats wearing earrings of thick gold and the symbol of the udjat eye upon their chests. Their faces are serene. I can see the detail of carved whiskers on their long muzzles. Their eyes are like huge blank almonds, fixed forever on some distant place. I lower my eyes respectfully as I pass them.

Inside the air is cool, and heavy with the pungent smoke of incense. My eyes take a few moments to adjust to the darkness after the sunlight. Around me the room is alive with the music of the goddess. Her percussion is the purr of a thousand cats, her choir a multitude of mewing kittens. Her children have made music for her here almost since the beginning of time.

The light here is dim and flickering. It comes from tall candles the colour of sun-bleached straw. This is the outer shrine of Bast. I look around me and see that the room is full of cats. They lie in niches on the walls, on the floor, even draped over the feet of the statue of Bast's sacred cat that rears up at the back of the shrine. Some of the cats wear jewelled collars that glitter in the candlelight. They are lovingly tended by barefooted women. The cats watch with lazy interest as I approach the inner shrine of their mother.

I stop for a while in front of the huge basalt statue of a seated cat, which is the sacred animal of Bast. She is tall and beautiful, her eyes inky shadows in the candlelight. At her feet are many offerings; flowers, incense, jewels and intricate carved alabaster perfume jars form a mound around her. I have flowers in my hand. They have appeared suddenly as if from nowhere. I lay them before her as I pass by.

To the right of the statue is another smaller doorway. It leads into a long corridor, lit with flaming bowls of oil on the floor. I can see that there are paintings on the walls, but all I can make out in the dim light are smudges of ochre and black.

At the end of the corridor is an arched portal carved in gold. As I approach it, the music becomes louder and louder. There are

11

voices now, singing their accompaniment to the feline sounds. The music is gentle and lively at the same time. It makes me want to dance. I step through the gilded arch into the heart of Bast's temple.

At once, my vision fills with the massive golden staircase that rears before me. Its steps are covered with cats. Some sleep, some groom, others lie watchful, petted by the hands of the priestesses. The atmosphere here seems to vibrate with life. There is the heady scent of wine on the air and its taste is on my lips. Women dance and spin around me and I dance with them. I dance for her that she might speak with me.

At the top of the staircase is a beautiful golden statue of the goddess as a cat-headed woman. The carving is so perfect that I can see her fur, her whiskers, the slitted pupils of her eyes. It seems so real, as if the statue were alive but sleeping. Bast wears a long, carved robe that bares her breasts. The sculptor has captured the fluid nature of the material as it falls in golden pleats to the floor. In her hands she holds a metal sistrum and an ankh carved of lapis lazuli. Her eyes are bright crystals that glitter and shine. Around her graceful neck is a wide necklace of intricate carvings. At her feet her children too are carved of gold for there are tiny golden kittens playing in the folds of her dress.

I close my eyes and speak to her. The words come to me, familiar and strange at the same time. They are words that I have spoken countless times for I have always been her priestess. Other sounds fade away until it seems as if there are only the two of us in the room. Slowly, I raise my eyes to look at her.

She is no longer a golden statue. She is alive, a living, breathing goddess, standing before me on a staircase that is not gold but pink, polished granite. She begins to walk down the stairs towards me, the carpet of cats parting to let her through. She is smiling. Her eyes are those of a kind mother or sister, they seem to radiate light. Her dress is no longer gold but fine turquoise linen. Her sistrum makes music as she walks.

When she reaches the bottom of the staircase I reach out to her and I see that my arms are covered in soft fur, my nails are curling claws. I am her daughter, cat-headed and beautiful. It is her gift to me.

Bast is not a goddess who inspires fear in me or demands sacrifice. She is the kind mother, the cherished sister. I visit her temple often: when I have questions to ask, when I have problems I cannot solve alone and sometimes when I just need a mother to talk to or I feel like going home.

Illustrations

Credits

Ruby: 9, 10. Yuri Leitch: 11, 12.

All other images are from the authors' collection

Introduction

Cruel, but composed and bland,
Dumb, inscrutable and grand,
So Tiberius might have sat
Had Tiberius been a cat.

Matthew Arnold

The cat, she has many faces:

She slinks deep through wet undergrowth at the dark of the
moon seeking prey.

She is eyes without a face, glowing like neon in the dark of
lonely streets.

She is the howls of sexual frenzy that splinter the breathing
night.

She is the watchful one upon the wall, soaking sun.

She is our companion of the hearth, wreathed in purrs with
smiling slitted eyes.

She is the breath upon our faces in the dawn, and the knead-
ing of needle-armed paws against our flesh.

She is the one who walks by herself, yet follows us throughout
the day about the house.

She is the disdainful one, yet she also comforts us in times of
despair.

She is a creature of the moon and darkness, the witch's
familiar, and she is a devotee of the sun, sprawled on baking
flagstones.

She is the warrior, the huntress, the doting mother – she is all
of these and more.

The cat has been both worshipped and reviled throughout human
history. Perhaps no other animal evokes such extremes of reaction.
The cat is herself a creature of contradictions – she could be said to
have two faces. She is a creature of the night – of that we have no
doubt – yet what other animal adores the sun as she? It is difficult
to equate the aloof creature, who sometimes appears to be deaf
and ignores our voice completely, with the purring, head-butting
attention-seeker who marches across our books and newspapers
when we are trying to read, or gazes with such love into our eyes
when she deigns to sit on our laps.

Scientific minds shudder in horror at the thought that cats might
have such traits of personality, and try to put down all aspects of
their behaviour to instinctive reflexes, yet anyone who has loved a
cat will know the scientists are wrong.

Who would argue that an animal possessed of such mysterious
grace and enigmatic behaviour, let alone such sheer beauty, is not
a creature of magic? Cats have been associated with witchcraft and
the supernatural for hundreds, if not thousands, of years. And
nowhere has the cat played such a prominent role in religion as in
the beliefs of ancient Egypt. Many modern witches, pagans, ritual
occultists and practitioners of the ancient Egyptian religion own at
least one cat, if not many more. It therefore seems odd that the
goddess forms of the cat have rarely been deeply examined in
magical literature. Even though it is fairly easy to acquire material
about other Egyptian gods and goddesses, very little has been written about Bast and Sekhmet, the deities who, as domestic cat and
lioness, could be said to represent the two faces of the feline in
certain respects.

We ourselves have been cat-lovers since childhood, and practitioners of magic since our teens. But although we might have called
upon Bast occasionally, when her aid was needed to help with a
cat's health and well-being, we never considered working with her
intensively as we did with other deities. Our temple group came

16

together naturally through friendship, and was comprised of people who had all trained in different magical traditions. Then someone suggested we work magically together, and Bast seemed the obvious focus of our initial group ritual, as she was a goddess with whom we all empathized and felt comfortable.

When we performed our first rite to Bast, we were unprepared for the exciting, and sometimes amazing, voyage of discovery that followed. It seemed that once we had awoken this frequency of energy within ourselves, we sparked off a series of events and synchronicities that led us to learn about Bast, and her leonine contemporary Skehmet, in unexpected depth and detail. It seemed that with our first tentative steps, we merely scratched the surface of a whole hidden tradition, but once that surface had been breached, information came flooding through.

At first, we felt that Bast and Sekhmet were different aspects of the same goddess: one the gentle, benign lady of the hearth, the other a fierce huntress to be approached with respect and a certain amount of caution. However, our studies led us to understand that this was not the case. The ancient Egyptians' view of gods and goddesses is often misunderstood. We found that they believed in one god, or universal force, who has many different names or faces. Bast and Sekhmet are just two of these, and although they share some attributes, others are very different. We came to view them as two distinct entities in their own right; linked in certain ways, yes, through being part of the universal energy, but not opposite aspects of the same force.

We worked in two directions to discover more about these deities. There was the hard research of visiting museums and libraries and talking to people who had knowledge we did not, while from a more visionary viewpoint our group undertook many sessions of visualization, during which we projected our minds back to ancient times and attempted to glean information psychically. While certain details could be verified as based on historical fact, we have no sure way of telling if *all* the results of our meditations were real or imaginary. But the rich imagery that came through was indispensable in creating vivid, moving and effective rituals.

In this book we aim to provide, for the first time, practical information for interacting with the goddess forms of Bast and Sekhmet, and with their many feline and leonine contemporaries. We shall reveal our own experiences of communing with these goddesses, including meditations and rituals, and we shall show how to create a personal temple and write rituals and visualizations, whether working alone or forming a temple group.

It is important to stress at this point that the system we have developed can only ever be *based* on the beliefs of ancient Egypt. We cannot hope to reproduce in their entirety the rites and mind-set of this vanished race. The only evidence we have to go on is the often very formalized texts derived from the walls of tombs and temples. We have to appreciate that much of what is shown in these paintings must be stylized and representative rather than clear reportage of a way of life. We cannot ever see into the mind of an ancient Egyptian and learn for ourselves the way they thought, lived and believed, even though through meditation we can attempt to glean inspired information about the way things might have been. Much of the evidence for mundane daily life has been lost, mainly because the Egyptians used incorruptible stone only in their ceremonial buildings. Houses, and even palaces, were usually constructed from mud bricks which have been destroyed over the millennia.

Even the great temple at Bubastis, the centre for Bast's worship in the later history of Egypt, is now no more than levelled ruins, although at the time of writing we understand that a German team plans to reconstruct what remains of the city. We have accounts from the Greek historian Herodotus, who recorded the appearance of this magnificent complex and certain aspects of the rites conducted there, but hardly anything in concrete terms from the site itself.

In developing our magical system, we incorporated several techniques and skills which we had learned and used before, such as constructing a cone of power, visionary questing, meditation, visualization and colour magic. Although these can hardly be regarded as ancient Egyptians techniques (although colour did play a great part in their rituals), we found they fitted very comfortably into our work.

We felt it would be inappropriate, if not impossible, for us, as modern practitioners of magic, to try and reproduce to the letter the way in which the ancient Egyptians worshipped and worked with magic. Not only are we very different from them psychologically and culturally, but some concerns that drove the Egyptians do not have the same relevance for us. A large part of the Egyptian belief system revolved around the underworld and the afterlife, as well as the yearly inundation of the Nile upon which their livelihood depended. Modern misunderstanding has led many people to believe that the Egyptians were actually preoccupied with death, but again we have to remember that most evidence left to us consists of the carvings and inscriptions on tomb walls. There are no personal diaries of common people for us to puruse. In those times, early deaths must have been more prevalent than they are now, but the Egyptians must have been equally as concerned about love, money, work and childbirth, things with which we today are consummately preoccupied! These timeless concerns do provide a link between the past and the present, but the lives we lead now are very different to those lived in Ancient Egypt.

There are priestly instructions on the wall of the Temple of Horus at Edfu which say: 'Do not carry out the divine service according to your own fancy. Of what profit, then, is it for you to gaze upon the ancient writings, if you have taken the ritual of the temple into your own hands?' These words are often quoted to suggest that no modern practitioner has the right to tamper with ancient practices or texts; they should remain as they were originally, and not be changed. Obviously, in writing this book, we have written new rituals to the goddesses, and some readers might take issue with this. But our reasons for doing so are twofold.

First, we cannot help thinking that the Edfu text once came from the mouths, minds and hands of men, very much as the Judaeo-Christian Bible did. Perhaps this proscription was not just religious, but political. History tells us that the priesthood of Egypt was very powerful, in a political as well as a religious sense. It is feasible that they would have taken measures to safeguard that exclusive power. The inscription might derive from divine inspiration, but then again, it might not. We have no way of knowing. That said, if people now want to stand by its sentiments, we respect that.

Our second reason for devizing new rituals is that we believe that for ancient deities and beliefs to have relevance and context in a modern society, they deserve to be kept alive by reinterpretation. We accept that not everyone will agree with this view, but nevertheless we feel it is valid.

We think that everyone has the right to their own spiritual beliefs and are responsible for them. We do not think that anyone should have ultimate responsibility for anyone else's beliefs. We want to make our feelings on this clear from the start.

We do not see our rites in terms of adoration of the gods, but frameworks through which we can interact with the universal energy, of which deities such as Bast and Sekhmet are but frequencies. We interact with these frequencies in order to develop ourselves and understand more about our species and our culture, as well as effecting changes in our reality. Obviously, because so much energy and belief have been invested in these deities over the ages, we feel it is equally important to approach them with respect.

We know we are not alone in resonating with the beliefs of ancient times and feeling empathy with the deities who presided over them, particularly those associated with the cat. We are all perhaps drawn by the apparent noble elegance of the Egyptian people. Their mysterious god-forms have power because they have the ability to affect us, whether with inspiration, fear or curiosity. And from personal experience, we can assert that deities such as Bast and Sekhmet can help us, and do have relevance, even for those of us who are far removed in space and time from their point of origin.

We have attempted to collate as much as possible of the fragmented material available, so that we can develop rites of the cat which are pertinent to our modern lives. Gods and goddesses could be said to need humans to live, as much as humans interact with them to create beneficial changes in their lives. If a god or goddess has no followers, perhaps he or she ceases to exist. Bast and Sekhmet are certainly still alive for many people. Our own frustration at being unable to find one comprehensive source of information about them and their worship inspired us to write this book. We gathered the material piecemeal, as we needed it, but now hope to inspire others by presenting it in a unified form. We feel that this process is ongoing and dynamic: there is still more to be discovered, remembered and imagined.

1

Pawprints of the Gods

Like poets, cats lead us along the margins of the everyday, visible world. By following in their footsteps we can slip behind the looking glass, to find, as often as not, the reflection in the mirror is our own image. He who knows the cat surely understands himself a little better.

From *The Secret Life of Cats* by Robert De Laroche and Jean Michel Labat

The lure of the cat

For most of us, our first encounter with the feline gods of ancient Egypt is through the typical statue of a seated Egyptian cat, as

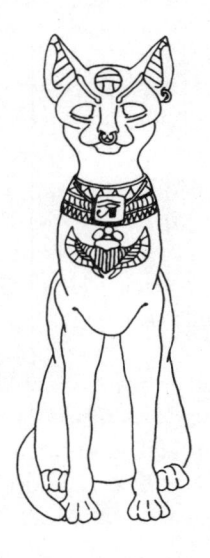

21

exemplified by the bronze Gayer Anderson cat on show in the British Museum. From this, we come to learn that the cat was held sacred in ancient times, although it might not be until much later that we discover the name of Bast and the fact that she was venerated as a goddess.

As children, we may have heard stories at school about how it was illegal to kill a cat in ancient Egypt, and how Roman soldiers had been executed for disobeying this holy law. Most of us will have been intrigued by the concept of mummies and pyramids, and from films and books we may have learned that the gods of the Egyptians had animal heads: birds, cats, jackals, rams.

Children can go through a stage of being fascinated, if not obsessed, by all things Egyptian. For some of us, this fascination persists into adulthood. We are drawn to ancient Egypt, aesthetically and culturally. Our interest may simply involve wanting to read more about these times, but some of us are touched in a spiritual way; we feel an affinity for the mysterious gods of the Two Lands and believe that if we could commune with them we would be able to experience the divine.

Some people believe that they are reincarnated souls from ancient Egypt, and we are in no position to dispute this, but we do not have to have lived in those times to feel close to the Egyptian belief system. It might feel so alive for us because it was powerful and dynamic, and because it is still relevant. In Chapter 2 we will look at how the ancient Egyptians regarded natural energy, with which we work in magic today, and at certain similarities with modern practices.

The religion and magic of ancient Egypt have survived millennia, and although a great many of the gods are now virtually forgotten, they can still intrigue and inspire us. Many of us are drawn specifically to the feline goddesses Bast and Sekhmet, probably because the cat, as a domestic animal, is now more popular than it has ever been.

Cats at home give us comfort, delight our senses with their beauty and grace, and bestow their love and trust. Perhaps it is not surprising that many writers have said that they prefer one good cat to any number of lovers. Cat-haters might say that cats are cruel and aloof, but although we cannot deny our feline friends can possess those qualities, those of us who have lived with them know that we have to earn their respect, and once we have it, it is unlikely to be withdrawn. We could say that cats do not suffer fools gladly, and a relationship with a cat can be more meaningful than those we enjoy with other animals. Affinity with a cat goddess could be seen as a natural impulse for all cat-lovers.

The cat in Egypt

In ancient Egypt cats were regarded as sacred and were often bedecked with jewels and invited to feed from the same plates as those who cared for them. If a household cat should die, all the inhabitants would shave off their eyebrows. They were believed to be sacred to Bast and a personification of the sun. Diodorus tells us that cats were fed on bread, milk and slices of Nile fish. The Greek historian Herodotus gives an account of how Egyptian families might rescue a cat from a burning house, even if it meant precious possessions would be lost.

However, the Egyptian attitude is not quite as benign as we might think. We know that they took a very dim view of foreigners harming their cats, yet from the innumerable mummified remains of cats found in various burial complexes around Egypt, a different picture emerges. A great many of them are of a similar age and died in the same way – they were usually found with a twisted or broken neck. This would suggest that they were sacrifices of some kind, which could have been bred in the temples for this purpose. But perhaps sacrifice is not the right word. Given the Egyptian view of death and the afterlife, by killing a sacred cat a priest would in a way be deifying it, so that it could speak to the gods for him. Worshippers might have been able to 'buy' a cat, which was then summarily slaughtered and preserved, but which in a spiritual sense could act or speak on the petitioner's behalf with the gods. A spell has been found that describes how to turn a live cat into a 'praised one' by drowning it. The cat's body was then fitted with inscribed metal tablets called *lamellae* and mummified. Once this ritual act had been performed, the magician could invoke the cat form of the sun god to take action against his enemies. It is possible that some ritual killings were performed so that the cat could act for the devotee on the spiritual plane.

Another, less spiritual, explanation for the large number of mummified cats is that they could be the results of large-scale culls, when the numbers of temple cats became unmanageable.

With our modern sensibilities, it is hard to equate any of these explanations with a view of the cat as sacred and inviolable. Even the most fervent modern-day worshipper of Bast would find abhorrent the idea of killing their beloved animals as an act of devotion or magic. We can only accept that the unsentimental views of the ancient Egyptians – and their beliefs concerning death – were very different from our own.

Sacred cats

Three felines in particular appear to have had cults based around them: the cat, the lion and the lynx – although it is not completely clear from surviving evidence whether the last was a lynx, a leopard or a cheetah. Lions may well have been worshipped because of their strength, power and beauty, and because of their association with solar deities such as Ra and Horus. They lived in the desert, where it was believed the sun died each evening and was reborn each morning. While people might have feared the dark, because they could not see what demons might be hiding within it, they believed that lions could see just as well in darkness as in light. They were therefore regarded as valuable protectors during the night hours. People even had representations of lions carved into their beds.

There was a cult centre for lion worship, in the form of the god Mahes (or Mihos), at Leontopolis in the northern Delta. Leontopolis literally means 'Lion City', but sacred lions were kept at temple complexes throughout Egypt. There were far more lion- and lioness-headed deities than were depicted as having the head of a domestic cat.

The cat was sacred to the goddess Bast, and this cult is also very ancient. The first representations of cats begin around 1950 BC, when they were often depicted as accompanying people, as in scenes of Egyptian noblemen hunting with their cats in the marshes of the Nile, or seated ladies whose cats lay beneath their chairs. The cat was certainly regarded as a protective animal, which most likely stemmed from its prowess as a snake-killer. The sun god Ra could manifest as a male cat, when he was known as Mau or the great tom cat. In this guise, he defeated the serpent-fiend Apep, who dwells in the underworld.

The lynx was called Maftet or Mafdet and there was a goddess of this name, who was renowned for killing snakes and scorpions with her claws. Her scratch was lethal to snakes and, symbolically, the barbs of the king's harpoon became her claws for decapitating his enemies in the underworld.

Cats are reputedly immune to snakebites and, coupled with their fearlessness of snakes, this made them indispensable in Egypt, where venomous bites were common and often deadly, especially for children and older people. Mafdet is described as 'leaping at the necks of snakes', which has led to the suggestion that she could take on the form of a mongoose. (Mongooses and genets were also regarded as sacred animals.) In one epithet, she is described as wearing braided hair, which could be a metaphor for the segmented arachnoid bodies of scorpions she had killed. Mafdet appeared in literature and wall carvings sporadically throughout Egyptian history, and it has been suggested by some Egyptologists that she may have been the first goddess to appear in the guise of a feline.

It seems clear that the worship of feline deities began very early in Egyptian history, although it is more difficult to pin down how they actually developed. Aker was one of the oldest known lion gods, in legend he guarded the Gate of the Dawn, through which the sun god had to pass each morning. Another primordial goddess was Tefnut, goddess of moisture, and sister/consort of the air god, Shu. She also possessed a lioness-headed aspect, and according to one legend was the first daughter of the creator god, Atum.

There are literally hundreds, if not thousands, of Egyptian gods, demons and spirits, almost as if they were continually being invented.

The sacred cat outside Egypt

Egypt was not alone in seeing felines as magical animals. The cat has ever been cast as a witch's familiar in Europe and America, and often suffered persecution because of it. The Celts of western Scotland worshipped a cat-headed goddess called Skiathach (or Scathhach), who was very similar in nature to Sekhmet. Middle Eastern countries such as Mesopotamia also had anthropomorphic cat-headed deities as part of their religions, and Japanese mythology includes tales of supernatural felines. The goddess Freya in Norse legend was often accompanied by cats. But for many of us, the most alluring of all these deities and spirits are still the Egyptian Bast and Sekhmet, with their lithe bodies, exquisite dress and jewellery, innate nobility and inherent grace and power.

There were numerous other cat- and lion-headed gods and

goddesses in Egyptian religion, who might have had different names and functions in different regions, or extremely specialized duties to do with the afterlife. Some of them remain only as anonymous figures on tomb paintings, while others still have vague stories attached to them. For the most part, these deities are neglected, their names and occasionally their temples known only to Egyptologists. In Chapter 5, we list as many of these gods and goddesses as we have been able to discover, but we appreciate that the list is far from complete.

The puzzle of the past

The mythology of ancient Egypt is fragmented. Unlike the myths of the Greeks and the Romans, which catalogue all the acts and relationships of their deities and have survived intact, it is more difficult for us to piece together all the stories about the Egyptian gods. The most information we can get about a deity is quite often the names by which he or she was invoked or the circumstances in which he or she was appealed to. There are several different versions of the creation myth, and quite a lot of material about the goddess Isis and her consort Osiris and their immediate families. But myths about Bast are non-existent, and there is only one detailed story about Sekhmet. The goddess Hathor and Sekhmet seem to be interchangeable, yet their characters are very different. Hathor is a benevolent goddess associated with love, music and dancing (very similar attributes to those of Bast), and the animal with which she is most closely associated is the cow. Lioness-headed Sekhmet, on the other hand, is often portrayed as a ferocious lady to be approached with extreme caution.

As we shall see later, gods can have many different faces, different parents, different children, different functions. The geography of Egypt is partly responsible for this confusion. Similar deities were worshipped all over Egypt but were known locally by different names. Hence Bast, Hathor and Sekhmet were sometimes different aspects of the same goddess, who had been subjected to local preferences. So it is impossible to impose a rigid, chronological framework upon Egyptian mythology, with so many stories and characters overlapping and interchanging. All we can do is collate the known material and try to draw a coherent picture from it.

The names of God

The best way to make sense of all this conflicting information is to keep in mind that the Egyptians saw the divine principle as one force with many different names. It could be everything, everywhere and all at the same time. The Egyptian word for god was *neter* or *netjer*, and this term included all the various representations of divinity: one god, many different aspects, both male and female. Because *neter* is one thing, an almost incomprehensibly huge idea, it can have immeasurable guises, immeasurable functions. It can be in countless places at the same time. It has no limits.

2

The Goddess Bast

I am born of the divine She-Cat, conceived beneath the sycamore of the enclosure by the seed come from on high that my divinity may never be denied. I am born of the sacred She-Cat, but I am also become a son of the sun.
From *The Book of the Dead*

Bast's origins

Bast was worshipped from the most ancient times, and her earliest form is lioness-headed. It was not until the first millennium BC that she was worshipped in the form of a lissom woman with the head of a domestic cat. The seated cat statues which are so typical of Egyptian art were not actually representations of the goddess herself, but of her sacred animals. They often had scarab beetles on their foreheads or chests, and this represented Bast's connection with the sun god Ra.

During the Twenty-second Dynasty, the pharaoh of Egypt made Bast a national goddess, and even though this later cat-headed form became more popular than her previous manifestations, she never ceased to have a lioness-headed aspect. Her cult lasted for over 3,000 years, and it could be said that in some ways it never died, for even now Bast has her devotees and worshippers.

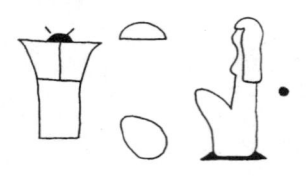

Bast was known as the Lady of the East and as such was one of the goddesses of the four directions, along with Sekhmet (west), Nekhbet (south) and Wadjet (north). Of these goddesses, only Nekhbet, who was associated mainly with the vulture, did not have a feline aspect. There have been many variations on Bast's name – Pasht, Bastet, Per Bastet, Bubastis – although it is now clear that some of these are the result of mistranslation and misunderstanding. At the present time, the spelling 'Bast' is taken to be the correct one. *Bastet*, for example, literally means, 'she of the city of Bast'.

The hieroglyph of the name includes the pictogram of a sealed perfume jar. It has also been suggested that the perfume jar may itself have been worshipped as a fetish before Bast took feline form. This image might refer to the importance of perfume in her worship or to a suggestion of purity in her cult.

Images of the goddess

The centre of Bast's worship was at the city of Bubastis, capital of the nome of Am-Khent on the north-east Delta. Bubastis, now known as Tell Basta, lies in ruins, with a modern Egyptian town built over a large area of it. To our knowledge, no life-size or greater representations of Bast, in any form, have survived intact, although a great many smaller bronzes and statues have been recovered and can now be seen in museums around the world. (In particular, the reconstructed shrine to Bast in the field Museum of Chicago is well worth a visit, should you ever get the opportunity. The statue of Bast as a seated cat-headed woman is the largest we have come across, perhaps a little less than half life-size, and exquisite in its detail.) But this lack of evidence does not necessarily mean that larger statues did not exist. Bast's sacred city is mentioned in several early writings, including the Bible, where it is referred to as Pibeseth. In his *Histories*, the Greek historian Herodotus tells us that a statue of the goddess existed in the main temple shrine at Bubastis, but although he describes how it was carried out among the people as part of Bast's festival he gives us no detailed description of her. In visualizations on the past of Egypt, many people who concentrate on Bast have picked up imagery of huge cat-headed statues, but much as we would like to believe that these are psychic 'photographs' of history, we have to bear in mind that they may only be subjective.

Another important site was near the capital city of Memphis, where Bast had a temple complex called the Bubasteion. One of her titles, Mistress of Ankhtawy, originates from here as Ankhtawy is another name for Memphis.

Bast's lineage

No stories have survived about Bast's mythological life. As with so many of the Egyptian gods, we know of her characteristics but not her exploits. We have to consider that, unlike other ancient cultures, the ancient Egyptians may not have placed great importance upon such legends. The stories might not just be lost, they might never have existed in the first place. In some regions, Bast was regarded as the daughter of the creator god Atum, in others as the daughter of the sun god Ra. We know that she had children – Nefertum, Khonsu and Mahes – and she might have shared a husband with Sekhmet in the creator god of Memphis, Ptah.

Nefertum is the beautiful young god of the primeval lotus blossom, who is generally depicted in human form, although there are some representations of him with a lion's head. Confusingly, in Memphis Sekhmet was also credited with being Nefertum's mother, as well as Wadjet, the cobra goddess of Buto in the Delta, who can also take on a leonine form. Nefertum might have had three mothers, but at least they all had something in common: a feline form.

Even less is known of Mahes (or Mihos, or Mysis). He probably evolved at Leontopolis, and is known to have had a leonine form. He was worshipped extensively throughout Egypt from the Middle Kingdom onwards. The pharaoh Osorkon II, of the Twenty-second Dynasty, erected a temple to him at Bubastis, his mother's sacred town. We know nothing of the circumstances of Mahes' birth, whether Bast was definitely his mother, who his father was, or what divine acts he perpetrated. In most respects, he is just a name, although it is possible his father was a form of Osiris known as An. He was said to dwell in the temple of Bast at Dendera.

Khonsu was only regarded as the son of Bast in certain areas of Egypt. His father was a form of Amun-Ra and his main attribute was that of a lunar god. The Greeks equated Bast with their own goddess, Artemis, who was also a moon deity, and because of these associations, some writers have concluded that Bast herself had a lunar aspect, especially when she was portrayed with the head of a cat. But in our opinion, this aspect must derive from the fairly late period in Egypt's history when it was under Greek rule.

Bast's nature

In later times, Bast, unlike the leonine goddesses, was seen as approachable, the cat who could be picked up and stroked. However, her earliest form is aggressive in aspect, as is only to be expected in a feline. Like Sekhmet, she could be known as an Eye of Ra, the fire of the sun, capable of ferocity and rapacity. But while Sekhmet could be said to represent this frequency more fully, we can see Bast's fierceness as but one aspect of her being. Budge, in his *Gods of the Egyptians* suggests that both goddesses should be regarded as 'a personification of the power of the sun, which made itself manifest in the form of heat'. He goes on to speculate that

Sekhmet represented the more fiery and destructive aspect of the sun, while Bast personified a milder heat that encouraged the growth of plants. In some inscriptions, Bast is also described as a personification of the soul of Isis, and was sometimes regarded as the feminine aspect of certain male gods. As Rat, she was a female counterpart of Ra, and as Temt, of Tem. She was also occasionally referred to as the Shetat, which means 'the hidden one'.

Some sources suggest that Bast represents fertility and sexual availability, as there are many tomb paintings of ladies with cats beneath their chairs, said to be a symbol of their sexual receptiveness. She was associated with childbirth, perhaps because of the way a mother cat cares for her kittens – and the fact that she might have continual litters of them. During the second century AD Plutarch wrote, somewhat mysteriously, that the Egyptian cat gives birth first to one kitten, then two, until the number seven is reached. He points out that this makes a total of twenty-eight, the same as the days of the lunar month.

Bast was associated with perfume, music, dancing and love. Her sacred musical instrument was the sistrum, a bronze rattle which was also used by worshippers of Hathor. We can imagine that her worship included celebrations of great merriment. Her festival was reputedly a riotous time, involving drunkenness and orgiastic behaviour. The nurturing instincts of cats, combined with their protective ferocity, fertility and unlimited nocturnal love-life makes it easy to see how Bast was a popular choice to help with human problems.

Nowadays, Bast has assumed more of a mother goddess aspect. While there is no doubt she has a side with teeth and claws bared, she is generally regarded as benevolent. Her rituals involve music, feasting and dancing, when she can be petitioned to grant boons. She can be invoked to help with problems concerning domestic life, work situations and success, as well as love, protection and good health, for the petitioners, their friends and families or their cats.

There has recently been lively debate over claims that Bast can also be regarded as a goddess of, among other things, lesbians, sex and cannabis. While anyone is free to interpret spiritual entities in whatever way they please, we ourselves have found no evidence at all to suggest such connections.

The Egyptians did not to our knowledge make any great distinction in sexual orientation. They were certainly not at all prudish about sex, so if Bast was a deity specifically connected with this aspect of human life it would have been depicted uncompromisingly in tomb or temple paintings and carvings – and it was not. People might have got drunk at her festivals, and uninhibited sexual behaviour may have followed, but this was not an official attribute of the goddess. No doubt such behaviour occurred at many other festivals too. The Egyptian gods were not regarded as deities of anything in particular. For example, there are no gods or goddesses or war, love, travellers or nature. The gods had certain attributes and aspects, but specialization is really part of different systems such as the Greek and Roman.

That said, we do not wish to proclaim that our view of Bast is the only right one. We believe that people should think and do what they feel most comfortable with. There should be as many interpretations of a deity as there are devotees; no two views will be the same.

As for whether it is appropriate to view Bast as a moon goddess or not, again it is up to the individual. Some practitioners might want to stick to the earliest forms of the goddess, while others may not. Even if Bast originally did not have a lunar aspect, she does now. It might have developed as late as the nineteenth century, when Victorian occultists were greatly interested in Egyptian deities, but even so, that is over a hundred years ago and a century of belief has brought that aspect into being in the minds and hearts of many practitioners.

For us, any visit to the Temple of Bast, through visualization, is a time of serenity, contemplation and pleasure. We see her temple as being filled with cats, who are cared for by priests and priestesses. There is no longer a dark side of sacrifice and bloodletting. The modern-day priesthood of Bast has reinterpreted the practices of the past to reflect the changing attitudes of humankind.

The festival of Bast

Bast's main festival took place during April and May, when people would travel along the Nile to Bubastis. The Greek historian, Herodotus, left an account of the festival, which gives us an insight into the activities. A host of men and women travelled along the Nile to Bast's city, packed into boats. We can assume that the festival-goers created the appropriate mood by consuming liquor along the way, as Herodotus recorded that the women shouted raucously at anyone standing on the banks of the river, started dancing, and even threw their skirts up over their heads, presumably to shock the onlookers. Music was also important to the pilgrims, as some of the women played castanets and the men played flutes, while everyone else clapped and sang along. Once they reached Bubastis, the pilgrims made elaborate sacrifices to the goddess and it was reported that more wine was consumed in the city then than at any other time of year. It was said that up to seven hundred thousand men and women converged on Bubastis for the festival – a huge amount even by today's standards. The children who accompanied the celebrants were not even taken into account for that assessment.

That Bast was a very important goddess there is no doubt, as the remains of her city attest. Huge blocks of pink granite lie tumbled upon the ground, and an extensive cat cemetery can still be explored. We can only hope that the German team who want to reconstruct the ruins will be able to do so, as we shall all then be able to appreciate and enjoy an approximation of what Bubastis was like in its heyday. Herodotus visited the city during the fifth century BC and was clearly impressed by what he found there. He said that although temples in other parts of the world might have been larger or more expensive to build, the temple of Bubastis was 'a greater pleasure to look at'. The city stood on a kind of island, because water from the Nile had been diverted to create two canals that swept around the walls. The canals ended at the gates of Bubastis, but they did not actually meet. They were a hundred feet wide and their banks were shaded by trees. The gate to the city itself was around sixty feet high, and covered in huge carved figures. The temple was situated in the centre of the city, and from the description Herodotus left, we can visualize how splendid Bubastis must have been. Bast's temple was approached by a wide paved avenue, flanked by immense trees, and surrounded by a low wall, again carved with figures. The whole town was raised higher than the temple itself so that everyone could gaze down upon it. The temple, constructed of red granite, was designed in a square, which enclosed a sacred grove. Hidden within the lofty trees was a shrine that contained the statue of the goddess. This alone was unusual in that even though there were other sacred groves in Egypt, and some of them contained shrines, no other was actually part of a temple complex. Generally such groves were situated outside temple buildings.

An invocation

To conclude this chapter, we'd like to quote from a beautiful invocation written by E.A. St George, which appears as part of a rite to Bast in her booklet *Ancient and Modern Cat Worship*. We feel it sums up Bast's attributes perfectly.

Thou art the power of the sun.
Let us not be overwhelmed by thy destruction.
Thou art concerned with the fertility of lands and the fertility
*   of woman.*
Thou art beauty, health and gentleness.
Thou dost comfort those men who are made mad by the moon
*   when thou walkest at their side in the shadow lands.*
Thou contendeth with the desert jackal, with the serpents and
*   with the rodents, for these are the creatures of evil who*
*   consume the soul of the world.*
But thou, O lady, art of the gods who protect this world.
Thunders and lightnings sunder the skies but thou returnest in
*   glory with thy father the sun.*
Thou canst blast and thou canst forgive.
Thou canst punish and thou canst reward.
Thou canst grant sunshine unto children.
Thou canst grant moonshine unto lovers.
Thou has died and thou livest yet.
It is whispered that if one man shall believe in thy power,
*   thou canst harken to the prayers of all mankind.*
Hear me, Bast the wonder worker.
Thou canst twist the skein and entangle the thread of destiny.
Thou art Sekhmet-Bast-Ra, the sacred, the beautiful, the lady of
*   music, the lustrous, the all powerful.*
The world rides upon the arch of thy back.
Thou art sacred.
Thou art venerated and called the lady of the east.
Be favourable unto us.
Protect us from all evil vermin who would destroy us.

Bast and Sekhmet

*Protect our lives that we may live in health and rejoice in thy
care.
Protect our deaths that we shall pass with thee through the
tomb chamber wall and come into the lands of light.
Be favourable unto us.
Be gentle unto us.
Show us the pathway to the greater gods.*

3

The Goddess Sekhmet

We were not ever of their feline race
Never had hidden claws so sharp as theirs
In any half-remembered incarnation;
Have only the least knowledge of their minds
Through a grace on their part in thinking aloud.

From *Frightened Men* by Robert Graves

As Bast was associated with the Delta (northern) area of Egypt, Sekhmet's region was mainly in the south. The temples there are more intact than those in the north, so we know more about their gods and goddesses. There is thus much more information available about Sekhmet than about Bast.

Sekhmet appears as a woman with the head of a lioness, wearing a sun-disc on her head. Sometimes her linen dress has a rosette pattern over each nipple, which is said to represent the knot hairs found on the shoulders of lions.

Sekhmet's name means 'powerful, mighty, violent' and, like Bast, there are several variations, such as Sekhet or Sakhmet. She too was seen as the daughter of the sun god Ra, and myth tells us that she was placed in the uraeus on his brow from where she would spit flames at his enemies. Her main temple was at Memphis. She was the consort of the god Ptah, and the mother of Nefertum.

Sekhmet and Hathor

Sekhmet had strong links with the goddess Hathor, although they were distinct entities. The best known of Sekhmet's myths shows the relationship between them.

Ra feared that humanity was plotting against him, having come to the conclusion that he was too old and frail to govern them any more. The other gods encouraged him to punish the ungrateful humans by unleashing the power, or fire, of his avenging Eye upon them. Hathor, Sekhmet and Bast were all known as the Eyes of Ra. The god sent Hathor into Egypt to exact retribution from the people. Once there she transformed herself into a lioness and became Sekhmet, and she slew everyone she came across so that the land became red with their blood. At nightfall she left the land to sleep, but she planned to return the following day to finish her bloody work.

Ra realized that Sekhmet had developed a taste for blood and had become unstoppable. It was all going too far, a full-scale massacre was in prospect. He needed to stop the slaughter. He instructed the high priest at Heliopolis to obtain red ochre from Elephantine and mix it with 7,000 jars of beer to create a red liquid that looked like blood, but had rather different properties. The priest spread the mixture over the land. In the morning, Sekhmet returned to Egypt to finish off what remained of the people there, and lapped up what she assumed was their blood on the ground.

The beer made her drunk, which effectively ended her rampage of bloodlust.

One of Sekhmet's titles is lady of the bright red linen. Although this may refer to the colour of the soil of her homeland, it also illustrates her warlike aspect, in that her costume or that of her enemies could be imagined as drenched in blood.

Both Hathor and Sekhmet were believed to have seven aspects of themselves. The Seven Hathors were mostly seen as benign, and would pronounce a person's fate at birth, which might be good or bad. Inevitably, people would object to some of the Hathors' predictions and the priests would then have to work magic in order to change their destiny. The Seven Hathors were also petitioned in love spells, and people used red hair ribbons, perhaps consecrating them as ribbons of the Hathors, to bind enemies or malevolent spirits.

The seven forms of Sekhmet, however, were never a force for good. They were known as the Arrows of Sekhmet and always brought trouble, especially in the form of illness. Other multiple manifestations (or *bau*) of Sekhmet were known as the Slaughterers of Sekhmet, and we can easily imagine how the people would have feared them. The Slaughterers were seen as messengers of the goddess and were most active at certain times of year.

The Egyptian calendar

The ancient Egyptians split their calendar into three seasons: the inundation, the planting and the harvest. The year was split into thirty-six ten-day periods, with five 'spare' days, known as epagomenal days, tacked onto the end. (The Egyptians did not devise a leap year system, so eventually the seasons must have become rather displaced.) These spare days were when the children of the deities Geb and Nut were supposed to have been born, and were seen as a dangerous and unlucky period; the chaos god Set's birthday was especially inauspicious. Collectively the five days were known as the Days of the Demons. People may have refrained from making important decisions and tried to avoid accidents on these days, just as Westerners did (and some still do) on Friday the 13th.

The epagomenal days occurred just before the annual inundation of the Nile, and must have been a time of tension and anxiety. If the Nile did not flood, famine would occur, and if it flooded too much, it would be a national disaster, people would be swept away and drowned, and their houses and lands would be destroyed. The inundation also had a spiritual significance in that it mirrored the cycle of cosmic renewal. If things went wrong, then the cosmic cycle might end. In any event, infectious diseases would have been rife during this time. The harvest season was accompanied by scorching heat, and the desiccated land and shrinking river would become the hunting ground of the 'breath of the plague of the year'. People used spells to avert the wrath of Sekhmet and her messengers. One spell tells of how they would tie pieces of red linen around their throats in order to protect themselves from the Slaughterers.

By New Year's Day, at the start of the inundation (and assuming that the inundation proceeded normally), the people would be in a mood of relief and joy. Life would continue for another year. As part of their celebrations, they would exchange gifts, and these generally took the form of small amulets of Sekhmet and Bast. People would wear these in the hope of appeasing the terrible side of Sekhmet, so that she would not inflict flood, plague or famine upon them.

The nature of Sekhmet

Because of the powerful and ferocious nature of Sekhmet, her Arrows and her Slaughterers, they could be invoked or appealed to by priests and workers of magic to act as weapons on their behalf. The ancient Egyptians were not squeamish about the terrible aspects of some of their gods, and did not believe that they should be avoided or shunned. Priests would harness the energy of these entities to attack their enemies (or enemies of the kingdom itself) and protect themselves. Sekhmet, for example, could be used to avert the Evil Eye.

Sekhmet is still sometimes seen as a representation of evil in modern Egypt. The statue of her in her shrine at the temple of Ptah in Karnak is said to have been responsible for the murder of seven local boys who were employed as basket-carriers by archaeologists. A few years ago, some Luxor locals, who believed their actions might stop the goddess walking at night, broke Sekhmet's beautiful statue into three pieces. Fortunately, it has now been restored.

However, the lioness goddess was not just seen as a warmonger and the vengeful eye of the sun god. Because she was believed to bring plagues, the priests performed a kind of sympathetic magic (which we shall discuss in Chapter 4), to ward off and heal infections and illness. In this role, Sekhmet was known as the Lady of Life, and many of her priests were also physicians. In times of plague, they might perform huge, large-scale rituals. During the reign of Amenhotep III, hundreds of larger than life statues of Sekhmet were created, thirty of which are now in the custody of the British Museum. It seems conceivable that such a massive display of respect and veneration to the goddess might have been to avert and drive out a particularly virulent plague.

Sekhmet also had a male form, known as Sekhmet Min. There is a representation of her in this aspect in the temple of Khonsu at Karnak, Luxor, which shows the king standing before her to invoke her mighty strength in Min form.

Sekhmet seems more complex than Bast, but probably only because more material survives about her. To the pharaohs, she was seen as a symbol of their prowess as warriors and their ability to succeed in battle. On one limestone fragment, she is shown apparently breathing her divine life force into the mouth of the pharaoh Sneferu of the Fourth Dynasty.

Sekhmet in modern times

As with many other Egyptian goddesses, Sekhmet has been reinvented in the twentieth century. Although she is still regarded as a powerful force, to be approached with respect and caution, we can perceive a 'watering down' of her aspects. In ancient Egypt, she was dangerous and ferocious, the bringer of plagues and retribution, the fire of the sun god's eye. This was no benign figure who could be adored and worshipped as a gentle mother, even though she did have a healing aspect.

Nowadays, many women in particular view Sekhmet as a source of strength, independence and assertiveness, and commune with her frequency when these attributes need to be augmented or instilled. In many ways, we could say that she has become the symbol of the modern woman. She is still approached as a healer, as a bringer of justice and as a guardian or protector, but the emphasis has shifted. If any system is to survive, it has to move with the times and adjust itself to suit the sensibilities of those who adhere to it. It seems a natural progression that Sekhmet has been transformed from what was almost a force of chaos into an icon of immanent female power. However, we feel it would be folly to ignore what Sekhmet really represented to the Egyptian people, and although some people may interact with her now in new ways, her more frightening aspects are still part of her. She is not a frequency of energy to be played with.

A prayer to Sekhmet

The following was translated by E.A. St George and is taken from her booklet *Under Regulus*. In our opinion, it sums up Sekhmet's nature and power.

> *Behold, I smell the earth before the mighty one.*
> *Behold how I have kept the vigil in the shrine of Sekhmet.*
> *Behold, I am the child, the child of Sekhmet, the lady of the*
>   *east.*
> *I am with her. I am one with her.*
> *I am Sekhmet and the flames of all those who praise her.*
> *I am the hand of the powerful goddess, wearer of the solar disc.*
> *I am the twice beautiful one, more splendid than yesterday.*
> *I am she who goes forth with Ra. I am she.*
> *My hair is the hair of Sekhmet, the golden one.*
> *My eyes are the eyes of the lioness.*
> *My ears are the ears of the goddess.*
> *My nose is the nose of she who can sniff out all evil.*

The Goddess Sekhmet

My teeth are the fangs, which can devour the darkness.
My neck is the neck of the divine goddess.
My hands are the hands with long claws.
My forearms are the forearms of the mighty one.
My backbone is golden and it shines with splendour.
My chest is the chest of the mighty one of terror.
My belly and back are the belly and back of Sekhmet.
My buttocks are strong, as the goddess.
My hips and legs are the hips and legs of the goddess.
My feet are the clawed feet of the lion goddess.
There is no part of me that is not of the goddess.
I am Sekhmet who cometh forth in the dawn.
I am the power of Ra by day.
I shall not be dragged back by my arms and none shall lay violent
Hands upon me, lest I destroy them utterly.
Neither man nor god shall hurt me, nor shall the living,
Nor shall the holy dead detain me.
Nor shall the demons destroy me in battle, for I am Sekhmet
And I shall eat off their faces.
I am she who cometh forth.
I am yesterday and I am the seer of millions of years.
I am the power of the divine judge.
I dwell in the east.
I am the lady of eternity, the unveiled one.
My name is created to defy all evil.
I am the flame that shineth in the sanctuary.
I am Sekhmet.

4

Temples of the Soul

My own belief is that the cat was created to encourage us to dream. I even suspect it knows the limits of our imaginations and plays on them, inspiring us to attribute to it a thousand and one marvels, thus adding to its mystery.

From *The Secret Life of Cats* by Robert De Laroche and Jean Michel Labat

Before we can begin to interact with Bast and Sekhmet, it is important to understand what we are doing and why, and also have an appreciation of how the ancient Egyptians worked their magic and performed their worship. It is easy to buy a book, read through it, then plunge headlong into performing rituals, but we feel it is vital that some thought and study go into the process beforehand.

Some people turn to ancient belief systems because they feel 'let down' and unfulfilled by modern conventional religions. They find comfort, inspiration and solace in deities that mean more to them than the stern and oppressive god of patriarchal belief. Others are drawn to systems such as that of the ancient Egyptians from a purely magical perspective. They are not looking for comfort so much as understanding – of themselves and the universe around them.

Magic and religion

Are religion and magic compatible, or are they mutually exclusive? Before we answer that question, perhaps we need to define the difference. By using magic, practitioners (whether priests, priestesses or anyone else with the relevant knowledge), seek to change, ameliorate or in some cases worsen mundane circumstances or events. To do this, they might invoke certain god-forms or spirits to act on their behalf or aid them in their tasks. Someone who adheres to the neo-pagan belief system of Wicca might address such Celtic deities as Cerridwen and Cernunnos. Magicians who favour high Enochian magic might invoke angelic forms. A shaman might commune with nature spirits or the spirit-forms of totemic animals. Practitioners of magic believe that if they perform ritual actions, with the appropriate sequence of words all in the right order, they can affect reality and achieve the results they require. It can be likened to trying to find the correctly shaped plug to fit into the socket of the universe, from where we can access the universal life energy that animates and permeates all living things. If the plug fits snugly, then the current flows unimpeded. We can look upon gods and goddesses as different frequencies of this life-giving energy. As humans, we work better with pictures than with abstract ideas, so perhaps this is why gods were created as convenient 'masks' for the frequencies. The 'masks' help us understand and commune with the unknown, the impenetrable and the formless.

But magic is not just about causing effects and achieving results. It can, and in our opinion should, involve a search for self-knowledge, whereby practitioners gain wisdom, not just about themselves, but about others and the world in general. If we are a mess inside, and do not understand what makes us the people we are and why we behave as we do, how can we hope to understand others, or indeed effect positive changes in the world? Self-knowledge comes from examining ourselves, and performing visualizations is one effective way of doing this. All that we are, all that we aspire to and believe in, exists within our minds. Meditating in a relaxed state can release buried thoughts and feelings which may have been subtly affecting our daily lives. Such information usually comes in symbolic form. In this calm, objective state, we are able to examine those thoughts and feelings, and perhaps work out how they originated. This aspect of magic is self-evolution.

In its pure sense, magic does not involve worship – the praise of an individual god or goddess, with the hope of swaying their favour on the practitioner's behalf. Religion, on the other hand, is all about worship. In the most rigid religions, adherents do not imagine themselves as having autonomy or self-responsibility, and the idea of practising any form of ritual to 'play god' with reality is seen as abhorrent or blasphemous. Religious people might feel they are subject only to divine will. Through prayer – and most commonly the medium of a priesthood – they can appeal to their deity in order to have their requests granted. It is more a case of '*please* do this for me' rather than 'I *will* this to be so'. The priesthood, as part of its obligation, is expected to provide moral education for its congregation. In many religions, there is also an emphasis on the concept of sin or ungodly behaviour, which practitioners seek constantly to overcome or, more accurately, suppress within themselves. If they do sin, they must then undergo the appropriate penance to be forgiven by the deity if not their peers. A sinful person is a bad person who invites the wrath of the deity and the censure of the community. The idea of what is sinful arises through generations of opinion, control and conditioning within the society that espouses each belief system, and what is sinful in one religion might not be in another. For example, we need only look at the strictures placed upon women in rigid forms of Islamic belief in comparison with the way women are viewed in the Catholic Church. We could argue there is just as much oppression in the latter, but it is unlikely that a Catholic woman would be punished simply for walking down the street with her head uncovered.

In magic, such ideas are mostly irrelevant. The correct ritual actions will work regardless of the political or moral codes of the practitioner. Magicians have to take responsibility for their own actions, and the force behind magic is impartial, even if human beings rarely are. We could say that magical belief systems do not have central, co-ordinating bodies that supervise the practises and behaviour of practitioners, although some organizations have arisen that seek to impose such structures, as in the various 'pagan churches' which have formed around the world. Magical systems can, and many do, also involve some form of worship, although we view this as distinctly separate from the working of magic. The reasons for this will be examined in more detail later.

Religion and magic in ancient Egypt

In ancient Egypt, religion and magic went hand in hand. The priests were regarded as specialists in magic as well as intermediaries with the gods. They were paid for their services and performed magical rituals as part of their daily duties. The majority of the priesthood were part-time workers who took on a priestly role for one month in four. For the rest of the time, they would pursue a different occupation. It is well documented in a great many sources that some levels of the priesthood also acted as government officials, so we can perhaps even say that religion, magic and politics went hand in hand. As with any political institution, it therefore becomes necessary for us to examine the motives behind some of the priestly proclamations, as we mentioned earlier with reference to the Edfu text (see Introduction).

As in modern magical practice, the Egyptian priests believed in the inherent power of words and images, which when utilized correctly possessed their own creative force. Egyptian priests were not expected to provide moral education. In the Egyptian religion, there was no concept of repentance, even if on occasion people's actions were seen as bad or sinful. For the most part, people were seen as being victims of fate, and the priests' job was to work magic on their behalf to heal their misfortunes. They would blame bad luck, illness or accident upon the malevolence of an angry deity, a malicious spirit or another worker of magic, but not necessarily on the sufferer's own actions or behaviour.

The priests were also very concerned with understanding and interpreting the true nature of objects and living things. They sought to discern correspondences, similarities and connections between them. These shared properties would include colours and the sounds of names. For example a plant of a certain colour, say red, might have a name that sounded similar to that of a fiery god or goddess associated with the colour red. Correspondences therefore arose between them, and that plant could then be said to share the qualities of that deity. For example, a bark such as red sandalwood would be one of the incense ingredients used to help invoke the presence of a fiery or solar deity, such as Sekhmet. Similarly, a plant that grows in or near water, such as the iris (orris root), would be an ingredient of a lunar or watery incense, used in rituals to invoke a moon deity, which in the Egyptian system could be Khonsu. We can see how the influence that the moon has on the tides gave rise to the correspondence between the moon and water. This is similar to practices of modern magic, much of which revolves around tables or correspondences between things that students of the art have devised over the millennia.

The Egyptians also believed it was possible to cause an effect upon one object by performing ritual actions on another which possessed the same qualities, sometimes called sympathetic magic. One example is creating a 'poppet' or wax doll in order to perform magic upon an individual, whether for good or bad. Although this practice has rather grim connotations in the modern world and is seen as a malevolent form of witchcraft or voodoo, the ancient Egyptians often used it in love spells. Small figurines have been found with their limbs bound behind them and their bodies pierced by nails. Although at first inspection this might seem the most aggressive form of spell, the text that survived with one of these figurines made it clear that it had been created to sway the affections of a woman towards the practitioner. Other figurines have been found that clearly preserve the memory of magical workings with a more hostile flavour, such as the conquest or binding of enemies. We might argue about the ethics of this, as the majority of modern practitioners avoid any kind of working that influences the will of another, in whatever capacity, but we should guard against making judgements against a people whose culture and morals were undoubtedly very different from our own.

In addition to the priests, who were affiliated to various temples, other magicians worked among the populace, perhaps providing everyday spells to deal with ailments or other problems. It is thought that magicians unconnected with a temple were not held in quite the same high regard as priests, although people undoubtedly used their skills, because they spent quite a lot of their meagre income on spells and amulets. It is also unlikely that secular magicians had access to the prestigious books of magic that were compiled by the priests, mainly because they would have lacked the education to be able to read them.

The energy of the gods

The energy or power that the Egyptians channelled in order to affect things was called *heka*. They believed it was the force that the creator deity used to make the world and that every time they worked magic they reconnected themselves to the primal creative process, something which is still relevant today. All gods and spirits possessed it, as well as kings, and individuals who were 'different' in some way, such as dwarves or disabled people. One of ancient Egypt's most popular deities was Bes, the leonine dwarf god of luck and protection. The revered dead were believed to possess *heka* in abundance, which made them powerful workers of magic, and they could be appealed to or appeased. There is plenty of evidence that many Egyptians wrote letters to their dead relatives and left them in their tombs. These letters might ask for help to deal with a problem, or even blame the ancestors themselves for some misfortune or another. The dead, to the Egyptians, never really went away, and were often feared in the belief that they envied the living and liked nothing better than to cause trouble. Female spirits in particular were held in dread, especially around pregnant women and young children.

The god who was considered to have the most *heka* of all was the ibis-headed Thoth, who was credited with inventing both magic and writing and was the patron deity of scribes. Thoth's temple at Hermopolis possessed an acclaimed library of magical texts and ancient records.

Workers of magic used *akhu*, which in one translation means 'magical power'. Confusingly, it also refers to a spirit of the dead once it has passed through various transformation stages in the underworld. *Akhu* spirits were the most powerful and possessed great *heka*. But, in its magical sense, *akhu* can be regarded as spells, enchantments and the ritual acts required to access the *heka* of the gods. Both *heka* and *akhu* were seen as impartial powers that could be directed towards creative or destructive purposes. If we can accept the gods as simply masks through which we can interact with the universal energy, we can see that the Egyptian priests used this energy directly to produce specific effects.

Many belief systems incorporate the idea of a universal, life-giving energy. The ancient Chinese called it *chi*, and it was the principle behind the practice of feng shui, which is still used today. In feng shui, objects are placed strategically in order to improve the flow of *chi* around a building, in the belief that it is beneficial for all who live in it; blocked *chi* causes pools of stagnant energy that can have detrimental effects upon the individual. Muslim sufis believe in a force they call *barraka*, which is an energy possessed to greater or lesser degrees by living things, places and objects, especially items regarded as strange or exotic. In the Western world we find a belief in earth energy, a network of linear channels of power that form a matrix throughout the land and gives rise to the concept of ley lines or spirit lines, and the power immanent in sacred sites. Wiccans cast a magical circle to raise the natural energy, which they will then direct towards their intention or desire. Different cultures have their own interpretation of this energy, with various attributes and terminology, but the Egyptian priests sought to perceive connections between things, so we can appreciate that their belief in *heka* is very similar to the concept of universal energy espoused by many modern pagans and magicians.

Heka was not just a force of magic, but a god in his own right. Although there is no evidence that he had major temples devoted to him, there were small shrines to him in Lower Egypt, with a priesthood. In *Magic in Ancient Egypt*, Geraldine Pinch tells us: 'Some Egyptian deities were merely personifications of abstract concepts or natural phenomena, and were never the focus of cult worship or private devotion.' The common people were probably drawn more to homely deities such as Bes, Tawaret and Hathor, whose powers would seem more pertinent to their lives, whereas the god Heka could be seen as falling into the former category. Stephen Quirke, in *Ancient Egyptian Religion*, says, 'The faculty that allowed the primeval deity to develop into the existing world was also identified as *heka*, a word often translated as magic and which denotes the intangible energy of creative power that defends the sun-god and man-kind from the forces of darkness.'

Many of Heka's priests were also doctors, and it seems almost certain that medicine was as close to religion as magic was. Doctor-priests would act like modern physicians in establishing the immediate cause of an illness or injury and prescribing the most effective treatment, but it was also their job to interpret the *ultimate* cause, which might well be the malevolence of a deity or spirit, or even a human enemy. Magic was then performed to deal with this ultimate cause.

The term *hekau* was used to denote anyone who practised magic. As well as Heka, there was a goddess associated with magic, Weret Hekau (or Urt Hekau). Her name means 'great of magic', which was an epithet applied to many other goddesses as well. Weret Hekau was usually depicted as a cobra, although occasionally as feline, and it has been suggested that the cobra-shaped wands used by magicians represented her power. Along with other goddesses, such as Mut and Bast, she was regarded as a kind of cosmic mother to the divine kings of Egypt. She was also seen as the powerful force latent within their crowns. This probably stems from her association with the image of the cobra on the forehead of the ruler, which could be named 'Weret Hekau'.

Idols and monsters

At first glance, it might seem that the ancient Egyptians were idolaters who worshipped their gods as statues. After all, how could the power of a god or goddess be immanent within cold stone? But the priests would make offerings of food, drink and incense, and recite invocations to animate the statues of the gods and goddesses with the *heka* of the relevant deity. Through the offerings and a certain amount of flattery, they coerced the gods into entering the stone. So we can appreciate how a statue could become a tool of magic. The priests did not have to visualize the gods as pictures in their heads, but could focus upon them as living beings, resident in the carving before them. (We use our own technique for animating statues with energy, which we will discuss later – see Chapter 8). Nowadays, Wiccans might 'call down the moon' into the body of one of their priestesses, thereby making her a personification of the moon goddess standing among them. Again, we can perceive the similarities between these two systems.

Much as modern magicians use different components to create a powerful incense, or combine certain ritual actions to produce a specific effect, the Egyptian priests also used their deities as ingredients of what we can look upon as magical recipes. In order to fine-tune the desired results of a ritual, they would sometimes invoke several deities at once, subtly combining their qualities. Carvings and drawings have survived which portray these compound gods – monstrosities with multiple heads, limbs and regalia. For the most part, these were probably 'one-off' creations, devised for a specific magical working, but the Egyptians were also fond of combining different forms on a more permanent basis. Tawaret is perhaps an example of one such goddess. She has the body of a hippopotamus with pendulous human breasts, the paws of a lion and the tail of a crocodile. We can imagine the power inherent in this form, as it combines such strong and feared animals. Tawaret was appealed to as a powerful protector during childbirth, which was a time fraught with dangers for both mother and baby.

There was a form of Bast and Sekhmet, when they were combined with the sun god Ra, which can only be described as bizarre. Sekhmet-Bast-Ra was represented as a woman with a man's head. Her arms were adorned with wings, and from each of her shoulders sprouted the head of a vulture. She possessed the phallus of a man and the claws of a lion. Both Bast and Sekhmet were also often combined with the names and forms of other gods and goddesses to produce composite deities. This might have been to do with regional preferences, when the major local deity was desired to have the qualities of a number of other deities.

Some practitioners of magic still use the technique of combining deity forms today, and we can appreciate how this might sometimes be useful. However, we feel it is important to guard against ending up with undesirable results. An awkward mixture of energy can not only be ineffective in magic, but also produce undesired psychological effects. The different frequencies can clash, and if that energy is filling the environment in which the practitioner is working, it is obviously going to be detrimental to him or her. It is important to be specific when invoking particular frequencies of energy with which to work magic, and unless the practitioner has a thorough knowledge and experience of the results of combining different energy frequencies, this practice should be avoided. In particular, we feel it is inadvisable to try and combine deity forms from different belief systems, unless you really know what you are doing and why.

In the later stages of Egyptian culture, when the country was often under foreign rule, its magic and religion became contaminated by elements from other countries and cultures, such as Greece, the Near East and Rome. The Egyptians seemed happy to mix and match their indigenous gods and goddesses with foreign deities, and clearly saw the correspondences between many of them – perhaps because they perceived all gods as different faces of *neter* – but we have found no evidence that they used any cross-cultural combination god-forms.

Ecstasy in magic

Many systems of magic incorporate the use of natural mind-altering drugs, alcohol or frenzied dancing to induce ecstatic states so that the magician can commune on a higher level with spirits or gods. The native shamans of South America use the peyote cactus, while practitioners of Voodoo use wild dancing accompanied by rhythmic drums and chanting to create an altered state of consciousness. Evidence suggests that the priesthood of ancient

Egypt might have used techniques that we can regard as shamanistic. In shamanism, altered states are often seen as a necessary part of magical work, and totem animal spirits play a very important role. We do know that Egyptian priests sometimes dressed themselves in leopard skins, which suggests totemic beliefs. In wearing leopard skins, the priests might have believed that they would share some of that animal's attributes. Then again, they might have just liked the look and feel of the pelts, and worn them for aesthetic effect. (A legend reveals how Set, the god of chaos, transformed himself into a leopard to attack the body of Osiris. The jackal-headed Anubis caught him and, to punish him, branded his skin. This is how the leopard got its spots, which were also equated with the stars in the night sky.)

A great deal of the surviving texts from ancient times suggests that the priests were often involved in work of a visionary nature. There is a lot of wonderfully vivid imagery of travelling in the spirit world, and the descriptions of the realm of the Duat, or underworld, are extremely detailed, as if the priests who wrote the stories about it had actually been there – perhaps they had, in their minds. There is evidence that, under ritual conditions, some of the priesthood used mind-altering substances occasionally, but this does not mean it was a frequent or common practice.

Some Egyptian magicians used child mediums in their work. The young people would lie down while strong incense was burned around them. Simultaneously, the magician might recite invocations in a chant. It was probably the combined effect of the thick smoke and the rhythmic chanting that caused them to go into a trance, when they would scry in bowls filled with water, filmed by oil. On other occasions people might gather together and, after indulging in wild dancing, chanting, clapping and singing, collectively undergo a visionary experience.

Today, we also practice such visionary work, although it is not necessary for us to resort to mind-altering substances or frenzied movement to achieve the desired state. By incorporating breathing techniques that mostly derive from Eastern systems, we can control our breath to change the state of our consciousness and help us reach for that higher level. Coupled with an unimpeded flow of energy within the body, these techniques can emulate the visionary ability produced by certain drugs or alcohol, with no detrimental physical effects.

Women and magic

Although we would all like to believe that priestesses filled the temples of Bast and other goddesses, we should acknowledge what might be a difficult truth for modern women. The official religion in ancient Egypt was run by the state, and women appeared to have few established roles within it, at least until the late third millennium. Few goddesses had priestesses to serve them, but one that did was Hathor. Her priestesses were generally ladies of noble birth, the wives of high-ranking officials. As Hathor was believed to decree the fate of all new-born children, it's possible that her priestesses had a similar function in pronouncing the future.

While women may not have led rituals, they certainly did have another purpose within the temples as musicians and dancers. Although this might now seem to be an inconsequential or frivolous role, to the Egyptians it was very important. In their rites, the priesthood sought to please their gods, and most deities were believed to enjoy the things enjoyed by humans. Therefore, graceful dancing and sweet music might have contributed greatly in persuading a god or goddess to enter and animate the sacred statue in the temple.

Women also sometimes took the parts of various goddesses in temple rituals of a dramatic nature, such as that of 'god's wife' or 'god's hand' in the rites of Amun. In our own group rituals and visualizations, we do see women in the temples, and we describe them as priestesses, more for convenience than anything else. However, there are correct terms you might like to use in your own rituals. The term *henutet* (masculine *henuty*) referred to a woman who worked in a temple, and is thought to mean 'servant'. It is not known what the *henutets'* actual duties were, although from inscriptions it is clear that none of them, either male or female, was high-ranking in everyday life. A female musician was known as a *shemayet* and this word was generally followed by the name of the deity for whose temple the woman worked. Therefore a musician of Bast would have the title Shemayet Bast. The woman who was in charge of a musical temple troupe was known as *weret khener*, which means 'great one of the troupe of musical performers'. This role was held by a high-ranking woman, usually the wife of a temple official.

So why did women not become lector priestesses and direct important rituals? Priests had to undergo many arduous processes of purification before they could take part in rituals, including thorough bathing in sacred pools, the shaving of all body hair and abstention from sexual activity. All bodily secretions were seen as impure. Because women menstruated and gave birth to children, and the blood of these processes was regarded as unclean, they were seen as particularly vulnerable to hostile forces or evil spirits, which would probably have been viewed as an unsuitable attribute for a temple official. This might be hard for modern women to accept, especially those of us who are drawn to the Egyptian magical system. However, so little information has survived into modern times, and it might be that the results of current research do not present the full picture. We shall probably never know the whole truth, but even so perhaps we should guard against rewriting history as a cosy, fictitious image of the past that fits in with what we want to believe now.

Even though women in ancient Egypt might not have had a major role to play in the temples, it does not mean they did not have a rich and complex magical tradition of their own outside them. Male magicians had many titles, such as priest of Sekhmet, scorpion charmer and amulet man, but there was one term that referred to a magic worker of either sex, and this was *sau*. Women who acted as midwives or who cared for the sick were probably regarded as magicians in their own right, as they were said to 'make protection' for those in their care. Figurines have been found representing women wearing the mask of Beset, the female counterpart of the dwarf-god Bes. It could be that they took on this deity's role in certain rituals, and these would not have taken place within any temple precinct. We can only surmise that women in local communities performed their own group rituals to their favourite deities, who were more concerned with domestic life than the grandiose schemes of war and politics.

References have also been discovered that describe certain women as *rekhet* or 'knowing ones'. These were wise women or seeresses who were credited with being able to make contact with the dead – an ability that could have had various functions in a magical sense, whether to ask for advice or information or to coerce an ancestor to work magically on behalf of the living. *Rekhet* were believed to be able to sense which particular deity or spirit was responsible for a person's misfortune or illness, just as the doctor-priests would do when they were establishing the ultimate cause of sickness.

Although fewer records have survived of women's role in magic and religion, it is likely that *every* community had their own honoured *rekhet* and *sau*. The Egyptians were not misogynistic. Women had legal rights and could own property. They were certainly not the restricted, cloistered females of Greek and Roman culture. It cannot be denied that some of the most powerful, and in some cases terrifying, deities of the Egyptian belief system are female. These goddesses were revered, respected and often feared by the entire population, regardless of their gender.

Women's exclusion from prominent roles in the state religion might explain the popularity of deities like Bes, Beset and Tawaret, who had no grand, official temples and could be approached by the general population rather than only priests. Similarly, when Bast became a more popular goddess, during the Ptolemaic period in the first millennium BC, it is likely that women worked with her magically in the home as a domestic goddess. After all, her own sacred animal, the cat, was undoubtedly an important presence in every household.

Scrolls and spells

Another reason why women might have been denied official positions in the temples was because few of them were able to read and write. The majority of magical texts were written for and by men, who were very protective of their secret knowledge. The magicians, both male and female, who worked among the general population would probably have used a largely oral tradition of magic, and details of it have been lost. Most of what we know today about Egyptian magic derives from what was preserved in stone and on papyri, and this was in the written script used by the temple priests.

Although we refer to magical 'books' of ancient Egypt, these were in fact scrolls, most often lengths of papyrus stuck together and rolled up, but occasionally parchments of calf vellum. These books were regarded as extremely esoteric, and certainly not for the eyes of common people. Some were said to have been found in secret places, such as forgotten tombs and hidden caskets, and to record the actual words of Thoth or legendary sages and priests. It is likely the priests considered their own magic to be the most effective and sacred, and they kept their knowledge secret in order to make themselves appear more powerful in the eyes of less privileged individuals. They often wrote down their spells in a kind of code, referring to their ingredients by alternative names in order to confuse any uninitiated person who might try to read them.

The Egyptians used several different kinds of writing scripts throughout their history. Perhaps the most familiar to us is the hieroglyphic script that includes pictograms of animals and objects. This script was considered the most important and sacred of all, and it was the one used for tomb and temple carvings. With hyroglyphs, the power of the words was matched by the power of the symbols themselves. The symbols were regarded as being so powerful, precautions had to be taken to prevent them taking on a life of their own. This was especially so in the case of those that represented living animals, such as birds and cats. In some tomb carvings, the symbols are purposefully disfigured, perhaps to prevent them being animated accidentally by someone reading them aloud. Once animated, the symbols might decide to leave the tomb and abandon their function as protection for the deceased within.

Hieratic script was a simpler version of hieroglyphs, and would have been more widely known among the educated populace. Although it was used for spells and rituals, it was also the script employed for writing letters and documents. Later in Egyptian history, following Greek rule of the country, another script was devised, known as demotic. This was a kind of hieratic shorthand. The last written form of the Egyptian language was Coptic and this was mainly comprised of the Greek alphabet, but with some demotic symbols.

There is a set of books which derive from this late period, written mostly in Greek and Latin, called the *Hermetica*, which were supposedly penned by Thoth himself. The Egyptians appeared to share a belief that is still prevalent today, thinking a book or piece of knowledge, is somehow more powerful and true if it is old. There are many modern books which purport to reveal the amazing knowledge of newly discovered ancient texts, claims which later often prove to be fraudulent. Similarly, it is doubtful whether all the stories attached to various Egyptian magical books are true, but the stories increased the mystique of the books, and therefore made their esoteric knowledge more desirable.

Early Egyptian spells or rituals were written mainly to be spoken aloud, with few instructions as to what actions should be performed, but as writing developed and rituals perhaps became more static, the instructions became ever more detailed and specific. As in many modern rituals, the spells provided 'stage directions' to tell the practitioner what actions to perform and the text itself which was the speaking part. Repetition of particular phrases was very important, and it seems likely that rituals and spells were chanted or sung to differentiate them from common speech. It was vital that the words were pronounced in exactly the right manner, especially those that were the secret names of deities and demons. The correct pronunciation was probably an oral tradition handed down to neophyte priests by their elders to maintain the secrecy of the knowledge.

Techniques of the art

The Egyptians possessed a rich tradition of varying magical techniques and we could easily fill a book describing them all. Written spells themselves had a variety of functions.

Some magical workings required the practitioner to paint relevant hieroglyphs onto a piece of papyrus, which would then be dissolved in liquid, often beer or water. The resultant mush was then consumed by the magician. In this way, they expected to absorb the *heka* of the spell into themselves. A variation of the technique involved pouring water over a written spell, collecting it in a vessel and drinking it. Quite often, these spells would be used by doctor-priests, and the *heka*-charged water would be given as a medicine to their patients. Similarly, powerful symbols could be painted onto the inside of a vessel, from which the patient would drink.

Hieroglyphs might be painted or tattooed directly onto a person's body. Sometimes sick people would have symbols painted onto their hands, which they would then have to lick off, thus consuming the *heka* of the spell to heal them. In some cases, doctor-priests might press a piece of linen painted with hieroglyphs directly against a wound, or give to their patient an inscribed scrap of linen or papyrus, which could be worn around the neck as a protective or healing amulet.

In other rituals, the practitioner might paint a symbol of Maat on the tongue. Maat was not only a goddess of truth and justice, but also the actual concept of cosmic order, of what was right and true. If her symbol was drawn on someone's tongue, he or she would be able to speak nothing but the truth. Whatever that tongue described, it would be brought into being in the world by the power of Maat.

Images of other deities were sometimes drawn onto the skin of a priest or his client. A spell or invocation would then be recited to draw the god or goddess down into the image, whether to heal, to give strength or perhaps even to make someone more attractive to a person they desired.

The Egyptians set great store by amulets and they were widely used, especially by women and children. Many amulets were worn as pieces of jewellery and could represent gods and goddesses, everyday objects or parts of the human body. Amulets were used as protection, but also to promote success in various ventures, be it in love, work or the conception of a child.

Within the temples, priests performed rituals which, in many ways, are similar to the way magical rites are still performed. We shall return to these practices later, when we discuss our own rituals, and illustrate how many of their techniques are not only relevant but still practised today.

A way of life

At the beginning of this chapter we talked briefly of the difference between magic and religion. As we cannot go back in time and enter the mind of an ancient Egyptian, we do not know what the common people really thought about the connection between the two, nor how much importance they placed upon self-knowledge. They probably did not think about it, and simply functioned in a natural way in their environment, without the neuroses and angsts associated with modern living.

In our time, perhaps as a result of millennia of magical study, the distinction between magic and religion has become more important; we also place more emphasis on understanding ourselves. In this book, we aim to present a reinterpretation of Egyptian magic to promote and expand the belief in the feline deities in a modern context, and for this reason we feel it is important to distinguish between dogma and the freedom that comes from self-responsibility.

Religion often provides a crutch or safety net for people who feel lost, vulnerable or uncertain. Religion has boundaries, creeds and rules which can make people feel comfortable and secure. Dogma is handed out by a priesthood, and believers only have to swallow this wholesale to be part of a community where they need never feel alone or frightened again. However, this may also lead to a fear of the wrath of their deity, and they may adopt extreme behaviours that they think their god will find pleasing. The deity is responsible for everything, an all-powerful force. In most religions, adherents do not have self-responsibility, i.e. the belief that the world they inhabit is largely created by them and they are totally responsible for what happens to them – that can be a cold, lonely position to be in and most people follow a religion to avoid feeling that way. They want reassurance, the idea that some mighty being above them will care for them if they worship it enthusiastically enough. Strangely, a great many religious people also have an irrepressible urge to communicate their 'salvation' to others, and become evangelical in their attempts to convert people to their beliefs. Perhaps this is because they see safety in homogeneity. If everyone believes in the same thing, there can be no threat from outside, which might prove those beliefs to be wrong or ill-founded. This tendency has led to instances of sometimes hideous religious persecution throughout history.

Magic, on the other hand, is actually *about* self-expression and self-responsibility. There could be as many magical systems as there are magical practitioners. Students of the occult have compiled thousands of books over the years from which we can draw knowledge and techniques, but we are free to interpret and use that information in whatever way we please. Although, as herd animals, we like to work together, and magical orders and covens have arisen from that urge, the world has experienced no grand inquisitors of the golden Dawn, no Wicca army, nor indeed any other oppressive magical fraternity – at least not overtly. The idea seems unthinkable. Through magic, we are able to communicate with the divine, and therefore experience true spirituality, but we do this from a position of freedom, and ideally without fear. Even if they are religious, most magicians assume responsibility for all their acts, behaviour and feelings. The majority believe that what energy they send out returns to them greatly amplified, which is why the manipulation of negative energy, most commonly called 'black magic', is avoided. Most practitioners would agree that their magic is a way of life, subtly permeating all that they do, but it need not necessarily be the entire focus of their existence, so that all they live for is the next ritual. Practitioners of magic are rarely evangelical about their beliefs, and in many cases tend to be reticent in revealing them to outsiders.

Over the last forty years, magical systems in the Western world have lost some of their esoteric status and have become more widely known and accessible. Serious practitioners are still arguing whether this is a good thing or not, and it has to be said that there are valid arguments on both sides. One of the arguments against this popularization is that, for many people, ancient belief systems have taken on the role of religions that have fallen out of favour. Magical rituals can be poetic, moving and dramatic, and performing or taking part in them can provide that warm, 'belonging' glow once associated with singing hymns in church. The idea of an all-powerful, nurturing mother goddess is particularly comforting, and we can see how it attracts those who feel a lack of that frequency in their lives. In this way, Isis, or even Bast, can replace figures like Jesus and the Virgin Mary, and be worshipped in the same way. Same meat, we might say, but different gravy. This is not necessarily undesirable; if we have to have religion, then surely it is better to ascribe to one that is healthy and life-affirming than to one that involves a strict dogma based on fear, guilt and sin?

But there is a risk that in choosing a religion associated with magic, the two can become confused. Those of us with a drive to worship a deity from a position of submission often want to feel as if we are subject to that deity's will because it removes the need for self-responsibility. The drive derives from fear. And if we are driven by fear, we are in no condition to attempt magic. In this book, we look upon the gods as frequencies of the universal energy, frequencies we can tap into and experience, and which we can respect and revere, but we do not advocate blind, unquestioning worship.

The Egyptians had what seem to us to be a strange attitude to their gods. While they were happy to praise them in order to coerce them into manifestation, they were not above threatening them either. Many spells have survived which promise all manner of dire consequences if the deity concerned does not fulfil the practitioner's wishes. These threats included the destruction of temples, the slaughter of sacred beasts, and perhaps worst of all, the deliberate refusal to acknowledge a god's existence. The Egyptians must have been very much aware that the gods depended on their human believers in order to exist, and did not see it as wrong to exploit that. This does not mean that the Egyptians did not respect the power of their gods, but they perhaps understood the true relationship between gods and men. This is a concept we should remember today. While most of us would no longer feel comfortable uttering threats to our gods and goddesses, the relationship between us and them should be one of mutual respect and accord. We are them and they are us.

While this is not a book devoted solely to the search for self-knowledge which can be seen as the first step of all magical endeavour, we do feel it is important that a few of the basic principles of this search are understood. When we stand before the gods, we show them our innermost selves, our true motives and our fears. Fear is the fundamental cause of all human dilemmas. It is what makes us insecure, vulnerable and lacking in self-esteem. The complexities of modern life, and certain of its philosophies, have estranged a great many of us from nature, so that we are unaware of the way we and our world function. And yet, despite this lack of awareness, we are all still part of the universal energy, as are the gods. It is the connection between us. If we stand before them incapacitated by the fears engendered by modern life, our personal life energy is blocked and cannot flow in the direction we desire. This can sometimes be damaging, both psychologically and physically. Therefore, we shall later discuss techniques and exercises designed to overcome these risks (see p104).

These techniques are not drawn from the Egyptian tradition, and therefore have quite a modern flavour, but the Egyptians did not live in such a complicated, confused world as we do. They were closer to the natural function of the planet, so we must presume that they were more in tune with the universal energy.

We feel it is important that the difference between religion and magic is understood by anyone embarking upon a magical path. Sometimes this path can make us feel very insecure and uncertain. Self-knowledge involves facing the raw reality of ourselves, peeling away the restrictive layers of conditioning and suppression we have experienced throughout our lives, in order to know who we really are and evolve as individuals. As we learn more about ourselves and how we function psychologically, spiritually and physically, so we become stronger, more whole, contented and fulfilled. Magic, a belief in Egyptian deities or religion cannot give us this on their own.

It might seem as though we are suggesting it's impossible for a practitioner of magic to experience spirituality, but this is not the case. To a magician, witch, priestess or whatever title we wish to adopt, religion should be *about* spirituality, about experiencing the divine – but not from a position of submission and fear, but one of confident, free awareness. We have already described what we believe the divine to be: universal energy. Natural religion involves understanding and experiencing this energy. We can call it *heka, chi, barraka* or anything else, but fundamentally it is a way of life.

Looking within: the mirror of truth

Before setting off upon any magical path, it is important that we ask ourselves a basic question: why do we want to do this? It might be because we sense that there is more to life than we know. It might be that we become aware of something within ourselves that is drawn to magic, almost as if we have practised it for many lifetimes. We might have a great affinity for the planet upon which we live and feel the energy that dances upon and within it. It might be because we are hungry for knowledge. As for attuning specifically to Bast and Sekhmet, it might be because we have a great love of and empathy with cats. There could be any number of reasons, but some of them we might feel less comfortable owning up to.

Magic, especially the Egyptian system, is seen as mysterious, alluring and empowering. For this reason, it is very attractive to those who feel vulnerable, weak and powerless, and who wish *they* were mysterious, alluring and powerful. If we feel we lack those qualities, it is most often because we have low self-esteem, and low self-esteem derives from fear. To put it bluntly, some of us all too often want to possess the mystique of the magician without the hard work, in order to appear more interesting to others. One of the disadvantages of magic becoming more accessible is that it has, for some, become an identity accessory that makes them feel strong, valid and worthy. They think that all they have to do is dress up in the appropriate clothes, light the right incense, burn the right candles, intone a few rituals, and suddenly they are creatures of mystery who inspire awe and sometimes fear. The plethora of books available on witchcraft etc. enables anyone to jump in and start throwing energy about, without the guidance of more experienced practitioners. But even if someone is using magic in this way, if they can be honest enough to admit it, they can turn the situation around. Magic should involve the desire and search for self-knowledge, and not be used as a crutch to prop up a floundering personality. If someone is armed with this desire for truth and acknowledges that they are approaching magic from a position of weakness, vulnerability or restlessness without being judgmental or experiencing guilt, then they are already on the path to self-awareness. Calm acceptance of our less desirable attributes actually gives us strength, and goes a long way towards changing them.

We can look upon ourselves as beings of energy, but if we are unaware of how that energy functions within us, we are not ready to try and manipulate it outside ourselves. As workers of magic we should constantly be asking ourselves why. It is how we learn about ourselves. Be honest. Ask yourself now. Why are you attracted to magic? Write down your responses. You might find you write a poem, or even something that later you will be able to use in a ritual. No one else will read it, so you can be as honest as you like. Date the page. It is the beginning of a magical diary. Even those of us who have been practising for a long time should review this question from time to time.

We have been on our own paths to self-knowledge for many years now; it is a journey that never ends. Our search began from very different directions. We both explored various aspects of magic, experienced crises and celebrations, made mistakes and achieved successes. We learned the hard way, from patient teachers, what magic should entail. Then a few years ago, our paths came together, and the Lady of Ankhtawy made her presence felt. Perhaps the time was right.

5

The Tribe of Shadows

The wonderful thing about the cat is the way in which, when one of its mysteries is laid bare, it is only to reveal another. The essential enigma always remains intact, a sphinx within a sphinx within a sphinx, like one of those Russian dolls.

From *The Secret Life of Cats* by Robert De Laroche and Jean Michel Labat

As we have said, there were many other gods and goddesses who had feline associations in the ancient Egyptian belief system. Some of them are no more than figures and names on temple walls, while others are fairly well documented. We feel that our research into this subject is an on-going task. New information is coming to light all the time as archaeological excavation progresses.

To a large degree the feline deities of ancient Egypt have been neglected and forgotten. Bast and Sekhmet have enjoyed a revival both in pagan circles and in religious orders centred wholly around ancient Egyptian beliefs, but others, such as Tefnut and Pakhet, remain virtually unknown outside of scholarly circles. The legends associated with many Egyptian gods are also fragmented and incomplete. If we want to communicate with a deity such as the Greek Aphrodite, there are many tales and myths associated with her which we can use to enhance our rituals, and gain under-standing of her, but the same cannot be said of Sekhmet and Bast. It is tantalizing to think that once these myths might have existed, and that one day an archaeologist might rediscover them in some buried fragment or parchment, but for now we have to accept that what we have is all that remains, or perhaps all there ever was.

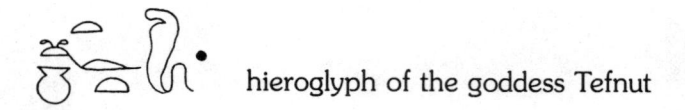

hieroglyph of the goddess Tefnut

We will be looking in more depth at visionary questing, through which we can expand upon the existing information and imagery associated with the feline deities in Chapter 22. Using this technique, anyone can take further the material presented here. This part of the work is interesting and exciting, but before immersing in it fully, it is important to have performed meditations and rituals to Bast and Sekhmet on a regular basis, and to be in tune with their frequency.

In this chapter, we list as many of the feline-associated gods and goddesses of ancient Egypt as we know about. The information can be used to check images and information picked up during visualizations. We know that our knowledge of the feline deities is not all-encompassing and that we will have to update the material, and we hope that readers with more information will contact us to aid us in this task.

Aker

Aker is one of the oldest of the lion gods. He was an earth god, but also guarded the Gate of the Dawn through which the sun god emerged every morning. His other attributes included being able to heal people afflicted by the bites of snakes, and if someone had swallowed a poisonous fly, he could neutralize the effects of that poison in the victim's stomach. When a pharaoh died, Aker was the god who opened up the earth's gate for the king to pass into the underworld.

There are later variations on this myth. The Egyptians believed that when the sun left the earth at night, he entered a kind of underworld tunnel beneath the earth. A lion god guarded each end of the tunnel. Together, these gods were known as the Akeru, or Akerui, primeval earth gods, older even than Geb, son of Shu and Tefnut (see below). Ancient texts indicate that they had a somewhat threatening nature. The Akeru were represented either as two lions seated back to back, or as one lion with two foreparts. Between them, they supported the horizon on which rested the solar disk.

They can be equated with Shu and Tefnut. Later still, the Akeru became Sef and Tuau, which means 'yesterday and today'.

The ancient Egyptians always saw lions as guardians and protectors. As lion gods guarded the gates of morning and evening, so statues of lions guarded tombs and palaces, protecting both the dead and living, keeping demons and human enemies at bay.

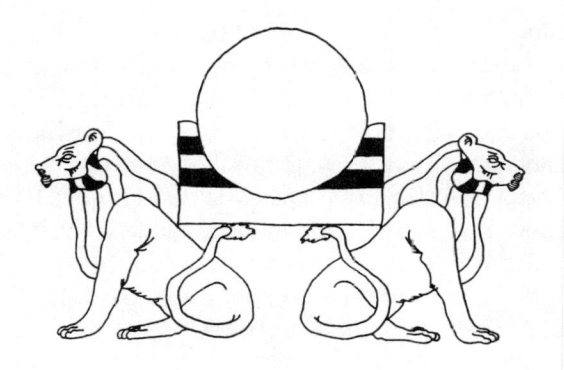

Apedemak

Apedemak is not strictly an Egyptian deity, as he derives from the culture of Kush, in what is now the Sudan. If Egypt is steeped in mystery and hidden treasures, the land of Kush is perhaps even more mysterious, mainly because it has not generated quite the same degree of archaeological and popular interest as Egypt itself and therefore less is known about it. What we do know is that Kush was seen as an enticing and exotic land of plenty by the Egyptians and many pharaohs sent expeditions south to bring back spoils of incense, animals and slaves.

Kush really came into its own as Egypt's royal dynasties fell into decline. Kashta, a great Kushite king, set out to conquer Egypt in the seventh century BC, a conquest which was completed by his son Piankhy around 725 BC. Some sixty years later, the Assyrians invaded Lower Egypt in the north and the Kushites were driven southward. Their civilization was finally vanquished by a rival African culture around AD 300.

For the later centuries of its existence, the capital of Kush was the city of Meroe, and the dramatic ruins of temples, tombs and palaces that still stand today are a testament to the once great kingdom that flourished there. Nearby lie the remains of the city of Naga, and here stands the Lion Temple, sacred to the lion god Apedemak. Meroe and Naga are now crumbling into the desert sands, but at one time the land would have been more fertile. What fascinating stories must lie buried beneath the numerous unexcavated sites. The names of the Meroitic queens alone inspire the imagination: Amanirenas, Amanishakhete, Naldamak.

It is possible that Egyptian kings of the early dynasties attempted to conquer the lands to the south, but there is little evidence to suggest that their victories were long-lasting. However, for centuries, the Kushites enjoyed a trading relationship with Egypt, and there is no doubt that they were influenced by Egyptian culture, if not vice versa. Certain Egyptian gods had temples in Kush, most notably Amun Ra. Apedemak, a lion-headed Kushite god, was absorbed into the Egyptian belief system. Alternatively, it has been suggested that Apedemak was originally a wholly Egyptian god who became more widely venerated in Kush.

It is fortunate that quite a lot of research has already been done on Apedemak, who can be viewed as a Kushite Mahes (the lion-headed son of Bast). He shared a number of attributes and qualities with Mahes. Like him, he was most often represented as a lion-headed man, holding a sceptre surmounted by a seated lion. However, Apedemak did have at least two other unusual forms. One was that of a lion-headed serpent, while the other was of a man in ceremonial dress, who is shown with three lion heads. There is some question over whether he actually had four heads, but only three are visible in bas-reliefs.

Apedemak was primarily a war god, and we can be sure that in the past he was invoked to bestow his blessing upon the outcome of battles. Warriors would have desired the god's strength and ferocity in combat. In one hymn he was described as 'one who sends forth a flaming breath against his enemies in this his name, Great of Power, who slays the rebels with [his] strength'. He was often depicted as wearing battledress of leather armour and carrying weapons, especially a bow and arrows. He was also shown slaying enemies or else holding on to bound captives, who were restrained with cords around their necks.

War was not Apedemak's only area of dominion. He was clearly very important to the Meroitic royal family, for representations have survived showing him being honoured by kings, queens and their children. In one hymn, he is addressed as 'Lion of the south, strong of arm; great god who comes to him who invokes him; bearer of secrets, mysterious of form who is not seen by any eye'. In another instance, he is described as a kind of heavenly provider, with the words 'one who provides nourishment for all men in this his name of He Who Wakes Intact'. Another, perhaps less important role was that of solar deity. In his three-headed aspect, these benign and provident qualities are emphasized. In one carving, he is shown with four arms. Two of them are offering bunches of flowers or perhaps corn to the King and Queen of Meroe, while his other two arms support those of the royal couple, whose own arms are raised in praise of the god. In another carving, Apedemak holds the sceptre of a king in one hand and a bunch of corn in the other. A representation of him survives from the pharaoh Akhenaten's city of Amarna, in which the queen Nefertiti is shown making offerings to him.

The Egyptian goddess Isis was often regarded as the wife of Apedemak, while Horus was his son. In this way, the Meroites substituted Osiris for their own god. However, in some instances, Tefnut was depicted as his wife.

His cult involved specially bred temple cattle, and also veneration of the African elephant. Sacred pilgrimages were made to his main temple, which was a vast complex at Musawwarat es-Sufra, in Butana, north of the sixth Nile cataract.

Ari-hes-nefer

He was a lion god. He may have been a form of Mahes (see below).

69

Asthartet

Asthartet derives from the Syrian goddess Asthoreth, who is associated with several other deities, such as Ishtar, Hathor and Isis. There are many correspondences and attributes of this goddess, which are often confusing and contradictory, but we shall adhere to the description of her given by Budge in *Gods of the Egyptians*, where she is represented as a lioness-headed woman. In Egyptian texts, Asthartet is referred to as 'mistress of horses, lady of the chariot, dweller in Apollionopolis Magna [Edfu]'. She is shown as a lioness-headed woman standing in a chariot, drawn by four horses that trample over the prostrate bodies of fallen enemies. Her head is surmounted by a sun disc. In one hand she carries what appears to be a whip, while in the other she holds the reins of the horses. It is believed her cult became established in Egypt round about the time of the Eighteenth Dynasty, but it continued in the Delta up until the Christian era. A letter survives that was sent by Tushratta, King of Mitani to the pharaoh Amenhotep III. In it he refers to 'Ishtar of Nineveh, lady of the world', which was a name of Asthartet. The king suggests that the goddess's worship in Egypt is going into decline and pleads with Amenhotep to do something about the situation, to increase her influence tenfold. Whether Amenhotep did this has not been recorded, but her cult certainly survived far longer than either king.

Asthartet had two main attributes. Primarily, she was a terrifying and destructive goddess of war, controlling the maddened steeds that drew her chariot over the battlefield. Horses were not used by the Egyptians in this manner earlier than about 1800 BC, which gives some indication of when Asthartet's worship may have started. She was also, however, worshipped as a moon goddess, which suggests a more tranquil and compassionate side to her nature.

The Egyptians never regarded the horse in quite the same way as they did animals such as cats, lions, baboons and jackals, in that there are no representations of a god having an equine-headed form. This may be because of the horse's comparatively late introduction into Egypt. However, Asthartet can be regarded as a patron goddess of horses, who may be approached to request protection for these animals.

Atet

A goddess of the ancient city Henen-su, in Lower Egypt, who was perhaps a female counterpart of Ra, she was reputed to have killed Apep, the great serpent of darkness, in the form of a cat.

Bes

Bes was one of the most popular gods among the common people of Egypt. Although he did have a warlike aspect, he was primarily a cheerful and benign god, associated with domestic matters, as well as laughter, dancing and general merrymaking. He was the lion dwarf, most likely of African origin, even though his name is Egyptian.

Bes had an almost comical, grotesque appearance. He was small and squat, with a great shaggy head of hair like a lion's mane. His nose was flat and beneath it his tongue protruded as if it were too big for his mouth. He had long arms and short, bowed legs, and his body was adorned with a lion or panther skin, whose tail trailed down behind him. He was generally shown wearing a crown of tall feathers, like ostrich plumes, which resembled a tribal head-dress. His ugliness was probably regarded as a deterrent to evil demons and spirits, in much the same way as gargoyles on Christian churches. The Egyptians did not mince words in addressing the dwarf god. They referred to him in such terms as 'great dwarf with a large head and short thighs', or else 'a monkey in old age'.

In paintings, Bes was often shown full-faced rather than in profile, which is unusual in Egyptian art. The only other deity represented in this way was the foreign goddess, Qetesh, and, occasionally, Hathor.

In his aspect of god of music and dancing, Bes was shown playing a harp or a tambourine. Sometimes, he was depicted standing on one leg as if frozen in the middle of a dance. The clamour of his music would also have helped drive away evil spirits. According to one legend, the god was said to have used his musical skills to ensure that the goddess Hathor remained in good spirits while she travelled, reluctantly, from Nubia to Dendera.

When he was wearing his more warlike aspect, Bes carried knives, or a sword and shield, and wore a military tunic. In this guise he was said to represent the destructive force of nature. Occasionally, he was shown with outspread hawk's wings, and sometimes carried a sign, called *sa*, which means protection.

Many household artefacts remain that bear Bes's image, from hand mirrors to make-up pots, and pillows. He was associated with restful sleep, and with joy and pleasure. Women were especially fond of him as he was supposed to attend them in childbirth. In general, he was regarded as a protector of babies and young children. In this aspect, he was often accompanied by another popular deity, the hippopotamus goddess Tawaret. Whenever a woman experienced problems in labour, for example, spells would be recited to Bes and Tawaret. It was not just the common people who turned to Bes at these times. Many tomb and temple paintings and carvings remain which show that he was present in royal birthing chambers too.

Bes was reputed to bring good luck to families and to protect them from the common threat of snakes and scorpions. He may well have had a sexual aspect too, and his presence in carvings and paintings in bedrooms might have been to ensure that a satisfactory sex life took place there.

It seems most likely that the cat and lion deities derived originally from other areas of Africa, and Bes more than any of them seemed to keep certain aspects of his place of creation. He was like a pygmy shaman, complete with ceremonial dress of animal hide and feathers. Pygmies were especially favoured by Egyptian kings and queens, who liked to have them at their court, and perhaps some of Bes's attributes derive from the capering court jester. Dwarves were also employed in this manner by ancient Western royalty.

Our group has done many rituals to Bes, whom we regard mainly as a god of good fortune, especially when associated with money. The rite given later in this book (see Chapter 19) can be used specifically – though not with disrespectful frequency – at those times when money is tight. We have found that Bes is quite happy to refill the coffers when it is sorely needed.

As well as ensuring good luck, Bes can be approached for fertility or childbirth, or simply as a means of lifting the spirits. Laughter is, without doubt, the best medicine for anyone feeling miserable, so we can see how invoking this cheerful deity might be beneficial to those who are depressed.

Beset

Beset was a lioness-demon, a feminine form of Bes. Figurines of her show her as having the normal proportions of a woman rather than being dwarf-like, although like Bes she has a mask-like face that resembles a lion. One surviving representation of her is a wooden figurine dating from the second millennium BC. It wears a Beset mask and holds metal serpents. Whether this is actually a representation of the goddess or of a woman taking her role in a rite is uncertain.

Hathor

The worship of Hathor, the cow goddess, can be traced back to very early times. The cow was seen as a symbol of fertility in an agricultural society and images of a bovine goddess have been found in pre-dynastic graves.

Hathor is one of the best known Egyptian goddesses. She is a daughter of Ra and her name literally means 'mansion of Horus', which is thought to be a reference to Hathor as 'Lady of the Sky'. In this role she was seen as the sky in which the falcon flew. Her main temple was at Dendera in Middle Egypt and was dedicated to the triad of Hathor, Horus and their son Harsomtus. The temple is famous today for its Hathor-headed columns, which are all crowned with reliefs of her as a woman with bovine ears.

She is usually depicted as a front-facing woman with the ears of a cow, or as a woman wearing a crown of cow horns and a sun disc. This image is one that was often found decorating sistra and mirrors. Interestingly, though, she has also been represented as a lioness. She has connections with both Sekhmet and Tefnut and shares many of Bast's attributes.

Like many of the more familiar leonine deities, although Hathor's nature is mostly benign, she does have a destructive side to her character. In some versions of the famous myth in which Sekhmet slaughters mankind and is stopped by becoming drunk (see Chapter 3), it is Hathor whom Ra first sends into the desert to kill humankind. Once there, she transforms into the raging Sekhmet. In other versions, such as the one given by Lewis Spence, Hathor and Sekhmet are the same deity known as 'Sekhmet-Hathor'.

Hathor is also associated with the primal lioness goddess Tefnut (see below), most notably in the myth which tells how Hathor/Tefnut, having become estranged from her father Ra, wandered off, sulking, into Nubia. Once there she became enraged and transformed herself into a fire-breathing lioness. In this state she relished the drinking of blood and fed on the flesh of both humans and animals that crossed her path. Ra missed her, however, and sent her brother, Shu, and the wise god, Thoth, to bring her home. Even Thoth had difficulty in persuading her to return home because she had acquired a taste for blood and hunting. Eventually he bribed her with promises of unimaginable new temples and riches and she was reunited with her father amidst great celebration. In some versions of this myth, Hathor/Tefnut leaves Egypt because she has been prevented from destroying mankind.

Like Bast, music was very important in the cult of Hathor and the sistrum was sacred to her. The drinking of wine and beer was also a part of rituals to her as she, like Bast, was seen as a goddess of love, pleasure and dancing. She was particularly revered by women and presided over birth.

Hebi

This is a lion god mentioned in Budge's *Gods of the Egyptians*.

Hekenth

Hekenth is a lioness-headed goddess of the seventh hour of the night.

Hert-Ketit-s

A lioness goddess of the eleventh hour of the night, Hert-Ketit-s was in charge of one of four terrible pits or chambers. Her chamber was called Hatet, and it was filled with the bodies of fiends who eternally dashed out their own brains with axes. Hert-Ketit-s stood by the side of the pit, belching fire into it from her mouth. After the fire had done its worst on the fiends within, the goddess chopped them into bits with an enormous knife she held in both hands.

Heru-neb-mesen

This is another lion god mentioned in Budge's *Gods of the Egyptians*.

Huntheth

She was the lioness-headed goddess of the tenth hour of the night.

Ketuit-ten-ba

This was a cat-headed god who ministered to Osiris in the second hour of the night.

Mafdet

Unlike the other deities discussed in this chapter, Mafdet (or Maftet) was not based on lion or domestic cat imagery. There is some confusion about exactly what animal she was, but she was certainly feline. Different sources claim she was a cheetah, a lynx or a leopard. Her name means 'runner', which seems to favour the idea she was a cheetah, but she is most popularly regarded as a lynx. She was certainly a ferocious goddess, as were most of the feline deities. In the *Pyramid Texts*, she is described as killing a serpent with her claws. The mere touch of her claws was apparently lethal to snakes. She reputedly leapt upon the necks of serpents and was also famous for slaying scorpions. In one instance, she is described as having braided hair, which could symbolize the bodies of scorpions and snakes that she killed.

There is little doubt that Mafdet is a very ancient goddess, predating both Bast and Sekhmet. The details of her worship have mostly been lost, although a representation of her does appear on a vase that was found at a royal tomb in Abydos, which dates from between 2950 and 2800 BC. It is likely that she is of African origin.

Mafdet is mentioned twice in the *Book of the Dead*. In one chapter she is reported as cutting off the head of a serpent, while in another she is called upon to prevent the deceased from being bitten by snakes in the underworld. The following is taken from E.A. Budge's version of Chapter 24: 'Oh Serpent! I am the flame which shineth upon the Opener of hundreds of thousands of years, and the standard of the god Tenpu, the standard of young plants and flowers. Depart ye from me, for I am the divine Mafdet.'

It seems that Mafdet could be either male or female, being referred to in different places as a lynx goddess or a lynx god. In our own group's encounters with this deity, he has so far manifested in our visualizations as male, a guide through the realm of shadows, an opener of the way. We have yet to ascertain whether this interpretation bears any resemblance to original Egyptian belief.

According to *The Witches' Goddess* by Janet and Stewart Farrar, Mafdet's title's are 'lady of the castle of life' and 'slayer of serpents'. Regarding the former title, as far as we are aware, castles were not a common feature of the Egyptian landscape, so perhaps the title would be better translated as 'lady of the palace of life' or 'lady of the house of life'.

Mahes

When we first began our studies, we knew little of this god, other than that he was the lion-headed son of Bast (sometimes of Sekhmet too), and had a temple at Leontopolis. However, we now know more about him, which has enabled us to design visualizations and rituals. We have learned that he was a much more important god in ancient times than we had previously believed. The men in our temple group are especially interested in this deity.

Mahes, also known as Maahes, Mihos, Maihesa (the wild lion), Ari-hes and Miysis, was reputedly a god of healing as well as a protector of the innocent. He also shared the qualities of many other leonine deities in that he had a fierce and aggressive aspect, being shown mauling the enemies of the king. It has been suggested that his name might mean 'true before her', which helps confirm an association with Maat, in that he is an upholder of the divine truth. Maat is both a concept and a goddess and represents cosmic order, truth and justice. His main centre, Leontopolis (ancient Taremu, modern Tell el Muqdam) is in the Delta, 50 kilometres north of Cairo, but he was worshipped throughout Egypt from the Middle Kingdom onwards. The pharaoh, Osorkon II of the Twenty-second Dynasty, erected a temple to him at Bubastis, the town sacred to his mother. Edouard Naville first excavated at Tell el Muqdam in 1892, but more recently, in 1992, an American archaeological team from the University of California in Berkeley has conducted an investigation of the site. They have unearthed many lion bronzes, statuettes and stelae, and we understand that one of the directors of the investigation is currently putting together a book about their discoveries, which will include a catalogue of all the known Mahes stelae.

The Ashmolean Museum in Oxford exhibits two bronze statuettes of Mahes. One of them shows him wearing a tall crown flanked by tall plumes, while in the other he is bareheaded. In the Field Museum in Chicago, there is a splendid statuette of him, seated on a throne and elaborately crowned.

We do know that Mahes was worshipped extensively throughout Egypt and in Meroe and Nubia, where he was closely associated with the god Apedemak (see above). Strabo wrote of an Egyptian 'City of Lions', and it seems almost certain that Tell el Muqdam is the site of this settlement. The cult of Mahes appears to have been most active during Ptolemaic times, which coincides with Bast's popularity as a cat-headed deity, rather than her earlier lion-headed form. Another Greek scholar, Aelian, wrote: 'In Egypt, they worship lions, and there is a city called after them . . . . The lions have temples and numerous spaces in which to roam; the flesh of oxen is supplied to them daily . . . and the lions eat to the accompaniment of song in the Egyptian language.'

Leontopolis was occupied by the Persians, (525–330 BC) and the Californian archaeological team working there have deduced that the artistic representation of lions suggests a strong Persian influence, exemplified by the coloured paste inlays and snarling mouths of the statuettes they have found. It is also possible that the Persian kings honoured Mahes, because they identified with the power of the lion. A powerful Egyptian individual named Nesmihos, whose black granite tomb has been known since 1889, had great influence in the Persian court. He was a prince, a courtier and a sealbearer of Lower Egypt, as well as royal scribe for the temple of Mahes. His name, and that of his father, Pedinihos, clearly derive from the name of the local god. As investigations continue into this site, we hope that more will be learned about the god himself.

In E.A. Wallis Budge's book, *The Gods of the Egyptians*, the author lists a number of lion gods, two of which are Ma-hes and Ari-hes-Nefer. Aris-hes is another name for Mahes, so these names could be variations of the same god – or they could be completely different entities. His epithets include 'great of roaring, great of strength, powerful of arms.' He was also known as 'the raging lion'. While his usual appearance was that of a lion-headed man, wearing a crown (in various forms), he was also depicted as a full lion.

We see Mahes as a god who may be approached in respect of

healing, whether of mind or body, and also as a source of protection. He can also be petitioned in respect of truth and justice. His image was often placed at the entrances to large temples as a form of guardian. He has the strength of the lion, but perhaps not the ferocious power of the lioness. Lions are notoriously lazy beasts, who are quite happy to let their numerous wives do all the hunting work. Therefore, we see Mahes' leonine power as less energetic than Sekhmet's; a slow, inexorable, confident force. Lions, in their beauty, seem well aware of their own majesty. Mahes can provide protection, a massive impenetrable wall of strength, in contrast to Sekhmet, whose protective power is much more active and fiery.

Mau

Apep, the great dark serpent, was slain by Ra in the form of a cat, Mau, the great tom cat. One text tells us:

> I am the cat, which fought hard by the Persea tree in Annu on the night when the foes of Neb-er-tcher [a form of Osiris] were destroyed. Who then is this? The male cat is Ra himself and he is called Mau by reason of the words of the god Sa, who said about him, 'Who is like [mau] unto him?' and thus his name became *mau* [cat].

This is a play on the words for 'cat' and 'like', which sounded the same.

Mekhit

In most respects, Mekhit, or Mehit, is very similar to Tefnut (see below) in that she is a lioness-headed goddess who is sometimes known as an 'Eye of Ra'. Like Tefnut, she left Egypt and fled to Nubia, from where she had to be brought back, in this case by a warrior and hunter god called Anhur, or Onuris. The name Anhur means 'the one who leads back the distant one'. Mekhit's name means 'she who has been completed'. The word Mehit, another form of this goddess's name, can also be used to refer to the Eye of Horus that was gouged out by Set, and subsequently healed, or 'completed', by Hathor.

Once Mekhit had come home, she became Anhur's consort, and statuettes exist in museums that depict them together. Although there is one instance of Anhur represented as a lion-headed man, he is generally shown as fully human. He usually holds a spear, but in some cases he carries a rope, which perhaps refers to the way he managed to capture the prodigal Mekhit. We have yet to find mention of any cult centres specifically devoted to Mekhit, but her husband Anhur had a temple in the Delta at Samannud, which had the ancient name of Sebennytos.

Menat

This lioness goddess, who was worshipped at Heliopolis, is mentioned by Budge.

Menkert

She was a lioness-headed goddess of the tenth hour of the night.

Meretseger

Meretseger is primarily a cobra goddess, but she does have a leonine aspect. She was popular particularly with the labourers and artisans of the village now known as Deir el-Medina. At one time, this place was the settlement where those who worked on the royal necropolis lived permanently. Meretseger was supposed to inhabit a mountain that overlooked the Valley of the Kings in western Thebes, which is known as Dehenet Imentet, or 'the peak of the west', an epithet which she shared. Hymns have survived which honour the 'lion of the peak'. During the New Kingdom era, she was regarded with great respect by all who inhabited or worked in the Theban necropolis area. In her snake aspect, Meretseger is generally depicted as a coiled cobra, although she can also be shown as a cobra with a woman's head, and with a human arm sticking out from the front of its hood. In her leonine aspect, she can be depicted as a lioness or as a lioness-headed woman.

Meretseger's name means 'she who loves silence', which seems apt for a goddess who presides over a typically quiet area – the tombs of the dead. The workers who venerated her have left stelae behind them, which tell us that they regarded Meretseger as a dangerous yet merciful goddess. She was reputed to have extremely venomous stings, and would strike out and blind anyone who committed a crime or uttered falsehoods. When her anger was aroused she was known as a 'raging lion'. It has been suggested that the working conditions in the desert necropolis, where dry dust must have been a continual problem, might have contributed to the deterioration of workers' eyesight, and for this they would have to blame a local deity or spirit. Scorpions and snakes would also abound in such an area.

However, despite her association with injuring people, Meretseger was also regarded as a healer. No doubt, when workers were stung by scorpions or bitten by snakes, they would have appealed to her for help. It is said, however, that the goddess would have to be absolutely sure a person repented of whatever wrong he had committed before she would aid him. One draughtsman who created a stela describing Meretseger concluded it with the words 'Beware the peak of the west!'

Miuty

In the *Book of Gates*, Miuty (also known as Mati or Meeyuty) is a cat-headed god of the eleventh division of the Duat or underworld, who carries two sceptres, one in the shape of a serpent. He is the guardian of the gateway to this division; the gate is called Mysterious of Approaches. Along with all the other gods of this region, he could never leave his appointed division of the underworld or ascend to heaven. His duties included placing a white crown on the heads of gods in the train of Ra as the sun god passed through the Duat in his boat. Miuty also had to weep for Osiris after Ra had passed out of the underworld. His soul was said to stay with the god always, even if his body had to remain in the Duat. He also had to 'raise up Maat' and establish it in the shrine of Ra. Along with his companions, Miuty 'fixed the period of the years, which those who were decreed for the Duat should pass there, and the period of those who were to live in heaven'. Another inscription tells us that Miuty and his companions 'tore their hair in grief before the great god in Amentet, for although they drove away Set from the pylon, they themselves were not allowed to enter into the heights of heaven'.

In the *Book of Caverns*, Miuty appears again, watching over Ra's bound enemies, while in *The Litany of the Sun*, Ra himself manifests as Miuty and also as the 'great tom cat'.

In the tomb of Seti II, many gods are depicted on the walls, and one of them is a cat-headed deity, in mummified form, called Mauti. Given that Meeyuty and Mauti both bear a resemblance to the Egyptian word for cat, *mau*, it is feasible that this rendition is a version of the same god. In the same tomb, there is a depiction of a large seated cat, which looks like a male, which has the name Mau-aa.

Mut

Along with her husband, Amun-Ra and her son Khonsu (the moon god), Mut was part of the Theben triad of gods. She was also known as Muit and Mauit. In the temple at Thebes, she appears in many wall carvings and is called 'the mistress of the nine bows', which symbolizes her and her husband's role as protector of both the pharaoh and the land. One meaning of her name is 'mother', and it was said she had not been born of any woman, although she could give birth herself. However, *Mut* can also mean 'death' or 'vulture', and she was associated with goddesses such as Nekhbet, the vulture-goddess of Upper Egypt. From her temple at Thebes come the epithets 'Mut, the great lady of Ashert, the lady of heaven, the queen of the gods'. She was also known as 'lady of the life of the two lands' and 'lady of the house of Ptah'. She is generally depicted as a woman, in a red or blue linen dress and the double crown of Egypt, carrying a lily sceptre. However, she sometimes has the head of a lioness, and has been associated with Sekhmet and Meretseger. Her sacred and symbolic animals are the lion, the cat and the vulture, although she is more commonly associated with felines than vultures. Her sanctuary in Thebes was called Isheru and the hiero-glyphs for this name contain the symbol of a recumbent lion. It was at Mut's temple that the pharaoh Amenhotep III erected a great many statues of Sekhmet.

In the New Kingdom, one of the great festivals of the Egyptian year involved carrying Amun's statue up the Nile on a sacred barge to his wife Mut's temple. This was the Festival of Opet (confusingly another name for Tawaret – see below). At the same time the pharaoh and his queen would conduct secret, sacred rituals, which may have had sexual connotations, connected with the god's annual conjugal visit to his wife.

As with many, if not most, Egyptian goddesses, Mut's name and attributes could be joined with those of other deities, and in Mut's case this certainly included Bast and Sekhmet.

The Egyptians would not have regarded Mut as a mother goddess in the same way that mother goddesses are revered in the modern Western tradition. She was more properly seen as a symbolic mother of the pharaoh, along with other goddesses such as Hathor and Isis. However, for the purposes of modern reinterpretation, she could be approached as a benevolent, nurturing deity. Here is the cat which can be picked up and stroked, which is more likely to purr than spit and scratch. She can be seen as a patroness of women, especially mothers, as well as a protectress and a righter of wrongs.

Some of her titles are 'mistress of heaven', 'the great sorceress' and, like Sekhmet and Bast, 'Eye of Ra'. In the *Book of the Dead* she is referred to as 'she who maketh souls strong and who maketh sound bodies'.

Nefertum

Nefertum, also known as Nefer-tem, was the son of Sekhmet and her husband Ptah, the god of creativity. The three of them form what is known as the Memphite Triad, as they were the primary divine 'family' of Memphis.

The word *nefer* in Nefertum implies that he was associated with great beauty and perfection, and he is generally depicted as a young man with a lotus flower on his head which sprouts two tall plumes. He was the god of the primeval lotus blossom, specifically the blue lotus from which the sun was believed to rise. In the *Pyramid Texts*, Nefertum is described as the lotus blossom before the nose of Ra. Part of his worship might have involved devotees breathing in the scent of the sacred lotus.

As is typical with Egyptian deities, he can claim more than one mother, as Wadjet, Pakhet and Bast are also reputed to have given birth to him. His father is generally regarded to have been Ptah, so he can be seen as the full or half brother of Mahes. In some instances, he is depicted as a child sitting upon a lotus blossom, like a young sun god, while occasionally he is shown as a man standing upon the back of a lion.

For our purposes, the most interesting depictions of Nefertum are those to be found in the temple complex of Sety I at Abydos. Here there is a vaulted chapel dedicated to Nefertum, and the representations of him are of a lion-headed man. This is regarded as a very unusual form of the god and suggests strong associations with Mahes. On the northern wall of the chapel, a relief shows Sety burning incense and pouring a libation in honour of the god. Nefertum stands before the pharaoh, holding an eye of Horus against his chest in his left hand. Upon his head, a falcon perches, crowned with a lotus flower. On the southern wall, Nefertum is shown as a lion-headed mummy, again with a lotus-crowned falcon on his head. The chapel walls are carved with hymns to Nefertum, as well as other pictorial representations of him. He is said to 'protect the two lands, and make to live the common people of Egypt and their children'.

We regard Nefertum as being an aspect of the rising sun and representing beauty, purity and perfume, similar in some respects to Bast. This is not a god of divine wrath or purging power, but a more gentle character. Because of his depictions as a beautiful child, he could perhaps be approached in respect of the welfare of children, especially for their protection. Otherwise he can bestow tranquillity and serenity. In his presence, we can imagine ourselves in a divine garden filled with lotus blossoms and the soft light of dawn.

Neith

Neith is generally depicted as a woman wearing the crown of northern Egypt, holding either a sceptre or a bow and two arrows. However, she also had a cat- or lioness-headed aspect.

She was widely worshipped in Egypt, which because of the Egyptian habit of reinterpreting the gods locally, means she is a complex deity of many attributes and symbols. She is certainly very ancient and may well have Libyian origins. Her cult centre eventually became established at Sais, in Lower Egypt, where her temple was known as Sapi-Meht, which means 'Sapi of the north'. She was also worshipped in Upper Egypt at a place called Esneh, or Seni, and here she was sometimes represented as having a green lioness's head. One of her titles at Esneh was 'father of fathers and mother of mothers'.

It is likely that in Sais she was seen as a feminine counterpart of the father god Tem. Like him, she was reputed to have been self-generated, and it is generally believed that she embodied elements of both male and female in her nature. Her titles included 'the great lady', 'the mother-goddess', 'the lady of heaven' and 'queen of the gods'. She was also known as 'mother of the gods'.

Every year, a festival dedicated to Isis-Neith was held at Sais, which was described by Herodotus as the 'night of sacrifices' and the 'festival of the lamps'. On this eve, the entire population of the city lit lamps outside their houses, which were kept burning all night. The lamps were flat dishes filled with oil and salt, in which wicks floated. Even people who could not attend the festival, and lived elsewhere, marked this festival night by lighting lamps, so we can imagine that throughout the whole country, the towns and cities were illuminated by the flicker of sacrificial flames. Herodotus stated that there was 'a sacred tradition, which accounts both for the date and for the manner of these observations'.

On other dates mysteries were enacted upon a lake in Sais, but although Herodotus tells us he was aware of what went on at these events, he does not reveal the details, claiming that the rites must remain secret. It is probable that these mysteries were concerned with the death of the god Osiris, who was said to have been buried at Sais.

Herodotus surmises that the Mysteries of Demeter were brought into Greece from Egypt, and it is likely that these were based on the highly secret mysteries of Neith and Isis in Sais.

Neith was identified with many other goddesses who had feline associations, such as Mut, Sekhmet and Bast. Her symbols were mainly two arrows and a shield, but she could also be depicted with a strange symbol on her head, representing a shuttle. She is thus also associated with weaving. Her earliest aspect, however, is almost certainly as a goddess associated with war or the hunt. Budge suggests that in predynastic times she could have been identified with a local wood or hunting spirit. In some depictions, she is shown suckling a crocodile, which probably represents her son, the crocodile god Sobhek.

Another of Neith's aspects is associated with the magic rituals and ceremonies connected with preserving the dead. She was also said to have given birth to the sun, Ra, in the waters of the Nun and was in fact credited with inventing birth.

A legend associated with Neith concerns a dispute between the gods Horus and Set over who should be king in Egypt, which had gone on for eighty years. Ra and the other gods could not resolve the conflict and called upon Neith to advise them. She suggested that Horus should be crowned as King, while Set should be given two foreign goddesses, Astarte and Anat, as wives. The gods all concurred with her wisdom, except Set, who clearly did not think he got the best of the deal. In her letter to Ra delivering her advice, Neith mentioned that if Horus did not become king she would grow so angry the sky would crash into the earth; this may have partly swayed Ra's decision.

Strangely enough, by the Pyramid Era, Neith was known as Set's wife, and the mother of Sobhek. Some inscriptions describe her as the mother of Apep, or Apophis, the great dark serpent who was Ra's enemy. His birth was unusual in that it was supposed to have been occasioned by Neith spitting him out as saliva into the primeval waters.

In another of her aspects she was similar to Hathor, in that she was regarded as a sky cow goddess. She was known as 'the cow who gave birth to Ra', 'the spirit behind the veil, whom no mortal could see face to face'. Several queens of the First Dynasty carried her name, which shows her great antiquity, and one of her epithets was 'all that has been, that is and that will be'.

Pakhet

Just as Bast's main region of worship was Lower Egypt and Sekhmet's Upper Egypt, so Pakhet was worshipped in Middle Egypt, and had a temple which was cut out of the solid rock near the modern village of Beni Hasan in the eastern desert. A great many mummified cats have been found there, as well as thousands of mummified hawks. There are several different forms of her name, such as Pekheth, Pekhit, Pakht, Pasht and Pekh. For some time, modern scholars confused her with Bast before deciding that she was a separate entity. Like Sekhmet, she was lioness-headed and was seen as something of a ferocious goddess, for her name means 'the tearer' or 'she who snatches'. One of her titles is 'goddess at the mouth of the wadi'. A wadi is a dry channel between cliffs or rocks, which in certain seasons might become filled with water. Her temple is situated near the mouth of a wadi, and was constructed by the female pharaoh Hatshepsut and pharaoh Thuthmosis III of the Eighteenth Dynasty. The Greeks equated her with the goddess Artemis and her temple is known by its classical name, Speos Artimidos. At Beni Hasan Pakhet was seen as a local version of Hathor's fierce lion-headed form. Unfinished Hathor-headed columns in the temple complex attest to this. In an Ancient Egyptian work called the *Coffin Texts*, Pakhet is called 'the great', and described as a 'night huntress with sharp claws'. One of her surviving titles is 'lady of sept', which could be translated as 'lady of the star of Sothis [Sirius]'. She was identified with forms of the goddesses Isis, Hathor and Sekhmet. In one of the inscriptions at Beni Hasan, she is referred to as Horus Pakht, which along with the evidence of the mummified hawks found at the site, suggests she also had a connection with a form of Horus. It is clear from the remains of her temple that she was a goddess of great importance in ancient times.

Perhaps because of her association with wadis, we can view Pakhet as being another goddess who might be petitioned to ensure that the land became irrigated sufficiently during the inundation. Her name 'tearer' suggests she might also have had similar attributes to Sekhmet, in that her energy could be harnessed as a weapon against enemies or harmful spirits. This association with Sekhmet is made clear in her temple, where they share many of the same characteristics. Scenes depicted here show Pakhet pledging her support for Hatshepsut with phrases such as 'my fiery breath being as fire against thine enemies'.

Another scene shows Hatshepsut giving offerings of incense and libations to the goddess, and here she is rewarded with 'I give thee all strength, all might, all lands and every hill country crushed beneath thy sandals like Ra.' Such depictions are typical of Sekhmet, which suggests that these goddesses were local manifestations of the same deity.

Renenet

This lioness goddess was associated with suckling, and was said to bring babies their names. She also presided over the harvest and was present during the judgement of the souls of the dead.

Sebqet

This lioness goddess is mentioned briefly by Budge in *Gods of the Egyptians*.

Sesenet-Khu

Sesenet-Khu is a lioness-headed goddess who ministers to Osiris in the second hour of the night in the Duat.

Shesmetet

It is likely that this leonine goddess is actually a form of Sekhmet. One of her epithets is 'lady of Punt'. Punt was the incense region of Africa, so she might have originated in this area, or else was associated specifically with incense. According to the *Pyramid Texts*, she gave birth to the king, and in some funeral texts she is credited with becoming the mother of the deceased. A spell survives which was recited on the last day of the year, and in it, Shesmetet is invoked to protect against 'demons of slaughter'.

Shu

For information on this god, see Tefnut below.

Tawaret

The wife and companion of Bes, Tawaret was primarily a very ancient, pre-dynastic hippopotamus goddess associated with child-birth and pregnancy, when she would be called upon to protect women. When she is the wife of Set, she is occasionally regarded as an avenging goddess. Although she is usually represented as a hippo with the hind quarters of a lion, she is sometimes depicted with the head of a lioness, and brandishing a knife.

Tefnut

Although Bast and Sekhmet are better known today, Tefnut is an equally important goddess. She was the first female deity to be created by the primal sun god Atum or Tem, who can also be called Amun-Ra, or simply Ra. As we have said, the Egyptians have left comparatively few narrative myths behind them, but one that was developed and preserved in its entirety is that of the Atum creation myth.

The story goes that Atum masturbated and produced from his seed his children Shu and Tefnut. Shu was associated with heat and dryness, for his name means 'dry, parched, withered and empty', while Tefnut was a goddess of moisture, in particular the moistness of the sky. Another version of the myth suggests that Atum spat moisture from his mouth, which became Tefnut, and breathed air from his nose, which became Shu.

An ancient hymn to the sun god says: 'Oh Amun-Ra, the gods have gone from thee. What flowed forth from thee became Shu, and that which was emitted by thee became Tefnut; thou didst create the nine gods at the beginning of all things, and thou was the Lion God of the Twin Lion Gods.' The twin lion gods were Shu and Tefnut. Together they were sometimes known as the Aker gods, the lions of yesterday and today, facing away from one another. Tefnut represented the setting sun, while Shu represented its rising.

Shu is sometimes depicted as a lion or a lion-headed man, but his usual form is that of a man wearing upon his head one, two or four feathers. The symbol of the feather is the hieroglyph for his name. The Egyptians believed he was the space that existed between the sky and the earth, and he was therefore shown in sculptures and reliefs as a figure kneeling upon one knee, lifting up the disc of the sun with two hands. Sometimes he is shown without feathers on his head, but in their place will be found a decoration that represents the hind quarters of a lion. As well as personifying dryness, or dry heat or air, Shu was a god of light. He was light personified, who manifested in the rays of the sun by day and the beams of the moon at night. He was also regarded as life itself, because of the life-breath of Ra which gave rise to him.

Like her brother, Tefnut can be shown in pure animal form as a lioness or as a full human, but is most often depicted as a lioness-headed woman. She wears a solar disc on her head, frequently decorated with a uraeus serpent, and carries an *ankh* and a sceptre. Generally, she appears very similar to Sekhmet, but some sources say that Sekhmet always has rounded ears while Tefnut's tend to be squared off.

After their 'birth', Shu and Tefnut became separated from their father and were lost in the Nun, the vast primeval waters that existed before the world was created. Atum sent his eye to look for his children, and once they were found, he named Shu as Life and

Tefnut as Order, powerful natural forces.

Shu and Tefnut lay entwined with their father in the Nun, where he kept them safe from harm. But eventually Atum tired of this inert existence and asked the Nun how he could create a more congenial resting place for himself. The Nun said to him, 'Kiss your daughter, Order, put her to your nose; so will your heart live. Never let her leave you. Let Order, who is your daughter, be with your son, Shu, who is Life.'

Atum then asked Shu to support him while he held Tefnut 'to his nose', which we can suppose is a euphemism for kissing her, or perhaps something more. From this act, the Iunu, the first solid mound to rise from the waters of the Nun, came into being and Atum was able to rest comfortably upon it. The *Pyramid Texts* tell us that this primal mound was called the High Hill in Iunu, and that it was actually a form of Atum himself. Only when he appeared as, or on, this hill did the first light break over the eternal darkness of the Nun.

Shu and Tefnut became lovers and produced two children, Geb, the earth, and Nut, the sky. We can see in this myth how the Egyptians imagined the creation of the earth. First there was air (Shu) and moisture (Tefnut), and when these elements came together the world came into being, creating earth and sky.

The Egyptians often represented the universe by showing Shu standing with his arms raised to support the outstretched body of a woman. The woman is Nut, his daughter the sky, and she usually wears a long dress covered with stars. A man lies prone at Shu's feet and this is Geb, his son the earth. Shu separated earth from sky, which in the legend created problems.

While still in the womb, Nut had been in conflict with her mother, Tefnut, and when the time came to be born, freed herself violently. As Shu and Tefnut had done before them, Geb and Nut became lovers. Nut placed herself on top of the earth god Geb, and there are representations of this act in Egyptian art. Geb is generally shown prone, sometimes with an erect phallus, while Nut arches over him.

Nut becomes pregnant, but Shu, the god of air, became jealous. He put one foot on Geb, pinning him down on his back, while he lifted Nut aloft with his arms. He tore them apart, and through this act, the earth became separated from the sky by air.

Shu's jealousy knew no bounds. Eventually Nut gave birth to her and Geb's children, who were the sun, the stars and the planets.

She placed them on her belly to protect them, perhaps so that Shu could not reach them. Shu, however, was incensed that his cherished daughter had born children to her brother Geb. In his rage, he cursed her. He decreed that she could never again be delivered of a child in any month in any year.

Nut was naturally furious about this and decided she must do something about the curse. The legend says that she had another lover, Thoth, who among his other attributes was associated with time. She challenged him to a game of dice, which she won. She demanded from Thoth five extra days, which were separate from the normal year. This part of the myth shows how the Egyptians explained away the five extra, or epagomenal days, which they added to their calendar of three hundred and sixty days (see Chapter 3). On these days, as they were not part of the normal year, Nut was able to give birth again. It was said that on the first day she bore Osiris, on the second Horus (the elder), on the third Set, on the fourth Isis and on the fifth Nephthys. Eventually, Osiris married his sister Isis, and Set married Nephthys. Atum, his children, his grandchildren and his great-grandchildren became known as the Great Ennead of Iunu. 'Ennead' literally means 'a company of nine', but in Egyptian myth an Ennead sometimes comprised more, or less, deities than this figure. In some versions of the Atum myth the god has only four great-grandchildren and Horus the Elder is omitted.

It is tempting to think that this ancient story was partly based upon truth, not in the sense of supernatural beings performing supernatural acts, but in that it might have derived from a dim memory of an early dynasty of kings. The legend goes on to tell us that Shu became King of Egypt, where he ruled for many years. As he grew older, he lost his power, becoming weak in his body and his eyes. As he was no longer able to exert control, his followers began to fight amongst themselves. More importantly, now that his father had lost his strength, Geb was able to exact a revenge for the time when Shu had separated him from his beloved, the sky goddess. It is said that Geb also envied his father's kingship.

Perhaps seeking sanctuary from his warring people and his dangerous son, Shu departed to a heavenly realm, along with those of his followers who were still loyal to him. Once he had left the earth, darkness fell upon it and a terrible, howling wind sprang up. For nine days it was so dark that people could not even see one another. Then, after this time, the wind died down and the light returned. Geb chose this moment to ascend the throne of his father and everyone in the royal palace bowed down before him. He now became King of Egypt, while Shu took his place among the gods as an attendant of Ra or Atum.

Another legend continues the story of this royal/divine family, and is probably of later origin than the original myth, perhaps with Greek influences. It was said that once Shu had left Egypt but before Geb became king, Geb fell in love with Tefnut, his mother. He went to where she lived in the palace at Memphis, and here forced himself upon her. The story goes that he raped her with great violence, but was not punished for it by man or god. He simply became king in Shu's place, since by taking the king's wife for himself, Geb could become king. To him, it was apparently irrelevant that the woman concerned was his mother, and the part of the story that tells us he 'fell in love with Tefnut' does not exactly ring true.

At this point, the story ends; nothing remains to tell us what happened to Tefnut. However, there is another, very early surviving legend about her, which concerns the time when Ra ruled on the Earth as King of Egypt. Tefnut was known as the Eye of Ra, just as Sekhmet, Bast and Hathor were later on. This story is very similar to the legend of Sekhmet's atrocities against humankind.

For some reason, which was not recorded, Tefnut became estranged from her father and fled into Nubia, where she transformed herself into a lioness. She raged through the countryside, emitting flames from her eyes and nostrils. Viciously, she drank the blood and fed on the flesh of both animals and humans. It is conceivable that this legend speaks of a time of drought in Egypt, when moisture went away and was replaced by cruel, murderous heat, and the other gods had to persuade the goddess of moisture to return.

As time went on, Ra missed his Eye, and longed to see her again. He summoned Shu to him, along with Thoth, who was the messenger of the gods and famous for his eloquence. Ra must have known that he would need his powers of persuasion to draw Tefnut back to him. Ra issued the command that Shu and Thoth must go to Nubia and bring back his recalcitrant daughter. Before they set off on their journey Shu and Thoth disguised themselves as baboons, an animal sacred to Thoth.

Eventually, they found Tefnut in Begum. Thoth began at once to try and persuade her to return to Egypt. Tefnut, however, was not interested. She liked hunting in the desert and was perfectly happy where she was. Thoth would not give up though, and wove stories to show her how gloom had descended upon Egypt since she had left. The people clearly needed her. Thoth also promised that the game she so loved hunting would be piled high for her on the altars in Egypt. She would not have to hunt for herself again. The people of Egypt would do anything for her if she would just return home. Ultimately, wooed by Thoth's promises, Tefnut relented and returned to Egypt accompanied by the two baboons. All the way there, Thoth kept her entertained with stories.

Tefnut made a triumphant entry into the homeland, accompanied by a host of Nubian musicians, dancers and baboons. She went from city to city, amid great rejoicing, until finally she was reunited with her father, and restored to her rightful position as his Eye.

It was a common fear in many ancient cultures that when the sun disappeared at night it might never return. Similarly, when it lost its heat in winter, the people did not have the scientific knowledge to be assured of its return. Consequently, they constructed myths to help them understand these frightening processes. The return of Tefnut to Egypt symbolized the miraculous return of the sun, auguring a period of warmth and light after a period of darkness or a season of lifelessness.

In the *Pyramid Texts*, Tefnut is credited with creating pure water for the king's feet from her vagina. She was responsible for the pharoah's Delta residence and there created a pool for him. One of her titles is 'the lady of Heaven', while another is 'the distant one', which refers to the period when she was in Nubia.

According to Budge, Tefnut was originally a goddess of gentle rain and soft wind, and later became identified with other goddesses, of whom some if not all were associated with lionesses, such as Nehemauit at Hermopolis, Menhit at Latopolis, Sekhmet in Memphis and Apsit in Nubia.

Shu and Tefnut generally have to be regarded as one entity, as they were reputed to share a soul. Dendera was known as Per-Shu, which means 'the house of Shu', Apolloninus Magna was called Hinu-en-Shu-nefer, Edfu was 'the seat of Shu' and one name for Memphis was 'palace of Shu'. A part of Dendera was also known as 'the house of Tefnut'. We do not know whether there were statues of Shu and Tefnut in these cities, but it is probable that they were worshipped throughout the land in the form of lions. The people of Heliopolis kept sacred lions in the temple of Helios.

94

Tefnut did not venture into Africa just in legends. She became a popular goddess in Kush and Nubia, where she was credited with being the wife of local deities such as Apedemak and Arensnuphis. She was also known there as a wife of Thoth.

Some researchers now believe that the site of the sphinx in Giza is that of the first creation of the primal mound. At one time, it would have been surrounded by water, the sacred lake or Nun. Shu and Tefnut, as lions, guarded the eastern and western horizons. As lion of the eastern horizon Shu supervised the rising of the sun each morning, while Tefnut, the lion of the western horizon, guarded the sun by night. It has been suggested by the Egyptian writer Bassam El-Shammaa, with convincing conjecture, that at one time there were two sphinxes. The existing one was Shu looking out to the east, but there was another one which represented Tefnut looking out to the west, and has now been destroyed or buried. Perhaps if further study and excavations take place, evidence will be found to support this claim.

When we first began performing visualizations concerning Tefnut, our group was surprised by the rich imagery we received. We felt that here was a goddess eager to make contact, who in some ways yearned for human attention. The results of our initial quest into Tefnut are given later, but every person present received the strong impression that Tefnut felt she had been ignored long enough. We were all asked to return to her domain again, which we did.

For us, Tefnut is a goddess of knowledge, in that she has the wisdom of the source of creation. She is a teacher who can lead the way along the path of development or initiation. She cannot really be seen as a lunar goddess *per se*, even though she is associated with water and the sky at night. She is the setting sun, the evening, the guardian of the dark hours, the mistress of the primal waters.

According to Lawrence Durdin-Robertson, in his book, *Year of the Goddess*, 21 May can be regarded as a feast day to Tefnut. This is because in the Dendera Zodiac, Gemini, the twins, is represented by Shu and Tefnut.

Tutu

Tutu was a son of Neith, who was represented in two feline forms: one as a human-headed sphinx, and another as a lion-headed man. From inscriptions at Philae, we learn that he was 'great of strength, the champion, pre-eminent in Biggeh, great of roaring, strong of arms' and 'mighty of power, who is over the gods, and who overthrows Apep'.

Many leonine deities were credited with being 'great of roaring', and when this phrase is found in a god's name, it is a good indication that he had a leonine form. Tutu, in slaying the serpent Apep, is similar to Ra in his feline form. He could also have a wholly human appearance.

Urt-hekau

The name of this lioness goddess, also written as Weret Hekau, is very much associated with magic, and means 'mighty one of words of power'. This was also a title of Nephthys, so this goddess could well be an aspect of her. She was also said to be 'the protective power of the Eye of Horus', and had associations with Neith.

Usit

Usit was a lioness-headed goddess of the tenth hour of the night.

Wadjet

Wadjet, also known as Uatchet, Udjat or Edjo, is primarily a cobra goddess, similar in some respects to Meretseger. And like her, Wadjet has a lioness-headed aspect. Her name means 'she who is

green', and she was a protectress goddess of Lower Egypt as well as being one of the goddesses of the four directions, in her case north. She is the uraeus, the snake who adorns the royal crown of pharaohs, when she is shown rearing up in a protective manner. Wadjet is often accompanied by the vulture goddess Nekhbet, and indeed many of the crowns of Egyptian queens bore representations of both cobra and vulture.

6

Felines from the Mists of Time

Dreaming, the noble postures they assume
Of sphinxes stretching out into the gloom
That seems to swoon into an endless trance.
From 'Cats' by Charles Baudelaire

Apart from the gods and goddesses we described in the previous chapter, there are certain other feline-associated deities and super-natural creatures in the Egyptian belief system, and these are described in this chapter.

The Ogdoad

As we have seen, the Egyptians did not have one strictly defined creation story or body of myths. Although Ra or Atum is described in one legend as the first of all gods, there are other stories which contradict this. According to Budge, the Ogdoad, which comprises eight gods, is the oldest of all Egyptian divine companies, and existed in religious thought long before any others. They form the basis of the creation myth of Hermopolis, whereas the story of Atum, Tefnut and Shu derived from Heliopolis. Worship of the Ogdoad did not become as popular or widespread as that of the Heliopolitan gods, which suggests that the priesthood of Heliopolis ultimately had more influence and power than their Hermopolitan counterparts.

According to the legend of the Ogdoad, at the beginning of time only chaos existed before the world came into being. This chaos possessed four characteristics, which were personified by four pairs of male and female deities. Budge describes them as 'personifications of aspects, or phases, or properties of primeval matter'. Although they are represented in various physical forms, the males were generally snake- or frog-headed, while the females had the heads either of frogs or cats. This feline connection justifies their place in this book, but the story itself is fascinating and adds to our understanding of Egyptian myth.

The goddesses of the Ogdoad are seen as completely equal to the gods and not merely child-bearers, as later goddesses often were.

Nu and Nut

Also known as Nun and Nunet, the only clues we have as to what these gods represented are from the hieroglyphs of their names. Nu's name includes three vases of water and the symbol of outstretched heaven, which Budge suggests meant he was the god of the 'watery mass of the sky'. Nut was Nu's female counterpart, and her name includes the same symbols. This Nut is not to be confused with the daughter of Shu and Tefnut, even though she does possess certain similarities.

As with most Egyptian deities, Nu and Nut were portrayed in different forms. Nu had a human aspect, when he carried a sceptre, but he also appeared with the head of a beetle-crowned frog or a snake. Nut was also shown as being entirely human, but sometimes she was depicted as having the head of a uraeus – a snake – crowned by a disc, or else as having the head of a cat.

In the previous chapter, on the section on Tefnut, we described how the Egyptians believed that before the world came into being all that existed was a boundless primeval ocean, and that the sky, the air and the earth derived from it. This belief is also part of the legend of the Ogdoad. In this deep ocean existed all the components that would later form every kind of animal and plant, which had lain dormant in the fertile soup since the beginning of time. The watery mass was supposed to lie between the sky and the heavens above it. Nu and Nut represented this strange floating mass. We could call them the god and goddess of the primordial water.

Later, Nu's position shifted, as he was identified with both the heavens and the sky that lay above and below the primeval ocean. Later still, he became identified with the River Nile and the earthly ocean. His name is similar to the Coptic word for 'abyss' or 'deep'.

Budge suggests that Nu was the inert mass of watery matter

from which the world was created. Nut was the primeval mother, and in later times several goddesses were identified with her, such as Hathor, Mut and Neith.

Hehu and Hehut

Also known as Heh and Hehet, the characteristics of this pair have not been as fully defined as those of Nu and Nut. The Italian Egyptologist Lanzone believed they were personifications of the male and female elements of fire, but the actual meaning seems to be so rarefied and vague that it is difficult to judge. Like Nu and Nut, Hehu could have the head of a serpent or a frog, and Hehut the head of a cat or a frog.

Another Egyptologist, Dr H. Brugsch, equated Hehu with a god called Heh, whose name means an undefined or unlimited number. When this name is applied to the concept of time, we end up with the idea of millions of years. Brugsch also wrote of a god named Heh who, like Shu, personified the atmosphere that lay between heaven and earth. Yet another interpretation of this pair's name is 'god and goddess of infinite space', so their characters are not very clear.

Kekui and Kekuit

Also known as Kek and Kekhet, this pair most likely represented the male and female powers of the great darkness that lay over the primeval ocean. They have also been credited with representing both night and day. Again, we use Budge's interpretation; he cites Kekui's name as meaning 'the raiser up of the light' and Kekuit's as 'the raiser up of the night'. He goes on to tell us that Kekui represented 'that period of night which immediately precedes the day, and Kekuit the period of the night which immediately follows the day', which would mean dusk or twilight. Like the other members of the Ogdoad, they could have the head of a serpent or a beetle-crowned frog and the head of a frog or a cat respectively.

Kerh and Kerhet

Also known as Amun and Amunet, these gods are also surrounded by an aura of vagueness, in that no one really knows what they represented, though Egyptologists have had a stab at guessing.

They have been called the god and goddess of invisibility. Budge decided that as the word 'kerh' meant 'night', so Kerh and Kerhet represented the male and female powers of night. To confuse things further, he tells us they were also regarded as 'personifications of some apparently inactive owers of the primeval watery abyss, and may therefore be regarded as types of powers of nature in a state of repose, either before or after a state of activity'. Perhaps we can interpret this as meaning that they represent the potential for creation in nature, or the creative process before it begins to manifest and after its work is done. Like the rest of their company, Kerh and Kerhet could appear with the head of a frog (with or without beetle) or a serpent and the head of a frog or a cat respectively.

It is difficult to define exactly what these gods represented. Some writers have attempted to make the four pairs personify the elements as known in the Western tradition (earth, air, fire and water), but these attributes can only be tenuously assigned to them at best. It is perhaps truer to the spirit of ancient Egyptian belief to see them as personifying the universal energies from which all things come into being. Budge describes this quite poetically: '[They] stand for the primeval Matter out of which all things have been made, and primeval Space, primeval Time and primeval Power.'

The Ogdoad can be seen as the elements of chaos from which the world emerged. The first thing to be created was the primal mount of Hermopolis. An egg was deposited on the mound and from it came a mighty solar god who set about expanding creation.

Monstrous animal gods

As we have seen, the Egyptians were fond of creating composite deities, where the attributes and features of several gods might be fused together, in order that their separate characteristics could be united as a potent whole. Their gods usually had a quasi-human form, if not always fully human, but they also devised a bestiary of strange supernatural creatures which combined the aspects of different animals.

To the ancient people, the grace and strength of the lion must have seemed magical. Similarly, the serpent was regarded as unnaturally cunning and clever, whereas humans did not have those attributes to the same degree. People can only judge 'what is' by their own experience; to the Egyptians anything they did not have in their own make-up must have been supernatural in origin. It is no wonder that they ascribed divine connections to creatures that could kill them, such as snakes, scorpions, lions and crocodiles. Perhaps if the spiritual ruler of these creatures was appeased and worshipped, they would be less likely to cause trouble for humans.

The creatures described below may have been dreamed up as demons or spirits, or else they may be assumptions of exotic animals from far lands. Even in Western history, maps were drawn that included all manner of monstrous beings, such as hippogriffs, basilisks and manticores, which were supposed to live in foreign countries.

A nameless creature

There was a creature with no recorded name, which reputedly had the appearance of a leopard, although pictures we have seen suggest that it was based on a cheetah, for the shape resembles that animal more. From the middle of its back sprouts a winged human head, which represents the fact that the creature had human intelligence, coupled with the strength and grace of a feline.

Sak

Sak was represented as having eight teats, like a lioness. Her forequarters were leonine, but her hindquarters were those of a hoofed animal, probably a horse. She had a long tail ending in a spiked tuft, which resembled feathers or the petals of a flower. Her head was that of a hawk and around her neck she wore a collar from which a long spike poked out. She represented strength, agility, speed and perhaps the keen sight of the hawk.

Sefer

Sefer had the body of a lion, which was winged, and the head of an eagle, looking very similar to the griffin of Western beliefs. It had the strength of a lion and the swift flight of a bird.

Setcha

This creature had the body of a leopard and the head and neck of a serpent, combining the cunning of a snake with the lithe and powerful grace of the feline.

Sphinx

The best known of all composite animal forms, owing to the great monument which still lies upon the Giza plateau, is the sphinx. Sphinxes generally had leonine bodies and human heads, although some had rams' heads, (in which case they are termed criosphinxes) or hawks' heads (hieracosphinxes).

The sphinx is found in the mythology of other ancient cultures. In Greece, it had the head and breasts of a woman and the body of a winged lion. The Greek sphinx was a ferocious creature, fond of asking riddles. If anyone failed to come up with the right answer, she would devour them. In Babylonian mythology, the sphinx appears as a winged human-headed bull or lion, generally with a long beard.

Egyptian kings were often portrayed as sphinxes, to represent their royal power, their greatness and their function as protectors of the land.

Having established the names and attributes of the gods and other creatures, it is time to move on and begin to interact with them, specifically Bast and Sekhmet. But first, some knowledge of basic magical techniques is required.

7

Breath, the Purr of Life

When the inner senses are fully awake, we may see visions of extraordinary beauty, smell the blossoms of the Isle of Apples, taste ambrosia and hear the songs of the gods.

From *The Spiral Dance* by Starhawk

Before we become involved in full-scale meditations and rituals, it is essential to learn how to breathe correctly and visualize imagery.

The breath of life

Through breathing we absorb the energy of the universe. This could be said to be the basic building block of magic, if not of life. In order to work with this energy, it has to flow freely and unimpeded through our bodies, and one of the ways to achieve this is through breathing deeply and fully. All too often, the stresses of life cause us to breathe in a quick, shallow way; we rarely take time to sit down and concentrate on it. For a thorough study of life energy and how to understand and work with it, we recommend the book *The Inward Revolution* by Deborah Benstead and Storm Constantine. The exercises that follow are derived from this work, as they are the techniques used by the authors' temple group.

At the beginning of any magical working, you should take a few minutes to concentrate on your breathing. This helps alter your state of consciousness and also improves the flow of life energy within the body. If you are new to magic, some time should be spent practising the techniques outlined below before embarking upon any of the other exercises or rushing to the ritual working part. The exercises can be performed safely once or twice a day. They can be looked upon as the preliminary moves in a kind of 'psychic workout'. If you have not done work of this nature before, you need to tone up your psychic muscles. In the same way that physical exercise has to be built up gradually, it does us no good to try and perform long and complex visualizations without warming up or gaining flexibility and stamina. The best that can happen is that the results will not be very good, and the worst is that you can end up with psychic 'cramp'. Too much meditational work too soon can leave you feeling disorientated and even slightly depressed.

Just about every system of magic advocates the use of a magical diary. It is important to record the results of exercises, workings and rituals, not only so that you can see a progression in your work, but also as a reference book should you need to look back on or repeat anything. Some people like to use a beautiful book with blank pages, in which they neatly write up their entries, while others prefer to record the results of their work on computer. It really does not matter which method you choose, the important thing is that nothing is lost or forgotten.

If you think you will find it difficult to learn the instructions for any of the exercises that follow by heart, you can record them on a portable tape recorder and then play them back. Remember to talk slowly while you are recording and leave gaps where appropriate. Give yourself plenty of time to relax and experience the effects of the exercise. Alternatively, you can ask someone else to read the exercises out to you.

Do the exercises in a quiet place, at a time when you are not likely to be disturbed. The breathing exercises can also be performed in bed before you go to sleep, or else while you are in the bath. Make sure you are comfortable, and wear loose-fitting clothes. Make sure you feel warm, or cool, enough.

You can either sit with a straight spine in a comfortable chair or lie down. Choose whichever is best for you. Your torso should be erect when sitting, or comfortably stretched when lying down, to enable your breath to flow freely.

Bright lights can sometimes impede mental concentration, so it is best to do the exercises with the curtains drawn and the lights dimmed, or by candlelight. If you wish, you can play soft music in the background.

Breathing down

1. Lie or sit down. Close your eyes as if you are preparing to go to sleep. Breathe normally but slowly for a while.
2. Now listen to yourself breathe. Become aware of your chest rising and falling, feel the rhythmic movement it creates.
3. After a couple of minutes, begin to breathe more deeply, taking the breaths in through your nose and out through your mouth.
4. Continue to breathe as deeply as you can for another couple of minutes, listening to the increased noise that deeper breathing creates.
5. Try to concentrate on your breathing, keeping it as regular and deep as you can, ignoring any distracting thoughts that may come into your mind.
6. The next stage is to breathe in through the nose for the count of ten seconds, then out through the mouth for the count of eleven.
7. On the next breath, inhale for nine seconds and exhale for ten.
8. Now inhale for eight seconds, and exhale for nine.
9. Inhale for seven seconds, exhale for eight.
10. Inhale for six seconds, exhale for seven.
11. Inhale for five seconds, exhale for six.
12. Inhale for four seconds, exhale for five.
13. Inhale for three seconds, exhale for four.
14. Inhale for two seconds, exhale for three.
15. Inhale for one second, exhale for two.
16. Inhale again and gently hold your breath for the count of three before breathing out.
17. Resume normal breathing.

If you find starting with a count of eleven too difficult, just start at a lower number.

Practise this exercise until you feel adept at it. You may experience some physical effects, such as a tingling sensation that starts in the eyes and face and spreads down throughout the chest. This is nothing to worry about, as it indicates that your energy is flowing more freely inside your body. The idea behind doing this exercise is to relax, calm the mind and improve the flow of energy.

Record the results of the exercise in your diary. Write down everything you felt and experienced, as well as any thoughts you had about it.

Breathing up

This exercise is very similar to the first one, except that the breaths get longer rather than shorter.

1. Start by breathing deeply and regularly, again becoming aware of the sound and movement of breath in and out of the body.
2. This time breathe sharply in for the count of two and out for the count of one.
3. Increase the counts by inhaling on the next breath for the count of three and out for the count of two, then in for four and out for three, and so on.
4. As you increase the counts, your breath will change from short sharp bursts to deep inhalations.
5. As the inhalations become longer, so do the exhalations, but keep the out breath one count below the in at all times.
6. Do this until you have reached the maximum count for an inhalation you can manage. When you reach maximum inhalation point, breathe at that level deeply for as long as you can. You may start to feel that fuzzy feeling begin to spread from the mouth to the eyes, face and then the chest.

You can stop this exercise whenever you want to, although the longer you can manage it, the more effect it will have on the energy in your body. The best time to stop is indicated by a sense of dizziness. If at any point you feel light-headed, then stop the exercise by slowing down the rate of breath and gradually returning to a calm, regular rhythm.

If after this exercise you still feel over-excited or dizzy, slow your breathing right down by reverting to the breathing down exercise.

The point of this exercise is to enliven the energy in your body.

Again, record the results of the exercise in your diary.

Once a breathing exercise has been performed, your body and mind are in a relaxed yet enlivened, open state and you can then move on to the work in hand, whether that is a full-scale ritual or a simple meditation. Experience will tell you whether you need to do the breathing up exercise or the breathing down version before any given situation. A lot depends on your state of mind before you begin. If you feel tense and agitated, breathe down. If you feel lethargic and tired, breathe up.

Visualization

The next step in magical work is learning how to visualize. This involves using the imagination, but controlling it. When we visualize, we see ourselves in imaginary surroundings or are able to observe pictures in our mind that are not really there. It is similar to daydreaming, only more controlled. By closing our eyes and forming images of our choice, we begin to control our imaginations. As with dreaming, when you visualize you should be able to use all of your senses to experience what you 'see' around you.

The simple act of visualization can enable you to change reality. This might seem literally like magic, but if you can imagine that the energy in your own body is part of the universal energy, then you have the ability to affect energy outside yourself. It is like ripples in a pond. Any thoughts you have are expressions of energy in themselves. Through skilled visualization, you can direct that energy towards a specific effect.

There are a number of simple exercises you can do in order to improve your visualization skills. The first involves perceiving life energy as a white light. Once you feel proficient at this, you can move on to the next exercises, which will include more specific imagery. Skilled visualization involves more than just the sense of sight. In the exercises that follow, other senses will be brought into play, which will make all your magical work more immediate and vivid.

Before you begin any of the exercises, set aside some time when you know that you will not be disturbed. Make sure that you are warm and comfortable. You may find it much easier to begin visualizing in a darkened room with no background music – the fewer distractions you have around you, the easier it is to concentrate on forming the images. If you find that you cannot hold a picture in your mind and that you begin thinking of other things, simply spend a few seconds clearing your mind, then either start the visualization again or begin where you left off. Many people find learning to visualize quite difficult at first – they close their eyes and await an amazing vision, which never appears. During visualization, pictures rarely come to you in a flash of psychic inspiration. You have to use your imagination and your will in order to build them. To visualize well you have to learn to create scenes in your imagination. Once you have mastered this, the scenes you create often take on a life of their own and inspired information may come your way.

In most of the rituals and workings in this book visualization plays a large and crucial part. Obviously, when you perform a visualization in order to meet a deity in their temple, you should be able to visualize strongly, but the ability becomes even more vital when you are performing a ritual to effect some kind of change. It is essential that you are able to envisage the result that you require clearly and accurately.

The hidden light

This is the most basic of all visualization exercises, in which you will perceive your natural life energy as light. Once you can visualize it clearly, you will have more control over its flow within your body. Before beginning, perform the breathing down exercise.

1. Start by inhaling for a count of ten and exhaling for a count of eleven – or at a lower number if you prefer.
2. As before, reduce the count with each breath, but make sure you exhale longer than you inhale.
3. When you reach the count of one for breathing in, gently hold your breath and then resume normal breathing.
4. Now maintain a slow and steady rate of breathing, ensuring that it is still deep but gentle.
5. For a few moments, visualize that a cloud of radiant white, sparkling light is hanging over your head. Then imagine that when you breathe in through the nose, you are inhaling this light. Try to perceive the air going into your nostrils as a stream of white glittery light.
6. As you carry on breathing, visualize the light travelling up your nose and down through your throat into your chest. Try to not only see this light, but to feel what it would be like to breathe it. It might be cool or warm, or induce other sensations – it is up to your individual imagination.
7. Steadily continue to visualize the light going in through your nose and down into your body. Feel it expanding your chest

and swirling around within you. The inside of your body is best visualized as complete blackness, a dark void. Do not focus on the physical contents of it – organs, blood, bones and such like – but imagine it as empty and completely black. You are an empty vessel, like a bottle being filled with the radiance of liquid light.

8. Visualize the light going down further into your stomach area, into your legs and feet, and upwards and outwards into your head and arms. Observe it moving into and filling every area of blackness inside you.

9. When your body is completely saturated with this white light, imagine that when you breathe out through your mouth, you exhale dirty air. As the white light leaves your body, it changes from a sparkling mist to a foggy grey smoke.

10. Begin to imagine that with each exhalation, the white light inside you is beginning to diminish. It is being used up, expelled as dirty smoke. Continue to do this, seeing the white light becoming dimmer and dimmer, until you feel that it has completely gone from your body.

There is no time limit to this exercise. It can take as little or as much time as you need.

If this is the first time you have attempted a visualization of this type, you might find it difficult to keep the image consistent in your mind. Do not worry about this. It gets better with practice. To start with, you could practise visualizing the light only when you breathe in, or else when you breathe out. The exercise will become easier the more you do it, but it is not a good idea to attempt it more than a couple of times in each session, otherwise you might end up feeling a bit disorientated.

Write about your experiences in your magical diary.

This is actually a cleansing exercise, during which you take vibrant free-flowing energy into your body from outside, and 'clean out' any stagnant energy from within.

The Tree of Life

Similar to the hidden light, this exercise also helps you to enliven yourself with natural life energy from the environment. This time, the visualization aspect of the exercise is slightly more advanced. This is a classic visualization exercise, and there are many variations, but this version is a favourite of our own group. If space and the weather permit you may enjoy performing it outside.

In order to get the most from this exercise, try to sit up straight and stretch your spine gently. If you find this position uncomfortable to maintain unsupported, lean against a chair or the wall. If you find any part of it difficult to imagine, just concentrate on one image at a time until you feel you can picture it easily. Take as long as you need for each stage, before you move onto the next.

1. Begin by breathing deeply and slowly. Breathe in through your nose for the count of three, hold the breath for three and then breathe out through your mouth for the count of three.
2. Continue this for a few minutes until you feel calm and relaxed. When you feel ready, close your eyes and check that your spine is still straight.
3. Now try and imagine that your spine is the trunk of a tree. From its base you can feel roots beginning to extend down into the earth. At first they are only small, but they begin to grow quickly. Feel them growing into the earth beneath you, anchoring you. Really see yourself as a tree. Your arms are branches hanging at your side. Imagine that like real tree roots, the roots growing from you into the earth can draw up natural energy into your body. Visualize that deep beneath you, in the earth, is a reservoir of energy. When your roots reach it they can carry it back up to nourish you.
4. Begin to feel the energy rising up through your roots. Feel it as it rises up your spine like sap rising through the trunk of a tree. Each breath you take draws the sap up higher through the 'trunk' of your spine. As it rises, it seeps outwards and fills your whole body with energy. Concentrate on breathing deeply and pulling the energy up from the earth until it fills you right up to the top of your head. You may need to spend a few minutes doing this.
5. When you feel that the energy-giving sap has reached the crown of your head imagine that you have new branches beginning to sprout from the top of your head. See them grow, small and green with new leaves. Let them grow longer until they begin to sweep down again like the branches of a weeping willow.
6. Continue to visualize the drooping willow-like branches

growing until they are so long that they reach the ground beside you.

7. When they touch the ground visualize that you are part of a circuit of natural energy. You draw it up from the base of your trunk and return it through the tips of your branches. Spend a few minutes visualizing this clearly.

8. When you feel ready to end the visualization, imagine that you can suck in the energy from your branches as if you were sucking through a straw. Take a deep breath and suck it back in. As you do this imagine that as the energy leaves your branches they begin to fade away.

9. When they have gone take another deep breath and suck the sap back down the tree truck and let it flow back into the earth.

10. When all the sap has returned to the earth let the image of yourself as a tree fade. Visualize yourself sitting on the ground. You are relaxed and revitalized. When you are ready, open your eyes and return to normal consciousness.

This exercise may take some time to perfect but once you can visualize it clearly while maintaining controlled breathing, you are ready to try more advanced exercises.

All the visualizations that follow can be undertaken on their own or with any of the preceding exercises. As with any other work, remember to record your experiences in your diary.

The eye of the cat

1. Sitting comfortably, close your eyes and begin to breathe deeply and slowly. When you feel relaxed try to visualize a huge black screen before you. See it as a cinema screen, filling your vision.

2. When this is clear in your mind, see two pinpricks of pale green light appear on the screen.

3. Now imagine the lights expanding until they are no longer pinpricks but shining, almond-shaped cat's eyes. See the black slit of the pupil, the flecks of gold amongst the green. Concentrate on the image until it is clear. If you lose it or become distracted just wait a couple of moments and begin again.

4. Once you can picture the eyes easily, imagine that they slowly close and you are left with a blank screen before you.

Practise this exercise any time. Once you are proficient at it, you can make it harder by seeing the eyes blink, or imagining that the light varies and the pupils change from tiny slits to huge black discs.

The image of the cat

1. Start as before with some deep breathing until you feel ready to begin.
2. Close your eyes and visualize yourself sitting outside on a stretch of grass. This could be your own garden, a park you know well or even somewhere totally imaginary.
3. When you can see your surroundings clearly, imagine that you are watching a cat make its way towards you. It can be any cat, Siamese or tabby, long-haired or short, large or small. Try to see all of the cat, in as much detail as possible. What colour are its eyes? Are its ears tattered and scratched from fighting? What colour are its whiskers or the pads on its paws?
4. When you know everything about the appearance of the cat, visualize picking it up in your arms. Is it heavy? Can you hear it purr? Stroke its fur. How does it feel? Imagine that you are rubbing its chin. Does it close its eyes or stretch out its neck?
5. Hold the cat up close and smell its fur. Is it perfumed? Musky? Spend as much time as you need building up as complete a picture as you can.
6. When you feel satisfied that you are visualizing clearly, see yourself putting the cat down on the ground. See it wander off again across the grass until it disappears from view.
7. When you feel ready, open your eyes.

Record any impressions you may have in your diary.

You may find that the cat you see is one which lives with you, or one you knew which died. Other people who have done this visualization have ended up with a kind of cat familiar who appears to them regularly in other visualizations.

Experiencing the inner landscape

For this exercise you will again visualize meeting a cat, but this time you will follow it on a journey through an imaginary landscape. Practising this technique will help you create clear images of different surroundings, a skill required for the visualizations and rituals described later.

Repeat this exercise as often as you can, until you feel you are adept at moving through visualized landscapes and communicating with an entity you meet there.

As with the other exercises make sure that you will not be disturbed and then spend some time breathing deeply and clearing your mind of every day worries.

1. When you feel relaxed, imagine that you are standing at the edge of a wood. Ahead of you there is a small path that has been worn by the many feet that have walked upon it. The path leads in among the trees. Follow it.

2. Once you are surrounded by trees, stop and look around. What season is it? Is the foliage the lush green of early summer or the rich red of autumn? Is the ground covered in leaves or is there a carpet of verdant ferns underfoot? Is the wood made up of ancient oaks or tall pines? Take a few moments to take in your surroundings. Experience as vividly as you can the sights, smells and sounds of the wood. Reach out and touch the rough bark of the trees, feel the texture of the leaves. Visualize the horizon, the edge of your vision, as far as you can see. Then imagine you can see twice as far again. This really helps expand your perception.

3. When you feel that you have built up a really clear picture in your mind, imagine that you can hear a rustling in the undergrowth. Which direction is the sound coming from? Find the movement with your eyes as well as your ears.

4. When you can see which section of undergrowth is moving, watch it carefully. See a cat appear there. What does the cat look like? Build up a clear picture in your mind.

5. When you can see the cat clearly, you know that you should follow it. How does the cat communicate with you? Do you hear a voice in your head or is the communication in the way the cat looks at you? Follow the cat deeper into the wood.

6. Now spend some time visualizing your journey through the wood with your feline companion. Where does it take you? Does it want to show you something or does it have a message for you?

7. When you feel ready to end the visualization tell your guide that you wish to return to the beginning of the path. Imagine that

the cat leads you back out of the wood, to the point from which you began the visualization.

8. When you reach the edge of the wood, thank the cat for its company. See it wandering back into the undergrowth until you can no longer see it. You can only hear the faint rustlings as it moves away from you.

9. When you are ready, picture yourself back in your own environment and open your eyes.

The next time you perform this visualization, try imagining a different setting, such as an arid desert, a cool, dark temple or even a busy city park – anything that appeals to you.

By now controlled breathing and visualization should have become a little easier to master. If you are experiencing any problems do not become discouraged. Some people are naturally adept at visualizing, while some have to strive to 'see' anything at all. Do not worry too much if you find it difficult at first. With a little time and practice, anyone can learn this skill. You might find that you have a preferential sense. Some of our group tend to 'feel' things rather than see them. Others find their sense of smell or hearing prevails over that of sight. The most important thing is to pick up impressions which you can later interpret and analyse.

8

Bringing the
Sacred Home

The tools, the physical objects we use ... are the tangible
representatives of unseen forces. The mind works magic,
and no elaborately forged knife or elegant wand can do any
more than augment the power of a trained mind. The tools
are simply aids in communicating with Younger Self, who
responds much better to tangibles than to abstracts.
From: *The Spiral Dance* by Starhawk

Creating a shrine

When people first begin working magically, many like to create a
shrine in their own home to a favourite god or goddess, or build an
altar for general magical purposes. Apart from anything else, it is
practical to have a permanent location for your magical equipment.
In our case, shrines just formed around our statues because it
seemed natural to place candles or flowers next to them.

Your shrine or altar will usually form the focal point of any magical working, so it should be constructed in the room where you
perform rituals and meditations. Alternatively, you could create a
portable altar which can be erected when needed; equipment can
be stored in a chest or cupboard reserved specifically for that
purpose. Not many of us have the luxury of a separate room that
we can set up as a permanent temple, so we have to adapt an area
in our living room or bedroom to serve as a ritual space. If this is
the case, then your altar could be anything from a coffee table in
your living room to a dressing table or cupboard in your bedroom.

The first thing to do is to choose the space in the home that best
suits your needs. One important consideration is whether or not

you are comfortable with your magical equipment being visible to guests. Many people choose to tuck their shrine away in a cupboard that can be kept closed when not in use, or, if they share a home with others who do not share their beliefs, do their workings in their bedroom. This is entirely a matter of personal preference. We have tended to use our living rooms simply because there is enough space to accommodate our temple group without a problem.

Altar placement

There are traditional (and conflicting) 'rules' of magic in the Western tradition that state which direction your altar should face. However, we do not feel that these rules should necessarily apply when performing rituals to Egyptian deities. It is important simply to do what you feel comfortable with, what feels right to you. One point that you may want to consider, however, is that it was customary in Egyptian temples to 'wake' the statue by exposing it to sunlight. For this reason, you might consider placing your altar in a position that receives the sun in the mornings, so that you can 'wake' your statue with sunlight every morning in keeping with ancient tradition. If this does not appeal to you then you may want to consider magical directions when you choose a position for your altar. Here are a few suggestions.

The east is the direction of the rising sun, while west is the sinking sun, and both were important aspects of Egyptian beliefs. Bast and Sekhmet were known as goddesses of the east and west respectively, which could play some part in deciding where you position your altar, depending on what ritual work you are doing. The south is associated with the fierce heat of noonday, so could be used as the direction of the Eyes of Ra in their most aggressive aspects. However, if circumstances limit your options, you may have to imagine what we call a 'magical east' or a 'magical west', which might have no bearing on the true direction at all.

Magical equipment

Once you have chosen the position for your altar and have acquired the right piece of furniture for it, you will have to decide what equipment you want to use. In the Western tradition, this might involve acquiring a vast array of artefacts, including wands, ritual costumes and knives, but this kind of paraphernalia is not essential for the rituals we have devised. Some equipment *is* needed, but it can be made cheaply if you do not want to purchase expensive ready-made items. As you build upon the rites suggested in this book, you might decide to add certain other 'props' to the ones we suggest, but this is really up to you.

First, you will need a representation of the god or goddess towards whom your ritual or meditation is directed. To begin with, you will certainly need an image of Bast, and then of Sekhmet. You can acquire images of other feline deities later, should you take your exploration of them further.

Your representation of the deity is the vessel that will become filled with the *heka* of the goddess, enabling you to interact with them on a personal level. This representation usually takes the form of a statue. Figurines of Bast and Sekhmet can be purchased from certain museum shops or good occult suppliers; some sources are listed in the back of this book. As for statues of other feline deities, Bes is fairly easy to come by, while others are more difficult. For most of the lioness-headed goddesses, figurines of Sekhmet can be substituted. We have acquired a statuette of a standing male lion-headed figure which is available in various occult shops, where it is generally sold as a representation of Sekhmet.

However, statues can be expensive, and if funds are tight it is acceptable to have a picture of the relevant deity as the centrepiece of your altar instead. This could be anything from a museum postcard to a colour photocopy of a book illustration or, if you have the skill, a painting you have created yourself. You should choose whatever suits your funds or creative abilities. You could even use an ornament of a cat or a lion to represent Bast and Sekhmet. Many of our statues have come to us as birthday gifts from friends and relatives who are aware of our beliefs. When a member of our temple group has a birthday, the rest of us club together to buy him or her an artefact or piece of equipment that would otherwise be too expensive.

The next step is to acquire candle-holders and an incense burner. Again, these do not have to break the bank – beautiful holders may be lovely to look at, but at the end of the day candles on saucers work just as well as the most expensive candlesticks. Similarly, a heatproof bowl filled with sand is just as practical as the most ornate incense burner. What you use is entirely up to you. This kind of equipment does not have to be costly; there are always bargains to be found in ethnic shops or on market stalls, so have a look around.

You will need at least three candlesticks, two for the altar and one to hold your own votive candle during ritual work. In our group, we use very small candles, about 4-6 inches long, as our votive candles. This is because one needs to let the candle burn away completely, and it is unsafe to leave a large candle unattended after you have gone to bed; small candles burn away in an hour or two. They can be difficult to find, but suppliers are again listed at the back of the book. However, if you cannot find any, large candles can be cut into smaller sections. If, for any reason, you decide to put out a candle that has been used in a ritual, snuff or pinch it out with wet fingers rather than blowing it. Blowing out candles is said to be disrespectful to the gods! This is just a superstition, but we have found that pinching out a candle, with the possibility of burning oneself, somehow seems more significant an act.

You will need a selection of different-coloured candles. The most important colour will be that of our own colour ray, which we describe in more detail in Chapter 9. For altar candles, we use red, orange, gold or yellow for Sekhmet, and blue, yellow, silver, green or purple for Bast. The colour we choose for each occasion depends on the ritual we are doing, or on the result we are looking for.

For the incense, you will need some self-igniting charcoal discs and some appropriate loose incenses or, if you intend to make your own, the relevant ingredients. There is more information on this in the appendix and in the suppliers' list. If you really cannot obtain loose incense and charcoals, joss sticks can be substituted, or better still pure essential oils which you can burn.

The statue, candles and incense are all props which psychologically help you to enter the state of mind required for a ritual or meditation. It might be possible to visualize the statue of Bast in her temple without having one in front of you at home, and you might also be able to imagine the exotic scent of incense and the soft light of candles. However, the real scent of incense smoke and the flicker of candles in front of a statue really do make you feel as if you are casting off the mundane in favour of the magical. They therefore have to be regarded as valuable tools. Nothing can replace a room you have carefully prepared for ritual work. We are humans who interact with the world through our five senses, and if we can stimulate them, the experience becomes all the more real for us.

For many of the rituals in this book, you will need a cup, goblet or glass for the wine offering, and a bowl for the food offerings. A wine glass and a cereal bowl are fine, but if the objects are aesthetically pleasing, it augments the appearance of your altar, which again helps create the right sense of occasion.

Altar cloths from occult suppliers are a nice touch but they are not essential. Alternatively, you can make one from a silk scarf or an off-cut of fabric. The colours for Bast and Sekhmet are the same as for the candles.

The sacred rattle

For rituals, you will also need a sistrum, or rattle, but these can be quite difficult to come by. In the meantime, you could use something like a small plastic tub or a glass jar filled with beads, dried beans or pasta; it will do the same job. Both tubs and jars can be painted in the colours and symbols of your choice. If you have the skill, you could try to make an authentic-looking sistrum, as used in the ancient temples.

The sistrum was shaken to make music for a goddess. It was sacred, in particular, to Hathor, Isis and Bast. Sistra, which were known as *sheshesht*, were made of either metal or faience, which was fashioned into a loop shape and threaded with three or four small rods. These rods would be strung with small metal discs, so that when the sistrum was shaken they rattled together. It has been suggested that sistra with four rods were designed to represent the four elements, while those with three represented the Egyptian seasons. Sistra would often be decorated with a Hathor motif (a forward-facing woman's head with bovine ears), a picture of Bes or small kittens to represent Bast.

In the rituals of the ancient Egyptians, sistra were used most often in the temples of Hathor and other dual-nature goddesses who had dangerous aspects to their characters. A large part of the rituals to these deities was designed to pacify their perilous sides, and sistra were shaken to achieve this end. The sacred rattles were always shaken by women; it was one of a few female roles within the temple complexes. Queens often appeared in Egyptian art shaking sistra, perhaps to illustrate that they sometimes joined their husbands in ritual. Sistra are always portrayed in these pictures as being held in the right hand. The sacred rattles were also often given as wedding gifts, as when they were decorated with kittens they were seen as fertility charms. Sistra were also used until fairly recently in the rituals of the Coptic Church.

In modern rituals, sistra are useful in three ways. First, they can be shaken to aid the purification of sacred space, symbolically shaking up the atmosphere, enlivening it and driving away negative influences. Secondly, in many of the rituals in this book sistra are shaken to encourage the *heka* of a particular deity to enter into a statue on the altar. In addition, sistra can also be shaken to induce a trance-like state. Their percussion is an incessant rhythm, which helps to release the mind from the mundane.

Our group started off with home-made sistra of the bean and tub variety, but we have since found more authentic instruments in museum shops and occult and ethnic stores. Some occult suppliers sell sistra by mail order. Simple wooden rattles are usually inexpensive.

The living statue

The everyday role of the priesthood in Egypt was largely based around caring for the statue of the god that was kept in the temple shrine. It was believed that this representation served as a kind of earthly body that the god could choose to inhabit at any time. As a result, the priests tended to the statue as if they were tending to the god himself.

Many of these daily rituals were recorded in carvings on the temple walls and some are still accessible today. From them, we learn that statues were woken at dawn with sunlight and the music of sistra. They were offered food and drink and were anointed with perfumed oils and unguents. Priests censed them with purifying incenses and 'dressed' them with cloths of specific colours. At night, the statues were 'put to bed' and their shrines were locked until the morning when everything began again at dawn.

If you have a representation of a deity in a shrine or on an altar you may like to make offerings, perhaps not to the extent of those given by the Egyptian priesthood, but something small and simple. Members of our group feel that this constant 'topping up' helps keep the presence of the deity alive within the statues. We place vases of fresh flowers on our altars, as well as stones or crystals. Sekhmet has tiger's eye stones arranged around her, while Bast has pieces of turquoise or lapis lazuli. In some instances we have adorned the necks of the statues with beads of an appropriate colour. We also often give gifts of feathers or shells that we might find on our travels. Sometimes we anoint the statues with scented oils in thanks or in anticipation. You can put anything you feel is appropriate or significant on your altar. Several of us pick up any claws or whiskers shed by our cats and place these on the bases of our Bast statues. You may want your offerings to be more in keeping with ancient tradition, in which case, you could lay out daily offerings of food that would be suitable for your cat to consume afterwards. You could anoint your statues with perfumed oils or burn incense for them. Small libations of fresh water or cups of wine are also appropriate. And you may like to cover your statue with a special cloth at night.

Consecration

Once you have all the things you need to begin your magical work, you are ready to consecrate your tools. Consecration is a way of cleansing an object of past associations and filling it with new energy or intention. This usually takes the form of a simple ceremony whereby equipment is set aside for magical use, energized and sometimes blessed.

Consecration, or rather animation, was an important consideration for Egyptian priests. As we have mentioned already, the statues of the gods were considered to be their earthly bodies, alive with the *heka* of the deity, and were cared for accordingly.

Representations of gods or goddesses in Egyptian temple complexes underwent special ceremonies, sometimes known as the 'opening of the mouth'. During the ceremony, priests would coax the spirit of the deity into the statue, thereby changing it from an inanimate piece of stone into a 'vessel for the spirit' of the relevant god. Stephen Quirke, in his book *Ancient Egyptian Religion*, describes such a ceremony:

> [It] was performed on the first day of the first month ... It culminated in a procession escorting the sacred images of the deities worshipped in the temple, heading up to a chapel on the roof. There the statue could 'see' and 'join' the sun disc. This action activated the statue so that the Ba-spirit of the deity could see, hear and act through the earthly vehicle of the statue.

Barbara Watterson, in her book *The House of Horus at Edfu*, says that the most important aspect of this ceremony 'involved touching the mouth, and other parts of the body, with various ritual implements, notably a ceremonial adze [blade], while reciting formulae such as "I perform the Opening of the Mouth so that you may speak." '

The ceremony we devised for our own group is given below. The example given is the consecration of a statue of Bast as a protector of the home, which is an appropriate way to 'break in' a new image of the goddess, but this little ritual can be adapted to charge any magical tool with intention and energy. Once you have learned the basic plan, you can change the words as you think appropriate.

Now is the time for you to begin trying out the skill of visualization you have learned in the preceding chapters. As the consecration is simple and straight forward, it will not require a great deal of imagery. The idea is to put your intention into the stone. As you are doing it be quietly aware that you will soon be using it in a magical capacity.

You will need the following equipment:

- new statue or amulet
- a standard-sized candle of blue, purple or silver
- a small candle or tea light of blue or purple (or a plain one in container of relevant colour)
- Bast oil (see appendix), or flowery perfume oil
- Bast incense, or joss sticks or a flowery perfume
- a blue, purple or silver cloth (large enough to wrap the statue)
- a previously consecrated statue of Bast or sacred cat (if available)

Wrap your statue or amulet in the cloth until you are ready to perform the consecration. If you have one, place the previously consecrated statue on the altar. Light the large candle and the incense, and place these upon the altar as well.

Unwrap the new statue and anoint it with the oil, all the while visualizing energy going into it. If it is being consecrated for a specific purpose (in this particular example protecting a person or a place) visualize Bast performing this function. See her as a presence in your room, emanating feelings or protection and strength. Imagine that presence entering into the statue in your hands. If you want to, you can visualize this as blue light or smoke.

The words below are for a person working alone, but if the consecration is performed by a group the relevant changes to the wording can easily be made. Pass the statue back and forth through the incense smoke and say:

Oh, Bast, lady of Asheru, ruler of Sekhet-neter,
Ruler of the divine field, lady of Ankhtawy,
Life of the two lands,
Hear me,
Awaken to my presence.
May the heka *of your divine spirit enter into this stone.*
I open your mouth that you might speak.
I open your eyes that you might see.
I open your ears that you might hear.
Abide here in gentleness,
Abide here in serenity.
I ask that you protect this home
And all who dwell within it.
Protect my heart.
Protect my soul,
Protect my body,
And guard this threshold that none who intend harm may
   enter.
I ask this in your name, oh Bast.

If you are working in a group, the consecration should be shared as the statue is passed around the circle, each person saying his or her own words. People should say what they feel – there is no need to stick to the words above. If a new group is consecrating newly acquired statues, it might be a good idea to tape the ritual. Good ad-libbing can rarely be remembered accurately after the event, and the tape may be useful in expanding and personalizing your working consecration ritual.

Once the ritual is finished, place the newly consecrated statue before the old one (if you have one), so that the incense smoke can continue to waft over both of them. Put the small candle in front of the statues, the larger one to one side. Other Bast-related items, such as coloured stones or flowers of an appropriate hue, can also be placed around the new statue. Place there what you feel is relevant and pertinent to give the statue power and energy.

Replenish the incense until the charcoal has burned away. If the statue is to be given to someone else, wrap it in the cloth again, which should remain around it until the gift is received. If the statue is to remain where it was consecrated, it can be left for a full day on the altar, before using it for its desired purpose. In some cases, you may wish to work with the statue straight away; it really depends on the circumstances.

Once you have consecrated your equipment you can arrange your shrine as you like; it is a matter of personal taste. But do set this area aside now – it will seem more special if you do not use it as a home for coffee cups or magazines.

9

Colours of the Gods

Colour is intrinsically valuable in magical work as it is in healing. Each colour reflects a different symbolism or representation.

Every person and every animal incarnates under the influence of some ray or another.

From: *Lords of Light* by W.E. Butler

We have already mentioned the importance of colour in ancient Egyptian magic. For example, it was thought that plants of a similar colour shared certain properties. In the same way, the priests' ceremonial robes would be of a particular sacred hue, and this code extended into the colours of their equipment and the ingredients they used in their spells.

It is difficult for us to know exactly what colours they used because, for example, the Egyptians had one term that referred to all the reds, yellows and oranges. These were all seen as 'fire shades', and were therefore relevant to solar or fiery deities such as Sekhmet. But red was also seen as a potentially evil colour, perhaps because of the unpredictable nature of the fiery deities. The feared god of chaos, Set, was reputed to have red hair. When the names of Set and other chaotic deities and demons like him were written down in magical texts, the priests would often use red ink for the purpose. 'Doing red' to someone meant performing a powerful magical working against them, a spell that might be seen as 'evil'.

Black and green were regarded as very powerful colours, and black in particular was used frequently in magic. These shades were associated with regeneration, rebirth and growth in general. Even today, black is seen as an especially magical colour, being linked

126

with all things shadowy and mysterious, while green is known as a 'pagan' colour, the hue of nature and earth magic.

The Egyptians regarded shades of blue and turquoise as heavenly colours, strongly associated with the gods and their divine realms. Bast was often shown as having a robe of green or blue. Some modern practitioners depict her as dressed in purple.

Obviously, the colour of a deity's costume has importance because it symbolizes aspects of his or her nature. Bast, as a goddess of fertility and love, would naturally wear colours associated with these concepts. Blue is the colour of strong passion and creativity, while green, associated with the heart, is seen as representative of generosity and kindness. Purple is not only the 'royal colour', but is linked to spirituality and intuition.

It is as important today as it was then to have a grasp of the meaning of colours and their correspondences. For instance, we can feel naturally that using the soothing colour blue in a ritual to Sekhmet would not be appropriate, nor does it feel right to associate Bast with the more aggressive colour red.

However, in order to interact with the energy frequencies of certain gods, we need to be aware not only of their colour vibrations, but also of our own. We can visualize the gods as beings of energy that radiate different colours. But despite our physical bodies, we are also beings of energy. By breathing, we draw into ourselves the universal life energy. Electrical impulses fire in the human brain, enabling it to think and to carry out functions within the body. We have this nebulous thing called a soul, which nobody understands fully. Does it reside in our bodies or out somewhere in the realm of the gods? At the same time, we are firmly anchored in the physical world through our flesh. The gods, on the other hand, are wholly ethereal. They do not have physical bodies and cannot talk to us face to face, in the same way we talk to our fellow humans.

It therefore seems clear that in order to communicate most effectively with the gods, we should utilize a kind of communication that they can perceive and understand. And this is where our own colour frequencies come in.

Many people believe that individuals have an aura of energy around them which can be seen as a corona of coloured light. The aura indicates the state of a person's health, his or her mood and aspects of his or her personality. While we shall not discuss individual auras here, we will give an overview of what is known as colour psychology so that you can decide what your own predominant colour is, and how to incorporate it into your magical work.

The spectrum consists of seven colour rays: red, orange, yellow, green, blue, indigo and violet. Many magical traditions work with the Eastern belief that there are seven energy centres in the human body, each displaying a pure, vibrant colour of the spectrum. These energy centres are known as chakras, and the condition of the energy within them has a direct effect upon our health and well-being. Most people's characters and behaviour are dominated by one colour in particular, which could be said to be 'brighter' within them. In *The Inward Revolution* by Deborah Benstead and Storm Constantine, the authors provide an in-depth study and exercise programme concerned with the chakras, which we recommend to anyone who wants a full understanding of these concepts. But for the purposes of this book, we shall simply give the major correspondences of each spectral colour.

Read through the colour descriptions below, and then decide which best fits your personality. Do not just concentrate on the positive aspects, but be as honest with yourself as you can about the negative qualities.

You may think that two colours vibrate equally strongly in your aura, or that at certain times one or another predominates. Most of us can choose one colour to work with, but it is also acceptable to work with two or more, as long as you only use one at a time. For example, if you think you have a lot of blue and yellow, you might decide that for one particular magical working yellow is most applicable, while for another blue is best.

Red

Red is the colour of will and power. It is the colour of fiery and often warlike deities such as Mars, Sekhmet and Thor. If you have a predominantly red aura, or if the energy of your red chakra is particularly strong, you are likely to have a natural aptitude for leadership. You will be purposeful and direct, both in relationships and at work. You will usually be self-reliant and courageous, flamboyant and forceful. Quite often, people might say that they have a fiery nature, but that said, even if your anger is quickly kindled, it can also be swiftly forgotten. You will be seen as a strong person by others, and will not be easily frightened. You would be the first to

Eloise and Storm with a statue of Sekhmet in the British Museum. This is the celebrated statue near which many psychics and sensitives claim to have had visionary experiences

One of Storm's altars at home. Sometimes it's difficult to find representations of the more obscure deities. Here, the statue on the left, clearly male in dress and form, was sold to us as a representation of Sekhmet. We use the piece to represent Mahes, the lion-headed son of Bast. The middle statue is a gold leaf and marble statue of Sekhmet, while the piece on the right is a lioness-headed figure, which we have painted to represent the goddess, Pakhet

Eloise's altar at home, showing, left to right, a copy of the statue of Sekhmet at Karnak, a sacred cat of Bast, small statuette of the goddess, Bast, and a copy of a seated Sekhmet, such as those in the British Museum. Eloise's sistrum, incense burner and Bast candlesticks can be seen

We often paint our statues, and here are three of the ones that Storm has decorated, from left to right, Bast, Tefnut and Sekhmet

Eloise's shrine to Bast, showing the sacred cat of Bast, surrounded by offerings of feather, crystals, stones and cat claws. The statue has been draped with a necklace of lapis lazuli beads. The cat is flanked by small representations of Sekhmet and Horus, as well as other small sacred cats

Some unusual statues of male deities, which are often hard to come by. The piece on the left is a representation of the dwarf lion god, Bes. The seated 'scribe' cat and the striding male both came from Egypt

An authentic ancient Egyptian artefact (1500 BC) owned by Eloise. Small amulets of Bast and Sekhmet were often given as New Year gifts. This little amulet has a stone loop on the back, so that it can be worn as a necklace

Statues in Storm's collection. The piece on the left is a gold leaf and marble representation of Bast, used by Storm as the main focus of Bast rituals. The middle figure, again of Bast, is a 'one off', created by sculptor, Warren Hudson. The male statue on the right is used to represent the sun god, Ra, in cat aspect

Ruby's computer-generated interpretation of a temple of Bast

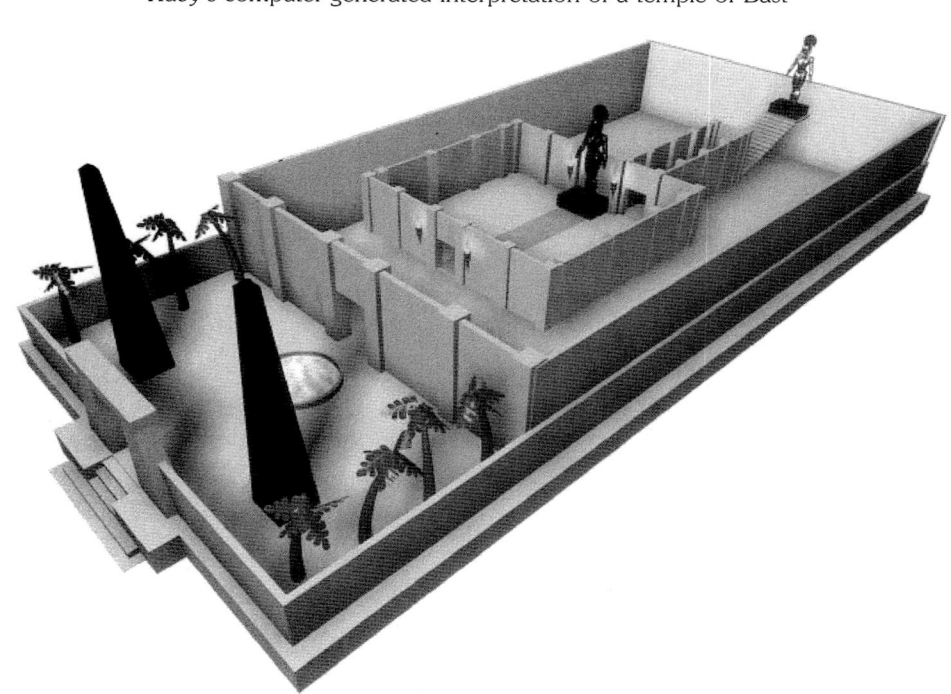

One of our artists, Ruby, performed several visualizations around Bast and Sekhmet with us. She was also inspired to create images of the temples she visited, as she visualized them. This is Ruby's interpretation of the underground temple of Sekhmet

Mask of the Lioness.

Artist Yuri Leitch was inspired by the cat goddess material to create a couple
of fantasy pictures. This illustration represents a woman wearing a lioness mask

Another of Yuri's fantasy pictures, showing the woman beneath the mask

investigate the creepy cellar in an old castle, while others are quaking at the door. Once you have made your mind up about something, it is likely that you will stick to it. Hence, you will be known as a loyal and steadfast friend, even if you do tend to speak your mind a bit too freely. You will inspire and organize activity in others.

All the colours have negative as well as positive aspects. Negative expressions of red can manifest in someone's personality as pride, arrogance, competitive ambition and a desire for power. Red people quite often refuse to accept that they are in the wrong, because they always tend to believe themselves to be right. They may be quite bossy. Sometimes they can also be downright nasty in their dealings with people, but they will then turn round in perplexity at the tears and upset they have caused and insist that the victim is overreacting, that the harsh words were 'just my way'. Their critics might say that they are too wilful and obstinate, and perhaps even selfish and cold-hearted. They can often be inflexible and resistant to change, especially if it is not on their own terms. Red also inspires materialism and overindulgence. Other negative aspects of a predominantly red aura include lack of consideration for others, intolerance, impatience and irritability.

Each colour has certain attributes and character tendencies within it, but there are also inherent *prospective* aspects too, characteristics which people might lack, but can aspire to developing within themselves. If red seems to be taking too much of an upper hand in your personality, you can work towards being more sympathetic and gentle with people, biting your tongue and trying to be more tolerant of others. You can work towards cultivating humility and patience, as well as learning to care for others without needing to be in control or possessive.

Orange

This is the colour of knowledge and reason, and therefore relates to the intellect. It is associated with airy and mercurial deities, such as Hermes and Thoth. If you are an 'orange' person, you will like to analyse things. Orange folk are natural sceptics, who need incontrovertible or scientific proof before they will believe in anything. They might be scientists or astronomers who shudder in horror at the mere mention of the word astrology. They are unlikely to tolerate people who lack objectivity, and will not be drawn towards subjective spiritual concepts that cannot be clearly defined. Faith will mean little to them; they always need 'proof'. In fact, it is unlikely that a person whose colour is overwhelmingly orange will even pick up a book like this. However, it is very rare, if not impossible, for someone to be wholly and totally one colour, and a little bit of scepticism and rational thinking is healthy, as it encourages challenges to the intellect, in which we can exercise our mental 'muscles'. Moreover, despite a lack of mysticism, a person in whose aura orange predominates will probably be inclined to be experimental and to think laterally, and as in the realm of quantum mechanics, this is the nexus where science and religion might one day collide.

If orange predominates within your aura, you will most likely have a keen sense of justice, enhanced by the ability to see all sides of an argument. You will have determination and perseverance in your work. People will think of you as having common sense and being an upright character. Dishonesty is not an orange attribute. Through your keen intellect, you will have a yearning to bring knowledge to others, and have the ability to communicate it in clear terms, even if those terms are coloured by your own – orange – mode of thinking. You will most likely be an independent person, happy in your own company, especially when you are investigating or studying something.

The other side of the orange coin is that it can lead to intellectual pride. Orange people sometimes cannot resist looking down on those they consider less intelligent and rational than themselves. They might even be thought of as narrow-minded, and they can certainly have a tendency to be prejudiced and tactless. They might tend to criticize others, and can have a very harsh temperament. Compassion might not come easily to them; in fact, they can be quite merciless in their dealings with others. Once they are upset, it is not easy for people to appease them and make up – they can hold grudges for a long time. Deep emotions might make them feel uncomfortable, and they are likely to despise those who give vent to emotional displays. Because they are so convinced of their superior intellect, they can appear sanctimonious, and can make a virtual religion out of reason.

The prospective aspects of orange include an ability to be sympathetic and feeling, to be able to love without prejudice, and to become more broad-minded in their consideration of others. A good maxim for an overly orange person is, 'Do not believe in anything, but do not disbelieve anything either.'

Yellow

This is the colour of awareness and active intelligence. It is the solar colour, associated with sun gods and divine kings, such as Christ, Apollo or Ra. If you have this colour predominant within your aura, you will be adaptable and possess understanding, dignity, grace and a great sense of compassion. You will have the ability to comprehend things clearly, but if there is a problem or situation, or some kind of knowledge, you do not or cannot understand, you really will not like it. Comprehension and understanding are paramount to a yellow person. Yellow people are effective communicators. They enjoy being at the centre of things, but as they are good co-ordinators, it is unlikely that anyone will complain about that. Although they do not like to be out of the limelight, they are not like the red ray person who just wants to dominate others. If they are in positions of leadership, they will place as much faith in, and importance on, the people they direct as they do themselves. They are team people, but always the leader of the team. If they can develop their self-awareness, it will reach into every aspect of their lives.

This solar colour confers a love of truth, a clear intellect and patience. If you have this colour predominating, you will have the ability to concentrate on learning, which derives from a desire for knowledge and a need to comprehend the world in which we live. You may well have a certain amount of cautiousness in your personality, but this is outweighed by your capacity for generosity, compassion and efficiency. Although you will have little personal interest in trifling issues or mundane worries, you will be tolerant of and helpful to others afflicted by them.

Yellow has the power to evolve. It includes the quality of mental illumination and the ability to bring abstract ideas into physical reality. If yellow predominates within you, you will probably speak and move rapidly. In fact, you will have great control over your physical movements, but this can lead to being zealous about fitness. You will be incapable of idleness, and you will appear to be constantly busy.

The sunny power of yellow seems to indicate almost perfect people, but yellow also gives rise to extremists who can easily become arrogant and narrow-minded. Another negative aspect of this colour is that it can lead to fanaticism in personal ideals. It is unlikely that a yellow person would adopt any of the universal religions, because they will be natural individualists, but any religion they do adopt may be personally constructed and perhaps somewhat eccentric. Eccentricity is, in fact, a yellow trait, whether positive or negative. Unlike red and orange, yellow people will not deliberately seek to humiliate or put others down, but they might have a tendency to justify their opinions and behaviour to others.

Are there any other clouds over the sun? Yes. You may be slightly neurotic and over-industrious. Like orange, you might be prone to intellectual pride. Your search for knowledge may leave you cold emotionally, leading to isolation and absent-mindedness. In extreme cases, the more positive aspects may be accompanied by obstinacy and self-importance. Perhaps the worst aspect of yellow is that it can, in some instances, give rise to a desire to manipulate others through scheming and deviousness. It may be that you will tell yourself you have others' best interests at heart, but sometimes the ends might not justify the means.

The prospective aspects of yellow are common sense, sympathy and the ability to 'let go'. Sometimes you might need to be able to accept that some things 'just are', without being able to understand them. This is especially important in relationships.

Green

This is the colour of love and emotion, and is associated with deities such as Cernunnos, Freya or Bast. If green predominates within you, you will most likely be among the healers, nurses, teachers and general 'givers' of humanity. You will be seen as a naturally genuine person who mixes well with others. People will instinctively like you, mainly because you are very sympathetic. However, you can get into hot water by trying to please everybody at the same time. You are an efficient peace-maker, who can help calm the troubled waters in any family or group of friends. You will be highly sensitive and experience emotions freely and often deeply. Love comes easily to you, and you are never usually short of friends. Green enables you to give easily to others – but you might stipulate that your generosity must be appreciated!

Green bestows a sharp perception which enables you to see

beneath the surface of things, whether individuals or situations. You will be able to see through people's masks, and will almost always sense the undercurrents in any group of people. You will always be ready to help others – sometimes to your own inconvenience – and can easily comprehend the subtleties of various circumstances and situations. You will naturally care about the welfare of others and will always be ready with a genuinely sympathetic ear that does not become tired, bored or exasperated.

With green dominating your aura, it is likely that you will be a calm person who radiates a sense of gentle strength. You will be kind and patient with people, (even when others feel the recipients do not deserve it), and will try to understand what causes a problem or a certain behaviour, in order to advise and help. This is where your natural intuition helps you greatly. In general, you will have a great affinity and love for nature and will walk through life with a fairly serene temper. Green people can deal with a rampaging red person when other colours have fled the scene in exasperation. They are faithful and loyal to their friends and loved ones, even under extreme circumstances. Another green attribute is endurance.

But all this gentleness and sensitivity has to have a downside. One green weakness is a tendency to be over-sentimental, and perhaps too sensitive for your own good. At times you may be seen as 'scatty' and impractical. You can easily be deflected from your purpose or views, changing them according to the company you are in. Another negative aspect is that you can appear over-fussy about your environment, which arises from a desire for clean and comfortable surroundings. Taken to extremes, this tendency can be neurotic.

Green people may recognize within themselves a lack of satisfaction with what they have attained in life. Even when their achievements are obvious to others, they might still feel that they have not accomplished anything. Owing to their innate sensitivity, feelings of fear and anxiety can be real burdens to them. In extreme cases, it can plague their lives with paranoia and worry, which leads to them becoming anxious and nervy. It seems tragic that those who possess the wonderful warm qualities of green should also be prey to the most debilitating conditions. The most negative aspects of green, perhaps because of its overwhelmingly compassionate positive side, are quite severe: despondency, poor self-image, self-loathing, a sense of inadequacy, depression, constant anxiety, self-pity, excessive self-effacement, inertia, ineffectiveness and materialism.

The prospective aspects of green are confidence, self-love, purposefulness, courage, a clear perception that is not clouded by emotion, self-awareness instead of just awareness of others, and the ability to give and love without condition.

Blue

This is the colour of wisdom and creation, associated with such deities as Athene, Neptune or Tefnut. If blue dominates your aura, you will be among the artists, tragic poets, sages and unconventional teachers of the world. Blue gives you a sensitivity to form, colour, mood and proportion, and brings the capacity to create easily and artistically. If blue is your predominating colour, you will often have excellent creative talents.

In its most positive aspect, blue can bestow exceptional wisdom. Through creativity, examining the universe through art, blue people may evolve a clear but deep understanding of others and the world in which we live. Whether they express these ideas in words, pictures, music, or simply ideas, the most talented can create harmony and true beauty, which can elevate the spirit, not just of themselves, but of others. However, if their creativity cannot be outwardly expressed, they might become extremely introspective.

When blue shines out from you, you can love with great passion. Love, to a blue person, is a great source of inspiration. This colour combines many of the positive aspects of the others, such as generosity, compassion, affection, devotion and quickness of intellect and perception, but as with the other colours, there are problem areas associated with it, and because of all that passion and creative energy, these can be quite severe.

One negative aspect of blue is inertia, and this may prevent you from expressing your abilities fully, which can lead to frustration and discontent. You may have dark days when you feel depressed and despondent, and are unable to be creative. At these times, it will be difficult for you to decide whether the former gives rise to the latter, or vice versa. You also have a tendency to be very lazy, which will also curtail any artistic endeavour. Whatever the reason for not expressing yourself, you will torture yourself about it. Others might see you as a natural pessimist who always thinks negatively. You can be impulsive and may often over-react in stressful situations. This can lead you to panic, rant, weep stormily or crawl into a dark place to hide. When episodes like this occur, people might roll their eyes and say you have an artistic temperament. You can be prone to greater or lesser forms of manic depression: hyperactive one minute, indolent the next.

Blue people can veer off into an isolated world of self-absorption or obsession. Their creative minds can lead them down some very strange roads, peopled with illusions and grandiose but impractical schemes. They can also become obsessive perfectionists. Their grip on reality may become weak, and they should be aware of the distinction between the imaginary and the real. Because predominant blue makes people absorb everything inwardly, they can take comments and criticisms personally, which in extreme cases can lead them to feel very paranoid. Their instinct to elevate things to a higher level can make them try constantly to become something or someone better. As a consequence, they can easily succumb to feelings of envy.

Blue people can be very manipulative with others, and stir up conflict in a devious way. They are equally adept at playing the victim or the oppressor, according to which gives them the best advantage in a situation.

The prospective aspects blue should work towards are serenity, positivity and confidence. You should seek to acquire self-control without having to suppress anything within yourself. You should strive for mental and emotional balance and guard against selfishness. You should love without obsession.

Indigo

This is the colour of devotion and idealism, associated with gods such as Pluto, Bel Marduk and Osiris. Of all the colours, this is the one that is least likely to influence someone wholly and completely. Those influenced by indigo are by nature very idealistic and nationalistic. They are the people who have the strongest religious convictions, which will involve intense personal feelings and emotion. Indigo is the colour of the saint, the mystic, the martyr and the evangelist, the priest and the fervid politician. We can see how religious wars and crusades can originate from its influence. Its positive aspects include a capacity for reverence, devotion, purposefulness, dedication, love, loyalty and intuition.

If you are dominated by indigo, everything will have to be perfect for you, or you will find life intolerable. It is vital for you to have a personal god to whom you can devote yourself, and this can lead to bigotry and fanaticism. In some cases it can lead you to persecute others in order to 'save their souls', for what you believe is the only true and right way.

If you are not a leader yourself, you will have a need to be blindly devoted to someone else. You will be prone to following gurus or preachers, and will ignore, if not despise, the intellect in favour of emotional and spiritual ideals. Your loyalty to a cause, good or bad, is zealous, and you will commit yourself with single-minded ardour and enthusiasm to anything in which you believe strongly. In love, you will be obsessive and possessive, and perhaps put your lovers on pedestals, only to be disappointed when they reveal themselves as human, with human failings.

Even though red might seem the strongest colour in the spectrum as regards its influence over personality traits, indigo is without doubt the most extreme. In some ways, it could be said to have more potential for destruction, as its influence can inspire corruption and emotional fanaticism. It gives rise to prejudice and self-deception. Influenced by it, you may experience cold anger towards those who do not share your ideals. Indigo people are rigid individuals who are not open to change, especially if it derives from someone else's opinions and ideals.

However, as we have said, very few people are governed by this colour alone. If you interact with someone who *is* strongly affected by its vibration, you might come away from them influenced by it yourself, but it is unlikely the effect will be lasting. It is also possible for some people to have indigo bubbling away permanently beneath another, more predominant colour.

The prospective aspects of indigo are strength, purity, serenity, compassion, truth, common sense, emotional balance, flexibility and tolerance, and love free of jealousy and possessiveness.

Violet

This is the colour of intuition, ceremony and order, and is associated with deities such as Ptah or Grim. Like indigo, it has a certain affinity with spirituality, but its expression is eloquent and graceful, without the narrow-minded zeal associated with indigo. If this colour is dominant in your aura, you will be among the healing shamans, benign mystics and open-minded priests or priestesses of this world. You will also be a natural organizer and, with your inherent love of pageant and ceremony, you will make a good theatrical producer.

Violet brings order through wise judgement and intuition. This is not the intuition of green, which empathizes strongly with others, but a more universal sense. While green ministers to the earthy aspects of caring for the body and the mind, violet is more concerned with spiritual care. It can create great innovators, because it inspires a higher intellect that can cross the boundaries of rigid, conformist thinking.

But not all violet people are great innovators. For most, violet will manifest as a need for ordered rituals in their daily lives, and they will be most happy with a safe and unchangeable routine. They might be prone to eccentric behaviour, and they can examine and accept alternative or non-conformist concepts and ideas without necessarily adhering to them themselves. Violet makes them open-minded and receptive.

This colour also inspires people to pay great attention to detail, hence the love of pomp and ceremony. If violet predominates in your aura, you will feel most comfortable with precision, ordered beauty and grace. In your work, you will want to become highly skilled, and will walk through life with great dignity.

If you become a healer, it will involve unorthodox methods, such as white magic or New Age and alternative therapies. If so, you will want to excel at your craft and be known as the best in the field. Although you will be naturally independent, your independence will not be coupled with the cold aloofness that prevents an exchange of emotion. In your love partners, you will seek those with whom you can resonate intellectually and spiritually.

The more negative aspects of violet mean that you can become pompous, sanctimonious and arrogant. You will not like situations where you feel you are not in control, and you loathe being humiliated. Discourtesy and rudeness offends you greatly, and you will not be prepared to take criticism from someone you consider to be less than yourself. However, you will be quite happy to criticize others, should you feel it is justified.

Your obsession with detail can lead to fussiness, officiousness and pettifoggery. You can be a proud and bigoted creature, fond of voicing your own opinions.

The mystical aspect of violet can lead to an obsession with omens and superstitions. You can become too involved in the secret and mysterious aspects of alternative spiritual beliefs and systems.

The prospective aspects of violet are humility, gentleness, and love with freedom of emotion and expression. You should work towards considering the body as much as the spirit.

Having studied the above descriptions, you should now be more or less sure of which is your predominating colour. If you are working in a group, it can be interesting to have a discussion about this. By now, you will probably be able to decide which colour dominates the auras of others in the group, so you can almost tell in advance who is most likely to argue the point!

In our group's magical workings, we use a candle of our specific colour in order to radiate it towards the deity with whom we wish to communicate. This is how Bast or Sekhmet recognizes us.

10

Opening the Way

The gate stands open, enter into light.
from *Apprenticed to Magic* by W.E. Butler

Group or solo work?

Before we discuss full visualizations and rituals, we need to decide whether it is better to work magically alone or with others. Generally, this is a matter of choice, but people are often forced to work alone simply because they have not come across like-minded companions to form a group. If you are in this situation and wish to change it, you should ask Bast to help you – you might be surprised at the results. Quite often, if you start off alone, you will find that when the time is right you will come across other practitioners 'as if by magic'. Then again, you might prefer to work alone. If you do, you can record the exercises and rituals on tape, or learn them as you need them, so that you do not have to refer to a book in the middle of a visualization. We have designed the visualizations and rituals so that they can be performed by a group, a couple or a lone practitioner.

If you do form a group, it is important that the members all get on together and trust one another. It is better to work alone than to rush into forming a group of people you do not really know. We speak from experience here. After a few wrong choices and upsets, we now always spend some time getting to know a potential new member in a social situation. Undertaking magical work should not be a hasty decision. It is vital that people appreciate what it entails and have a basic understanding of magical principles before they are thrown in at the deep end. Sometimes, the results of visualizations can be intensely personal. It is therefore important that group members feel comfortable with one another so that they can be open and honest. Looking inward, which is what visualization is, can not only give you a rich imagery of gods, goddesses and mythical landscapes, it can also introduce you to hidden aspects of yourself – unresolved conflicts, problems and anxieties – which can appear in symbolic form. Dealing with these things, and discussing them with trusted confidants, makes us stronger, wiser people. It gives us self-knowledge, which is part of what magic is all about. A magical group should be supportive of one another, tolerant and understanding.

You can therefore appreciate why some practitioners feel it is easier to work alone. Solo practitioners can please themselves as to what they do and when they do it. They can work at their own pace and all their results are completely private. They do not have to contend with arguments or personality clashes. Equally, however, they have no one with whom to share their experiences, no one to offer support or give an honest opinion when they feel confused about something they might have seen or felt.

On a practical level, a group can share the cost of buying equipment and the preparation of incense and food. Members can take turns in reading the visualizations and can work together, pooling ideas and images, to devise new rituals. Whatever the problems – and any collection of humans will inevitably encounter problems – nothing compares with the companionship that comes from working in a group. A feast is never the same if you have no one to share it with and it is always beneficial to have others around who will stop you taking yourself too seriously!

We have found, again through long trial and error, that the only way to have a successful working group is to ensure that no one broods or sulks in silence (or in selective complaining), but airs their grievances openly as soon as they can. We try to understand that no one is perfect and that if people work together for long enough, someone is bound to upset someone else, either intentionally or not. In the past, we have worked with groups which have simply fallen apart because people felt they could not speak openly about their feelings. Good communication can solve almost all problems before they become deeply entrenched. Discuss any problem together, not in cabals, for that only breeds dissension.

Purifying the temple

You should now have everything you need to work magically, including your personal purpose in becoming involved. You are ready for your first meeting with Bast in her temple, but first you should prepare yourself and your environment.

Before any ritual, ensure that the room you are using is clean and tidy. This will help you to feel in control, less distracted and therefore able to focus more clearly on your goal. Feng shui practitioners believe that if your home is full of unwanted clutter it signifies that your mind is cluttered too, and that you will be robbed of vitality and become less able to concentrate on the job in hand. Whether you believe this or not, before embarking on any important ritual or visualization it is best to prepare your surroundings carefully so that you will feel more organized and capable.

Once your temple area is clean and tidy, make sure that you have all the items you need close at hand. There is nothing worse than trying to light a candle halfway through a ritual only to discover you have left the matches in the kitchen. So check that you have everything you could possibly need.

In the majority of magical traditions it is customary to spend time turning the working area into sacred space, not just by physically cleaning it but also through acts of purification. The practice of the ancient Egyptians included sprinkling the floor with water and sweeping it with a special broom. This is an act performed by other traditions such as Wicca, when the practitioners use the familiar witch's besom.

In *The Temple of Horus at Edfu*, Barbara Watterson tells us that the purification ceremonies at the temple of Edfu incorporated the sprinkling of consecrated water, the burning of incense, the shaking of rattles and the opening up of the shrine to the light of the sun. The priests believed that once these preparations had been done the area would be set apart as a place that was pure enough for the god to reside in, and where chronological time had no meaning. In her book *Magic in Ancient Egypt*, Geraldine Pinch tells us that this space could then be used to 'return to the First Time and tap the energies of creation'.

We can gain a great deal of inspiration from ancient practices when devising our own methods and rituals. You might like to do the same as the priests of Egypt and ritually cleanse your temple by sprinkling it with water and wafting incense smoke around it before you begin your rituals. Perhaps you could enliven the space by shaking your rattle and light it up with sunlight by opening your windows. If you are performing your ritual in the evening, you could light your room symbolically by burning white or gold candles to represent the sun.

Alternatively, before taking your bath (see below), you can leave a few incense sticks burning in your ritual room and leave soft music playing, so that while you are away from the room it begins to assume the right atmosphere for the rite to come.

Bathing and purification

Once you have cleaned and prepared your temple, it is time for you to have a ritual bath. This is important, not only for cleansing yourself physically but because with a little foresight you can also cleanse yourself psychically too. Modern esoteric traditions all advocate some form of purification before embarking on any magical work. Even if bathing does nothing more than allow you some time to relax, it is valuable.

The ancient Egyptians placed great important on their priests being immaculate, believing that they were not worthy to serve the gods if they had not undergone a series of purifications. Barbara Watterson describes the purification of both priest and temple in detail. She tells us that the two most important aspects of physical purification were the washing of the mouth and the body. Priests would never enter the temple without having first cleaned out their mouths with natron, a simple mixture of sodium carbonate or bicarbonate and water. They would also wash their body in the sacred lake. Their hands and feet received special attention, since they would hold sacred objects and walk in sacred space. The removal of body hair is well documented, and from the Eighteenth Dynasty onwards, the shaving of head hair was also mandatory, with hefty fines being the consequence of laziness in this respect. Watterson also tells us that the priesthood was forbidden to wear clothes made of wool and leather, since fabrics derived from animals were thought to be unclean.

It is a good idea to try and set aside some time to bath before ritual work, but unlike the Egyptian priesthood, you will be no less worthy if you only have time to wash your hands and brush your teeth. As with everything else in this book, you need only do what you can.

Salt is traditionally a purifying substance so a handful of sea salt is far more beneficial in your bathwater than synthetic bath foams. We keep tubs of sea salt in our bathrooms especially for ritual baths. If you like you can also add a few drops of essential oil to your water. Use an oil to suit the purpose of your working. If you are doing a healing ritual or a quest for information rosemary is a good choice. If love is your aim then rose is perfect. If you just want to perform a meditation without a specific purpose or practise some of the preliminary exercises then you can use a purifying oil such as lavender or myrrh.

Take some time to relax in the bath and forget about day-to-day worries. Close your eyes and visualize that the healing water is washing away your fears and problems. Breathe deeply and slowly until you feel calm and centred. It is beneficial to take this time to work on creating a mood of calm confidence so that you approach the work in hand in a positive state of mind. This way you are far more likely to see results. A simple way of achieving a peaceful, meditative state is to regulate your breathing. You can perform one of the breathing exercises we described in Chapter 7, or this simplified version.

1. Breathe in deeply through your nose for the count of three.
2. Hold the breath for the count of three and then expel it through your mouth for the count of three.
3. Repeat this at least ten times and you should feel really relaxed.

When you feel ready let out the water and as it flows away imagine that all your worries have been absorbed by the water and are carried away within it.

After you have finished bathing, you may like to purify your mouth with natron in the manner of the ancient priesthood. If this does not appeal to you, then simply cleaning your teeth or using a mouthwash would be a suitable compromise.

Ritual attire

Clothing for ritual is a matter of personal taste. We do not wear special robes, but many people prefer to. Others choose to wear no clothes at all, in the belief that they block the natural flow of energy. The only considerations are that you should not wear fabric derived from animals and that whatever you do wear should be freshly laundered. Wearing something in your own colour is a good idea as it can help you send images of yourself to a deity, which is an important facet of many of our rituals. Ultimately, you should be happy and comfortable in whatever clothing you choose. Clean garments in a natural fibre, whatever their style or colour, are fine.

Some practitioners of magic believe you should not wear make-up and perfume during rituals, nor unconsecrated jewellery. However, our group likes to wear all three, and we have never noticed any deleterious effect, so we would again say it is a matter of personal choice. Even the simplest ritual benefits from a sense of occasion, and making an effort with your appearance may help to make it feel special to you. We all own small Bast and Sekhmet amulets that we wear for rituals, and while these are beautiful they are not essential. If you feel that you would like one, however, a list of suppliers of amulets and ritual jewellery can be found at the end of this book.

Setting the mood

It is important to set the mood for magic. Some people may regard music simply as another prop, since it is only our own energy, will and intention that effects magical changes, but we believe that such props are very helpful. We have already mentioned the shaking of sistra to purify and enliven a temple but this is not the only role of music in ritual. Playing CDs or tapes of soft, Egyptian-style music in the background during your rituals can make it easier for you to visualize musicians in a temple of Bast. As we have said, the gentle light of candles and the intoxicating aroma of incense can also help induce a sense of sacred occasion. If you find it difficult to step out of mundane reality, alter your state of consciousness and open yourself up to receive visualized images, then anything that helps you to achieve this state is extremely useful. For this reason, after you have cleaned your temple and either prior or after your bath, you might like to illuminate your ritual room entirely with candles, fill it with incense smoke, and relax there listening to music for an hour or so. Experiment and see what works for you. A glass of wine or so before a ritual is fine, but do not have too much. You can have a drink afterwards if you like, but keep a clear head for the working itself.

This preparatory hour or so is entirely optional. If you decide to forgo it, then before beginning your ritual you should light your incense charcoal and sprinkle the first few grains of incense upon it. Light the altar candles and spend a few moments sitting calmly before them. Start to play the CD or tape, if you have chosen one for the occasion. Make sure all your equipment is ready – we will indicate what is needed for each visualization and ritual throughout the book.

Anointing your candle

Anointing is a component of many of our rituals in order to imbue the candle with magical intention. This intention or energy is then released to do its work as the candle burns down during the working. To anoint a candle you will first need a suitable oil mixture. Recipes for oils are given in the appendix at the end of this book, but again you can purchase ready-made oils if you need to. Once you have chosen your oil and a candle of a suitable colour you are ready to begin.

Clear your mind and breathe deeply until you feel calm and relaxed. Pick up your candle and focus clearly on the result you want from your ritual. Then dip your fingers into the oil and, working from the end towards the centre of the candle, rub the oil into the wax. Work from one end to the middle and then turn the candle over and work from the other end to the middle. This method is important, because it ensures that all of your intention goes into the candle and remains there. If you just stroked the candle in one direction from end to end, all the energy would be pushed along it and then out through the tip. As you apply the oil, keep focused on what you hope to achieve. Let all your intention flood into the candle through your fingers.

When, after a few minutes, you feel you have completely charged the candle with your energy, place it in a holder until you are ready to light it.

11

The Cone of Power

Energy is ecstasy. When we drop the barriers and let power pour through, it floods the body, pulsing through every nerve, arousing every artery, coursing like a river that cleanses as it moves.

From *The Spiral Dance* by Starhawk

Before we begin any meditations or rituals, and after we have completed our breathing exercises, we construct a cone of power in which to work. This serves several purposes. First, it creates a special place, removed from the mundane, in which we can feel apart from everyday life. Secondly, it is constructed from the pure energy of our being, and therefore not only helps us with visualization but also enhances and enlivens any energy around us.

It can also act as a means of protection from unwanted energy, but should we require it, it can actually act as a beacon to energy entities – spirits, etc. – in the environment, which are drawn to it like moths to a flame. This is more effective out in the open rather than in a building. However, since this book is about communicating with deities of ancient Egypt rather than indigenous spirits, we will not go into that aspect of cone-building here.

The cone also acts as a vessel of energy that can transport us through space and time in our visualizations.

Because the cone is made of our energy, whatever intention we put into its construction will be its main focus. Consequently, if we are more concerned about its protective aspect, and pour our intention into that as we are building it, we will increase its potential for protection. If we are concerned mostly with the travelling aspect, in order to extend our minds back into the past of Egypt, that aspect of the cone will be enhanced.

Constructing a cone of power

After regulating your breathing, sit or lie comfortably to construct the cone.

1. First imagine a pinprick of light appearing on the ground behind you. It is going to travel around you in a clockwise direction as if following an invisible circle. The cone can be as wide or as small as you like. It can pass through walls and furniture, but it should encompass yourself, any other people present and the altar if there is one.
2. Imagine that the light begins to move around you at ground level. See it moving as clearly as you can. Hold that image in your mind until you feel it is fixed. The more energy and intention you can put into this process the more effective your cone will be.
3. As the light moves, your intention feeds it with energy, and it begins to grow in size. See it move more rapidly around you, picking up speed, growing larger and larger.
4. When it is about the size of a ping-pong ball, visualize it beginning to grow a tail, like a comet. It is a streaking ball of radiant blue-white light, whizzing around you at ground level.
5. See the ball moving so fast, it eventually catches up with its own tail to create a vibrating ring of vibrant blue-white light around you at ground level.
6. Keep this image firmly in your mind for a few moments.
7. Now, with the ball still growing, the ring begins to build upon itself like a snowball gathering snow as it rolls along. A wall is being built around you of blue-white light. Visualize that you can still see the expanding ball circling round, rising up and up.
8. See the wall grow up behind your back, your shoulders, your head. As it rises it begins to taper inwards to form the cone. Its apex will be high above your head.
9. Continue to build the cone until it comes to a point at, or just above, the ceiling.
10. For a few moments, keep the image of sitting within a vibrat-

ing cone of blue-white light. It is spinning around you, thrumming with energy.

11. Now see rays of light spiral in towards the centre at ground level. They swirl around and around to create a carpet of blue-white light beneath you.
12. As the light reaches the centre of the circle, it pushes up into a column, like a fountain. Concentrate on this image. See the light pulsing upwards in a column, and flecks of light raining down from it, just like water in a fountain.
13. Push the column right up to the apex of the cone. Feel the light raining down upon you, filling the cone with its radiance.
14. Feel the light pushing through your skin. Breathe it in. You are becoming part of the cone itself. Feel your body tingling with its energy. You feel relaxed yet powerful.
15. Once the cone is filled with light, and you feel you are totally part of it, imagine that the backdrop of the room behind it is fading away.

The travelling cone

You are now ready to do whatever work you wish within the cone, which might be consecrating tools, or some other minor operation that does not require actually visualizing going back in time. However, for most of the rituals and visualizations in this book, you will need to incorporate the following exercise.

1. After the backdrop of the room has faded away, imagine that all that exists is the spinning cone of light in a black void.
2. Now visualize that the cone is moving. Really try to feel that movement. It is your vessel, and it is going to take you back in space and time, to the ancient land of Khem, of Egypt.
3. Visualize the cone rushing through a black void. You may see stars and clouds of coloured gases. Feel the years stripping away, sense that you are going back in time.
4. Ahead of you, you see a jewel of light hanging in the void. As you approach it, you realize it is the Earth, but an Earth far older than the one you left behind. You rush towards it, down through the atmosphere towards the land of Khem.
5. Visualize the cone alighting in this land, at whatever location you have previously decided on for your ritual or meditation.

See a doorway open up in the wall of the cone. Stand up and walk through it.

It is a good idea to practise constructing a travelling cone a few times before you attempt the first full visualization of a visit to Bast's temple. So when you alight in your visualized land of ancient Khem, just take a few minutes to imagine walking around outside the cone, familiarizing yourself with the experience, strengthening your visionary 'muscles' and noticing anything that your senses pick up. Practise seeing the landscape, and experiencing sounds and smells as well. Try to feel the heat of the desert on your skin. Just let your imagination roam. When you feel ready, walk back to the cone, enter the doorway and sit down again.

All you have to do to return to your own time is reverse the process of travelling through the void. This time, see the backdrop of the land beyond the cone fading away into blackness. Then feel the cone begin to move again, but this time forwards in space and time. Feel the years mounting up as you travel.

Again, see a jewel of light ahead of you in the void, which is our own Earth. Visualize travelling back to your own land, your own town, your own house, or wherever else you might be doing the visualization. Imagine the cone landing in this place and the backdrop of the room appearing again behind it. Take a few moments to become fully aware of your physical body. Re-establish yourself firmly in the real world.

Dismantling the cone

It is very important to dismantle the cone correctly and patiently. This is so that no stray energy is left in the room, which can cause problems later on. If the energy you raised by constructing the cone is not properly dispersed, you might end up feeling agitated, depressed or tired. The remaining energy can become stagnant and cling to the environment, causing detrimental physical and psychological effects.

1. Begin to unwind the cone in an anticlockwise direction. Visualize the ball of light at the apex of the cone and see it reverse its spin. As it does so, the cone diminishes and the wall of light comes down. Imagine that all the energy is going back into the ball, including all the light that filled the cone.

2. Take down the cone until you have a vibrating ring of light around you at ground level. Then see that begin to break up, so that it is just a ball of light with a tail.
3. The tail gets shorter and shorter as the ball of light slows down. As it decelerates, it gets smaller.
4. Shrink and slow down the ball until the tail has vanished completely. Then see the ball shrink even further until it is a pinprick of light travelling slowly around you at ground level.
5. Slow down this spark of light until it comes to a halt and goes out.

You will get out of your cone what you put into its construction. There is often a temptation to rush this part of a visualization or ritual, because people are eager to get on to the much more vivid imagery that follows it. However, we cannot stress too strongly how important it is to take time with this part of a working – both constructing and dismantling – and to visualize it as minutely and carefully as possible. Not only does it help in altering your state of mind, removing you from the mundane, it also enlivens and enhances the energy around and within you, which is what you use to work magic. If this energy is flowing freely through your body and mind, your imagination has much more chance of picking up rich and meaningful imagery. Your intentions are given a powerful highway of energy to travel. As the saying goes, 'Intention goes where energy flows.'

The more people you have to build a cone, the more effective it is, although a cone constructed by a single person does the job required. We have constructed a cone with a group of three hundred or so people, and believe us, you could feel that vessel of light move!

A cleansing cone

Much as you used the breathing the hidden light exercise to cleanse your body, so a cone of power can be constructed to cleanse the environment, whether in the home or out in the open. Sometimes you might feel you want to cleanse a room, or even an entire building before doing your ritual work. You might feel that bad, stagnant energy is present – perhaps left behind by people who lived there before or as a result of a recent bad argument or sadness. It is always a good idea to cleanse a new home with this kind of cone before you do any magical work. Some people might even want to do it before they spend a night there! Negative energy does tend to hang around, clinging to the fabric of the environment, and it can sometimes affect you physically, by making you feel depressed, exhausted or anxious for no reason. Obviously, it is not advisable to attempt any magical or visionary work in such an atmosphere, as it will only enhance and amplify the negative energy already present. However, a cleansing cone effectively sorts the problems out.

1. Construct the cone, but once it is filled with light, imagine that rays of radiance push out from it, extending into the room beyond. See those rays fill every dark corner, expelling every shadow.
2. If you want to, extend the rays out into other rooms of the building, until it is completely filled with blue-white light. Visualize the rooms as clearly as you can, every detail. Nothing dark or negative can exist in this radiance. Visualize that strongly. See the atmosphere becoming clean and enlivened with positive energy.
3. Once the whole building is filled with this glowing light, draw it back into the cone, visualizing that the rooms are left full of positive energy behind it. Imagine that the furniture glows with it.
4. Draw all the light back into the cone, then unwind it as normal.

12

A Visit to the
Temple of Bast

Her eyes
Are made of charming minerals well-burnished.
Her nature, both by sphynx and angel furnished,
Is old, intact, symbolic and bizarre.

Charles Baudelaire

It is now time to extend your senses further. Before you perform rituals to the goddess, you should begin to build up your inner world, create the landscape where you will meet and communicate with Bast. You will go to visit her in her temple, and spend some time talking with her. For this visualization, which is an abridged version of our working rite to Bast, we do not use the scenario of the temple at Bubastis, but rather a simplified and idealized version of her shrine. For the full festival rite, which is given in Chapter 14, the visualization includes a trip down the Nile to the sacred city, with all the trimmings. For working rites, we feel more time should be expended on communing with the goddess than building up the environmental imagery.

If this is the first time you have attempted a long and detailed visualization, or if you still find visualizing difficult, do not worry if the imagery that comes to you does not seem flowing or continuous. It gets better with practice. If you find your mind wandering, and it is hard to concentrate on your surroundings, just relax and gently focus your inner eye once more. You can do this by imagining that you are closing your eyes and can see only blackness. Then imagine opening them again so that you can see your surroundings. You can take as long as you like to do this visualization.

If you are starting a temple group, you might want to perform this visualization together. In that case, we suggest that everyone attends to the ritual bathing part of the preparation at home beforehand, otherwise you might have to spend a considerable amount of time – not to mention hot water – while everyone gets ready. The group member who is hosting the evening should attend to the ritual room preparation before taking his or her own bath. It is best to do this before everyone else arrives, so that the group can spend some time together before the visualization. After this, everyone can enter the ritual room together, just before the lighting of the altar candles.

You might find it helpful to record the visualization on a tape recorder rather than memorize all the details. Alternatively, if you are working with a partner or in a group, one person can be designated reader for the occasion. In our group, we always share this role and appoint a different person to read at each meeting. When reading, it is important not to go too fast, so that people have plenty of time to visualize. When you reach a point where the group are left to wander off alone in their minds, give them at least five minutes to do this. The amount of time you spend in free visualizing is something that has to be decided within the group, but about five minutes is fine to start with. If you give people too much time, you will often notice them starting to fidget, so you will know that you should start speaking again. The more practised you become at visualizing, the longer you will want to spend doing it.

Obviously, once you are all familiar with the rites, the reader can simply recite the imagery from memory, which means that he or she can participate more. An accomplished reader can ad-lib during the visualization, making it more vivid for the participants.

If you are working alone and do not have a tape recorder, you can memorize the visualization by writing down the main 'landmarks' in longhand a few times. If you really do get 'lost' and need to check what you should be doing and seeing, come out of the visualization, read the relevant section, and then resume your meditation where you left off.

One image in this particular visualization is personal to us, and that is the golden stairs of Bast. As far as we know, the Egyptians did not have great flights of steps in their temples, but some years ago this image was seen by a psychic friend of ours following the death of one of our cats and for this reason we have always used it in our visualizations. If you want the temple of Bast to be more in keeping with authentic Egyptian temples, you can amend that part of the meditation.

The rite

Prepare yourself to meet the goddess Bast. Unplug the phone and lock the door. You do not want to be disturbed. Make sure your ritual room is freshly cleaned, warm and comfortable, the lighting low. On the altar, you should have a tall candle on either side of your image of Bast (one blue candle, one yellow). Place some flowers on the altar. Before or on the altar, lay out your incense materials, ready to be lit, along with a candle of your personal colour. Have paper and pen ready to write down the results of your visualization later (or, if you prefer, a small tape recorder to dictate into). Light some stick incense, so that while you are away preparing yourself, the room will start to become ready for your rite.

Then, by candlelight, take a lazy bath saturated with your favourite scents. You can have music playing to help you get in the right mood. As you soak yourself, imagine that you will soon be visiting someone you have always wanted to meet. You feel excited, and perhaps a little nervous. Through this meeting, your life will change, your horizons broaden.

After the bath, dress yourself in your ritual clothing, and if you wish, make up your face in an Egyptian style. Dab yourself with perfume, as Bast enjoys its fragrance. Now enter the ritual room and light the altar candles. Put on some soft music with an Eastern feel and burn your Bast incense.

Anoint your personal candle with the perfumed oil, from the ends towards the centre. As you do so, concentrate on putting your personality into the candle. It is through the light of the candle flame that Bast will recognize you. Breathe deeply for a few moments to enliven your energy, then light the anointed candle, and place it before the image of the goddess.

Start the rite by sitting or lying comfortably, and construct a cone of power around you. Breath in its white light to enliven your whole body.

When the cone is fully formed, imagine that the backdrop of the room is fading away. The cone is hanging in a black void, with you inside it.

Now feel the cone begin to move. You are rising up into the sky, leaving the earth behind. As the cone travels, it picks up speed. You can see stars flashing past, and planets, the coloured gases of immense nebulae. You are travelling back in time.

Presently, you see a brighter star ahead of you, winking with a blue-white light. The cone zooms towards it, and soon you see that the star is in fact the Earth, but in ancient times.

Visualize the cone dropping towards it, slowing down as it descends. You are moving towards Egypt. See the continents get larger and larger beneath you. With your mind, direct the cone to Egypt and make landfall.

Once the cone has landed imagine that a doorway appears in its side. Walk through it. Outside, you are surrounded by a desert of reddish sand. Nearby, you see the mighty pylon of a temple.

Walk towards the temple. Feel the heat of the sand beneath your feet, and the hot sun on your body. How are you dressed in this world? Take note of your surroundings. Use your inner eye to look around. What can you see? Although you are being led in this visualization, there is still plenty of space for you to add detail. No two people would ever see exactly the same imagery. Begin to build up your inner world. Make it real in your mind.

Now walk to the pylon and take a few moments to examine the walls rearing above you. Do they have carvings on them, or are they unadorned? Take a deep breath and smell the air. Incense smoke is drifting out from the temple; its heady aroma fills your nose. You can hear faint music – the bleat of pipes and the low beating of drums.

Enter beneath the shade of the pylon gate, cross a courtyard, and find yourself in a vast chamber of stone columns. It is quite dark, but on the floor there are bowls of burning oil that emit a flickering light. Here, the air is cooler and refreshing, and the smell of incense is complemented by a strong fragrance of exotic flowers. Perhaps there are people here – priests and priestesses – or perhaps you are alone. Again, spend a few moments looking round. Go to touch one of the columns; feel the rough texture of the stone beneath your fingers. As you look round, add your own details to the scene. Make it come alive for you.

Now walk across the hall of columns and pass through a doorway. You find you have entered a small shrine. Against one wall is a large black basalt statue of a seated cat, the sacred cat of Bast. The statue has golden earrings and a collar of faience. Bowls of incense smoulder before her and she is flanked by flickering flames. You see priests and priestesses in the shrine. They are surrounded by cats, some sitting on the floor, some lying in niches in the walls. The air is full of music of the cats, their purrs and cries. Pause to pay your respects to the sacred cat of Bast. You can talk to the priests and priestesses if you like. They may have something to tell you, or a gift to impart. Stroke the cats around you.

After a few minutes, say farewell to the priests and priestesses and leave the shrine by another doorway. You find yourself in a corridor with painted walls. Again, it is quite dark, but you can see where you are going by the dim lamplight glimmering on the floor.

Presently, the corridor opens out into a vast room lined with columns. Ahead of you, at the other end of the chamber, you see a flight of golden steps that lead up to a life-sized golden statue of the goddess. She is a cat-headed woman, carrying a sistrum, surrounded by kittens in gold. She wears a long sheath dress and a necklace around her throat, but her feet are bare. The steps are covered in cats, sleeping, grooming, playing. The room is full of soft but lively music, played by priestesses on flutes and drums and rattles. Other priests and priestesses dance sinuously to the music, like cats themselves. The floor is covered in petals and as you walk upon them, they release their rich fragrance.

Approach the foot of the stairs and gaze up at the goddess. Visualize the statue gradually coming alive. The eyes become living eyes, and slowly, the rigid gold turns to furry skin. See the goddess descend the stairs towards you, her eyes full of benevolence and peace.

While this is happening, cast your inner eye back to the room where your statue of the goddess stands before the anointed candle. Imagine that the light of this candle shines into the statue, which is an extension of the senses of Bast in the temple. Through the light of this candle, Bast can see your soul, and recognize you.

Spend some time speaking with the goddess. She is a friend to you. She may show you things, give you a symbolic gift or simply offer affection. She may have words of advice for your work to come, or ask you to do something for her in the real world. Let your mind wander freely.

After a few minutes, bow to the goddess, thank her for this audience, and say farewell. See her begin to retreat up the stairs. When she reaches the top she assumes her normal position and turns back into a sleeping statue of gold.

Now walk back through the temple, bidding farewell to the priests and priestesses, and all the cats. Go out into the desert and walk back towards the cone, which you can see shining ahead of you.

When you reach it, step inside and see the doorway sealing behind you. Sit or lie down for the journey home.

See the imagery of Egypt fading away outside the cone, until you are once again hanging in blackness. Feel the cone begin to move. You rise up into the sky and now travel through space, forward in time. Once again, see the stars flashing past, until you perceive the bright speck of light that is our earth. The light becomes brighter, until you can see the whole of the planet beneath you. Direct your cone back to your home and your ritual room.

When you have completed your journey, see the imagery of the room reappearing outside the cone. Then dismantle the cone, anticlockwise. When you are ready, open your eyes.

Once you have finished your visualization, you should write down or record as much as you can remember of what you saw, heard, smelled or touched. This can be transferred to your diary later. Over the months, as you practise visualizing, you will see how your impressions become more detailed and vivid. If you have performed the visualization in a group, you can tell each other what you saw before you write it down. Alternatively, you can pass a tape recorder around. (For groups, the latter method is probably better, especially if you have a member who is happy to type up the results for everyone.) This part of any meeting is usually lively and interesting. It is a good time to relax with refreshments, as everyone talks about what they have seen. Inevitably, there will be people who did not pick much up. It is important that the rest of the group do not let them get discouraged. Visualizing should not be a competition to see who comes up with the most stunning imagery and information. Some people are naturally more adept at it, but it is a skill that can be learned. We have also found that sometimes people are reticent to talk about what they have seen, especially when they have received information of a personal nature. Their silence should be respected. When they need to talk about it, they will.

You can repeat this visualization as often as you like. On each occasion, you will build up more imagery of your inner world.

One member of our group once said she was worried that she was wasting the goddess's time by simply going to see her and not doing any specific ritual work. But Bast is a part of ourselves. When we wake her up within us, she lives. We can talk to her any time. If we worry about wasting her time, perhaps it means we are not giving enough time to ourselves.

When you have been concentrating on the inner realm, it is important to ground yourself afterwards, to reassert yourself in the physical world. The best way to do this is through physical activity, and the best way to accomplish that with a group is to put on a favourite CD and dance in the ritual room. We always conclude our rituals with an impromptu dance session, and as Bast is a goddess associated with dancing, we feel this is entirely appropriate.

13

A Rite of Bast

With waving opalescence in her gown,
Even when she walks along, you think she's dancing.
Charles Baudelaire

You should visit the temple of Bast at least a couple of times before embarking upon a visualization that involves the manipulation of energy, which in simple terms means asking Bast to help you in some way and performing ritual acts to assist that, or approaching her on behalf of other people who need help.

Assigning roles

What follows is our habitual working rite, when we petition the goddess to aid us. When you become more proficient at this ritual, you should be able to do without the script being read or a tape of it being played. To prevent jarring interruptions in the ritual, it is best to be organized beforehand, and to make sure that certain people are in charge of particular aspects of the rite. Obviously, if you are performing the ritual alone, you have to be in charge of everything! As to whether a solo practitioner should speak aloud during the cone creation and visualized journey, this is up to the individual, but we certainly recommend that you recite the charges aloud.

In our group, we designate one person to construct and dismantle the cone of power, another to lead the visualization (whom we term the visualizer) and another to recite the charges (whom we term the charge-reader). One person makes sure the incense is replenished, while another ensures that the music keeps playing

160

and presses the repeat button on the CD player if necessary. These roles are swapped around from ritual to ritual. We all take part in the shaking of rattles and sistra.

It is important that the person who is leading the visualization does not rush it, so that everyone has time to visualize the scene properly. Similarly, someone who leads too slowly can ruin the atmosphere for the participants. A group needs to become familiar with working with one another to achieve the right balance, which takes practice, and sometimes requires patience. But as we have stressed before, practice makes perfect and even the least adept visualizers should be given the opportunity to improve.

The ritual can be adapted and changed to suit your needs. The more times you do it, the more you will probably think of little personal touches you want to add.

Clarifying your objectives

It is extremely important that everyone attending the rite is absolutely clear what they want to achieve from it. When you give Bast the pictures of your desires they must be as obvious and unambiguous as possible. Magic takes the path of least resistance. Do not just ask for help with money without telling the goddess exactly how you want to achieve that. Remember the story of the monkey's paw – if you just ask for money, you could end up getting it as compensation for some hideous, crippling accident. Be precise. If you want help with a job interview, see yourself walking into the interview room, and your potential new boss sitting behind a desk. Show Bast a picture of this person wearing a tag on their clothes with their name on it. Show this person smiling at you, liking you. Show yourself giving off positive energy. Then you could show Bast an image of the boss handing you a piece of paper, clearly marked 'employment contract' and with your name on it. See yourself signing this contract, shaking the hand of your new boss and everyone being happy.

In the case of simple money problems, show Bast an image of your bank statement, with a huge healthy balance on it. Then show her yourself, and your loved ones, all healthy, happy and smiling and deriving benefit from this state of affairs. Do not leave anything to chance.

One of our group members was very lonely, and asked for a new lover; she just wanted to be in love. Bast granted this request, but unfortunately our friend had forgotten to be clear about exactly what she asked for. She met the man of her dreams, but only weeks before he was due to leave the country for good. When he left, she felt worse than before she had met him. What she should have asked for was an *enduring* love affair, not just the experience of love itself. She should have visualized herself and her lover together in years to come, happy and secure. Again, this illustrates how you should be utterly specific about what you want.

Another group member wanted to leave shared accommodation and get a home of her own. Bast again granted this request: shortly afterwards our friend was asked to leave the house by her landlord, who wanted the room back for himself. It forced her to go out and find what she wanted, but perhaps was not quite the way in which she would have liked it to happen, as at the time it caused her a lot of stress and worry.

If dates are important in your request, show Bast a calendar with the day you are thinking of clearly marked. If your problems or needs are associated with a specific person, people or company, give Bast images of these with big labels on. A bank manager could have his title written across his forehead.

The above examples are the less successful stories; there are many more cases of wonderful things that have happened to members of our group when they have asked Bast for her aid. In particular, she can help with problems concerning cats. We have lost count of the number of times we have performed a ritual to ask for the return of a lost cat. In many cases, the cat has returned the very next day. People have been helped with their health, with their environment, with relationship problems and financial crises. The only limit to what can be achieved is the imagination.

It helps to imagine Bast as a discarnate entity with little comprehension of the reality of our day-to-day lives. She is a goddess; relationship problems, money worries and job fears hardly form part of her daily routine. In fact, the concept of time alone will mean nothing to her. We have to show her, then she can help us.

The rite

We include wine-drinking as part of our ritual. The descriptions of the festival of Bast given by Herodutus include stories of widespread consumption of alcohol in the form of wine and beer. Some people, however, may feel uncomfortable with the inclusion of alcohol in the rituals. The group or individual should do only what they feel comfortable with, and in the case of groups, it should always be a group decision.

Throughout the ritual we use the terms 'priestesses' and 'sisterhood'. These terms pertain to our own group, but they can be adjusted to suit your needs.

The version of the rite incorporates many of the Bast charges created by E.A. St George, some of which we have adapted to fit in with our own system and beliefs. Ms St George's words are particularly moving and evocative. The list of suppliers at the end of the book gives information on how to acquire her two booklets on Bast and Sekhmet, which include a beautiful selection of prayers and invocations, some of them translated from the original Egyptian.

Equipment

You will need:

- Bast statue or other image
- two altar candles, one for each side of the image: blue and yellow
- a goblet of wine
- a dish for offerings
- Bast incense
- Bast anointing oil
- rattles or sistra
- fresh flowers in blues, purples and white
- small candles, one for each member of the group in an appropriate colour
- food for the feast
- red wine or other appropriate drink

Preparation

Arrange the flowers around the statue of Bast and light the altar candles. Arrange the feast and the wine before the altar. Light the incense. Play soft music. The group should sit in a circle and anoint their personal candles with the perfumed oil, from the ends towards the centre. They should concentrate fully on what they want from the ritual, beginning to practise the strong images they will give to Bast later on, and put their intentions into the candles. When they burn, so their intentions will fly to the goddess.

The ritual

Begin the ritual with a breathing exercise to relax the particupants and enliven their energy. Now light the anointed candles which stand before the goddess.

Next, construct a cone of power. The cone is a travelling one, and the participants must visualize it leaving this world, travelling through space back in time to ancient Egypt, and alighting in the desert.

The visualizer now takes over, and says:

Step out of the cone and into the desert. Feel the warmth of the sun on your skin and the burning heat of the sand beneath your feet. In the distance you can see a vast temple rearing up to meet the sky. Begin to walk towards the temple, noting anything that you see on the way. As you draw closer you pass by an oasis pool surrounded by tall palm trees. Lionesses doze in the shade of the trees and as you pass by they lift their heads as if to grant you passage into the temple.

Walk on, past the lionesses, towards the temple. As you get closer you begin to realize what a massive structure it is. It is constructed of vast columns, which are intricately carved with symbols and hieroglyphs. Ahead of you there is a wide sandstone path leading up to the main entrance, which is flanked by two huge obelisks. These are constructed of rough golden sandstone and are so tall that they seem to reach up to the sky. Walk up the path and amongst the columns. Once you are in their shade the air feels cool and refreshing. It seems like a haven from the relentless heat of the desert. You can smell a strong fragrance of cut blooms on the air and the subtler scent of an exotic musky incense.

You find that you are standing in the outer courtyard of the temple. There are trees cultivated here and in the centre you can see a large circular pool. This pool reflects the burning gold of the sun in the daytime and the silver light of the moon by night for these are both aspects of the Goddess. There are temple staff around you, all going about their duties. Many of them smile at you in greeting but none approach you. It is as if you are expected here.

A Rite of Bast

At the back of the courtyard you can see a huge doorway which leads to the outer shrine. Walk towards it. Either side of this great doorway you can see that the walls are carved with pictures of cat-headed people and seated cats. You can reach out and run your hand over the warm stone. Feel the contours of the carvings beneath your fingers.

Step inside the shrine now. The room is dimly lit, let your eyes adjust after the bright sunlight outside. After a moment you can see that before you stands a statue of a great cat carved from smooth, black stone. It wears thick gold earrings and an ornately crafted collar of faience. At its feet lie offerings left by visitors to the temple. You can see many flowers and perfume jars, as well as statues and figurines. Priests and priestesses are in the shrine, tending a multitude of cats. The air around you is full of the music of the cats; their purrs and cries. Pause to pay your respect to the sacred cat of Bast, then walk on down a corridor to your right.

You are making your way towards the inner sanctum of Bast down a short corridor lit with flickering lamps and candles. At the far end the corridor opens out into a vast room lined by pillars.

At the other end of the room, so huge that it fills your vision, is a flight of golden steps that leads up to an immense golden statue of the goddess. She is depicted as a beautiful cat-headed woman. She wears heavy jewellery at her ears and throat and is swathed in a robe carved from gold. In her hand she carries a golden sistrum, her sacred rattle, and at her feet are tiny golden kittens. The steps below her are covered in cats, sleeping, grooming, playing. The room is full of soft but lively music, played by priestesses on flutes and drums and rattles. Other priests and priestesses dance sinuously to the music, like cats themselves. The floor is covered in petals and as you walk upon them, they release their heady fragrance.

Approach the foot of the stairs and raise your arms.

The visualizer shakes a sistrum three times.
The charge-reader says:

> *Oh, Bast, lady of Asheru, ruler of Sekhet-Neter,*
> *Ruler of the divine field, lady of Ankhtawy,*
> *Life of the two lands,*
> *We, your priestesses call to you.*
> *Hear our prayers.*
> *We come before you in love.*

We come before you in peace.
We come before you in joy.
And ask that we might speak with you.
May your essence enter into the statue before us.
And become your living body in this world.
Dwell here in gentleness, Bast,
And let your blessings be upon us.

The whole group shake their sistra, conjuring the *Heka* of Bast to enter the statue, both in the visualization and in the statue at home. Concentrate on this happening. When you feel a change in the energy of the room let the shaking die away. (A group may need a few attempts before they sense energy in unison but it will happen with practice.)

The visualizer resumes:

Now visualize that the statue before you begins to come alive. The eyes become the living eyes of a cat, and gradually the gold turns to furry skin. The kittens at her feet begin to play and the folds of her dress flow softly. The goddess begins to descend the stairs towards you, her eyes full of benevolence and peace.

While this is happening, you must cast your inner eye back to the room where your statue of the goddess stands before the anointed candles. Imagine that the light of these candles shines into the statue, which is like an extension of the senses of Bast in the temple. Through the light of these candles, Bast can see your soul, and recognizes you.

The visualizer shakes the rattles.
The charge-reader says:

Oh, Bast, queen of all cats,
Daughter of Ra,
We bring offerings to you
As symbols of our love and respect.
We offer food to the great goddess in the temple of Bast.
We offer drink to the cat of the heavens.
We offer incense to the gentle cat.
We offer love to the daughter of Ra.

Now burn some incense and eat the feast, but leave a small

portion of each item you eat for Bast. These morsels should be placed in a separate dish. The feast can be shared with any cats that are present. Pass round a goblet of wine (which can be refilled as often as you like), each person present splashing a little of it over the other offerings in the dish. Try to imagine that you are still in the temple rather than at home; the visualization has not ended.

After this has been done, place the dish of offerings on the altar before the statue. Now close your eyes and make yourself comfortable to return to the visualization.

The visualizer shakes the sistrum three times, and says:

See the temple clearly once more around you. Bast is standing before us, enjoying the offerings we have given her.

The visualizer shakes the sistrum three times again.

The charge-reader says:

> *Oh Bast, daughter of Ra,*
> *Divine cat, lady of all magic,*
> *Accept our offerings for they are given in love.*
> *Grant to us our desires and come to our aid.*
> *Reach out to us with gentle hands,*
> *And let your blessing be upon your priestesses.*
> *So it is spoken, so it is done.*

Each member of the group now visualizes clearly in pictures exactly what he or she wants from Bast. Imagine yourself as happy, carefree, loved and loving, but show it in pictures rather than words. After an appropriate time, the visualizer shakes the sistrum and the charge-reader says:

> *Oh Bast, queen of cats,*
> *Lady of love and pleasure,*
> *We offer you our humble thanks*
> *For all that you have granted to us.*
> *Continue to share with us your strength and your fire.*
> *Lend us your understanding, show us your wisdom.*
> *Give us the courage to be all that we may be*
> *And the ability to know ourselves as you know us.*
> *May we take with us from this temple a feeling of peace*
> *That will be with us in the days and weeks to come.*

May we feel enlivened and liberated from all care.
May you strengthen this sisterhood,
With love, unity and grace.
We ask this in your name, Bast,
Lady of Ankhtawy, lady of Asheru,
Ruler of the divine field,
Ruler of Sekhet-Neter.

Continue the visualization for a few moments. It is time for all present to commune privately with the goddess. She may have knowledge to bestow or gifts to impart. She may take you to other parts of the temple, or elsewhere in her realm. You may meet other people or gods.

After an appropriate time, the visualizer shakes the rattles, and the charge-reader says:

Oh, Bast, we thank you for this audience.
We go from your temple with your presence in our hearts.
We are your priestesses and will do all in our power
To protect your children on this earth.
When we make love, we will do so as an offering to you.
When we partake of delicious food and drink, we will do so as
an offering to you.
When we dance, we will do so as an offering to you.
When we sing, we will do so as an offering to you.
We give you our love and our gratitude,
Be forever in our hearts, Bast, even when we here present are
apart.

The visualizer resumes:

Now bow to the goddess, and see her begin to retreat up the stairs. When she reaches the top she assumes her normal position and turns back into a sleeping statue of gold.

When you are ready, bid farewell to the priests and priestesses, and to all the cats. Walk back down the corridor again. In the outer shrine it is time to have a few thoughts for your own cats. Perhaps you may like to ask for Bast's protection for them. You can also ask for her blessing for any other loved ones. When you have finished bow your head to the statue to show your thanks and continue on out of the temple.

A Rite of Bast

Make your way back through the outer courtyard and out of the huge entrance again. You can see the cone of power shining in the distance. Walk towards it, past the oasis pool and the lionesses. Once you reach it step inside and sit back down.

The person designated to construct the cone now brings it back to present space and time, and dismantles it. When this is done, he or she says, 'When you are ready, open your eyes.'

After the ritual

Once everyone has opened their eyes, it is a good idea for them to talk about their experiences. Some people might feel that their visualizations are too personal to discuss at that time, and this must be respected. In our group, we always tape the results of a working, and type it up afterwards as a permanent record. You may like to make a note of your experiences in your magical diary.

After the discussion, we always enter party mode. The first thing we do is dance for Bast. We play our favourite songs and usually sing to them – badly, it has to be said, but we are sure Bast does not mind that! On many ritual nights we have sat up drinking wine and talking until dawn. These are special nights, and everyone should enjoy them as they see fit.

The remains of the feast should be cast out over a garden or some other appropriate spot. During the following days, many of us also like to make some kind of donation to a charity associated with cats, whether in cash or simply a can of cat food in one of the many charity dump bins in pet stores.

This rite can be adapted for use as a simple 'thanks' ritual. Instead of asking Bast for her help, the time in the ritual apportioned for requesting boons can be spent simply thanking the goddess for past help and for her presence in our lives. We think it is as important to do this as any potent ritual to improve a situation or create opportunities. The aid of the gods should never be taken for granted.

14

The Festival of Bast

She's pale, and warm, and duskily beguiling;
Nobility is moulded in her neck;
Slender and tall she holds herself in check,
An huntress born, sure-eyed, and quiet-smiling.
From: 'To a Colonial Lady' by Charles Baudelaire

Bast's festival traditionally took place during April and May. The Revd Christina Paul, of the Kemetic Orthodox tradition, has researched the Egyptian calendar and its significant dates, and from her work we have discovered that Bast's festival began on 17 April. You could either celebrate the festival on this date, or perhaps some time during the following few weeks.

The festival rite

Our festival is not a working rite, but a ritual of celebration, so it is a time when people not of our temple group but interested in magic and the cat goddess in particular can be invited to participate. We have also joined up with other groups to celebrate the festival.

Herodotus described Bast's festival as a huge, drunken party at which more wine was consumed than at any other time of the year. While the excessive drinking is strictly optional we do believe that the festival should be seen as a special occasion and celebrated as such.

As part of this festival rite, we draw the hieroglyph of Bast's name on each other, on the forehead, the upper arm or the back of the hand. It is a good idea to practise this before the ritual.

Equipment

You will need:

- an appropriate feast for you and a feast for any household cats
- red wine
- Bast incense
- sistra
- a Bast statue
- purple, white and blue flowers
- alter candles of gold and silver
- Bast anointing oil
- one candle for each member of the group in an appropriate colour
- silver items, crystals and moonstones for the altar
- felt-tip pens or kohl pencils for drawing Bast's symbol

Preparation

Arrange the statue of Bast on the altar with the flowers and light the altar candles. Place the silver and moonstones on the altar around the statue and have everything else close at hand.

Members of the group anoint their personal candles with the perfumed oil, from the ends towards the centre. They should concentrate on putting a part of themselves into the candle.

Bast and Sekhmet

The ritual

The ritual begins with a breathing exercise to relax the participants and enliven their energy. Then light the anointed candles, which stand before the goddess. Construct the cone of power as normal and visualize the journey back to ancient Khem. The visualizer says:

The cone alights on the banks of the Nile, amid a palm grove. When you leave it, you walk down to the water, to a small wooden jetty. It is early morning and bright sunlight shines upon you. The air is fresh and the sun is warm but not yet hot. It is the day of the festival of Bast and you look forward to great celebration.

You see a boat sailing towards you, its oars cutting through the water. Its prow is adorned with the *wedjat eye*, the left eye of Horus, his lunar eye, once damaged by Set but restored by Thoth.

The boat is filled with people, who wave to you as they see you standing on the banks of the Nile. The boat veers towards you and draws alongside the jetty so that you may embark. You climb aboard, and the boat continues to sail along the great river.

As you travel up the Nile towards Bubastis, you join in with the merrymaking on board. Everyone is dancing, singing, clapping and drinking wine. You pass people on the riverbank, and some of the women on board shout out to them.

You sail to the Delta, and here you see the walls of Bubastis rising ahead of you. A canal leads up to the city and then branches into two streams to surround it. You cannot see the main gates, for they are on the other side of the city. You must travel up the canal to reach the great entrance.

Outside the city gates, you disembark and walk beneath the ceremonial arch, in procession with your fellow travellers. The city is in a mood of great celebration. Everywhere you look, people greet you as friends. Household cats are garlanded with flowers as they sit in doorways or lounge in the street.

Imagine that time has passed as you have journeyed up the Nile and it is now afternoon. The sun is high in the cloudless sky and the air is hot and humid. You walk to the great temple of the goddess, and enter the outer courtyard, which is laid with fresh sand. A sacred pool dominates the centre of the courtyard, surrounded by trees. The yard is filling up with people. Awnings have been erected so that people can escape from the heat. Temple servants move among the crowd, offering water. The air is full of the smell of flowers and incense. Strong fragrant smoke swirls around you.

Ahead of you are the pylons of the temple itself. Huge statues of seated cats adorn each side of it, and we can see many cats present. These are the temple cats sacred to the goddess Bast, and they are tended by her temple staff.

Now the crowd begins to quieten and you know that the ceremony is about to begin. Everyone raises their arms to the sky with their palms facing up and you do the same.

The charge-reader says:

> *Open the gates of the heavens.*
> *Raise the gate of the sky.*
> *Open the gate of the sky.*
> *Let the gods of old come forth*
> *And shower their blessings upon us.*

The visualizer resumes:

Now, in the dimness of the temple ahead of you there is a flash of silver. Gradually, the priests of Bast emerge in procession from smoky gloom. They are carrying an ornately carved plinth upon which stands the statue of the goddess. She is taller than life size and constructed of solid silver.

The priests bring the statue out into the courtyard for everyone to see. The women of the temple, who are dancers and musicians, follow them. These women are known as *shenayet*.

The visualiser shakes the sistrum.
The charge-reader says:

> *Oh, Bast, lady of Asheru, ruler of Sekhet-neter,*
> *lady of Ankhtawy, ruler of the divine field,*
> *Life of the two lands,*
> *We, your priests and priestesses, call to you.*
> *Hear our prayers.*
> *And awaken to our presence.*
> *We come before you in love.*
> *We come before you in peace.*
> *We come before you in joy,*
> *On this the day of your festival.*

173

The visualizer then resumes:

Now visualize yourself stepping forward and giving offerings to Bast, placing them at the feet of the silver statue. As you do this the whole crowd in the courtyard does likewise. Soon there are offerings of food, drink, flowers and perfume piled high around the feet of the goddess.

Now open your eyes and lay your flowers on Bast's altar in your temple at home and arrange your feast before her.

The group members lay flowers on the altar and the visualizer shakes the sistrum.

The charge-reader says:

We offer food unto the great goddess in the temple of Bast.
We offer drink unto the cat of the heavens.
We offer incense unto the gentle cat.
We offer warmth and love unto the daughter of Ra.
We offer her happiness and music.
We offer her a place in which to be reborn and spin once more
*   the destinies of men.*

The visualizer says:

Close your eyes again and return to your visualization. See the priests in the courtyard surrounding the statue. They perform ritual actions to persuade Bast to enter her statue. They draw her symbol on the sand in the courtyard and paint it onto the forehead of the statue. They offer her wine and anoint her with perfumed oil. The *shenayet* dance around them, singing and shaking their sistra. They are calling to the goddess with their music. Now open your eyes and draw the symbol of Bast on each other.

The group take it in turns to draw the hieroglyph of Bast's name on one another. When this is done, the visualizer shakes the sistrum again.

The charge-reader says:

Oh great Bast, lady of all magic, accept these offerings,
For they are given in love.
Great cat of the heavens

Dwell here in gentleness until the day
When all of us, your children, will greet the gods as brothers.
Dwell here in gentleness.
Let your blessing be upon this house.
Dwell here in gentleness and let your blessings be upon your
priestesses.
Dwell here in gentleness and stretch forth your hand to bless
your children.
So let it be spoken. So let it be done.

The visualizer says:

Now visualize that the statue in the courtyard begins to come alive, animated by *heka*. The eyes become living eyes, and gradually the silver turns to furry skin.

While this is happening, cast your inner eye back to the room where your statue of the goddess stands before the anointed candles. Imagine that your own statue is becoming filled with the *Heka* of Bast, so that the goddess stands before you in your own temple at home. Imagine that the light of your candle shines into the statue, which is like an extension of the senses of Bast in her temple. Through the light of your candle, Bast can see your soul and recognize you.

You can also feel the presence, strength and love of Bast entering your body, as her *heka* is drawn into the symbols you wear. Concentrate for a moment on this. Feel her energy filling you, enlivening you and freeing you from worry.

The visualizer then shakes the sistrum and the charge-reader says:

You are the power of the sun,
Let us not be overwhelmed by your destruction,
For you are concerned with the fertility of lands
And the fertility of women.
You are beauty, health and gentleness.
You comfort those who are made mad by the moon,
When you walk at their side in the shadow lands.
You, oh lady, are of the gods who protect this world.
Thunder and lightning strike the skies,
But you return in glory with your father, the sun,

175

Bast and Sekhmet

And your mother, the moon.
You can blast and you can forgive.
You can punish and you can reward.
You can grant sunshine unto children.
You can grant moonshine unto lovers.
You have died and yet you live.
It is whispered that if one man or woman should believe in your
*   power*
You can harken to the prayers of all the world.
Hear us, oh Bast,
You can twist and skein and weave the thread of destiny.
You are sacred and beautiful, lady of music.
You are lustrous and all-powerful.
And the world rides upon the arch of your back.
You are venerated and called the lady of the east.
Be favourable unto us. Protect us from all harm.
That we may live in health and rejoice in your care.
Be gentle with us and show us the pathway to the great gods,
The source of all creation.
Bast the divine, ruler of the night, goddess of love, infinite, all-
*   wise and all-knowing,*
Grant blessings unto us who follow in the ways of your many
*   priestesses.*
Great cat, who is the cat of the heavens,
Grant to us our desires.

The visualizer continues:

Now spend a few moments communing with Bast in your own way.
Now is the time to thank her for all that she has helped you with over
the last year. Perhaps you could thank her for the protection and
love she has shown for you and your own cats.

When everyone has finished, the charge-reader says:

Oh, Bast, queen of all cats,
Daughter of Ra.
We have brought offerings to you
As symbols of our love and respect.
Through us, may you experience their pleasures.

The Festival of Bast

Now eat the feast, but leave a small portion of each item for Bast. Do likewise with the wine. Try to imagine that you are still in the temple, rather than at home. The visualization has not ended. The household cats should also be fed their feast at this point, if possible.

After this has been done, place the remains on the altar before the candles and statue. The visualizer now says:

Close your eyes again now and return to your visualization. Imagine that the day is ended in Bubastis. The sun has set on the horizon and the sky in the west is streaked with orange light. The moon has already risen high. The festival is nearly at an end.

The visualizer shakes the sistrum.
The charge-reader says:

We will remember, oh Bast the immortal
That you are in the kingdom of the moon,
And your temple is wrought of silver.
Behold this altar, which is set with silver in token of the moon
See, oh perfumed one, how it is decorated with moonstones
And with crystals like the eyes of great cats.
We will remember, oh Bast, the white flame that burns upon
*   the altars of the moon*
Where Bast the gentle dwells among the veils of silver,
Wearing the crown that is great of horns.
We will remember the goddess who spins and weaves the
*   destinies of men.*
We will remember that beyond the moon, there are other ways
*   through trackless void*
And we will ask the great goddess of cats to guide our footsteps
*   there.*

The visualizer resumes:

Now the statue in the courtyard turns back into sliver as Bast's *heka* leaves it. Similarly, you feel her presence leave your body like smoke from the symbols you wear, but leaving a warmth behind that is a memory of her power. In our own temple at home your statue of Bast sleeps again until the next time you invoke her into it.

Torches are lit around the temple and in the courtyard the priests lift up the statue once more. They carry it slowly back into the inner shrine, followed by the *shenayet*. The crowd around you bow their heads as the priests pass by and you do the same. Then everyone stands silent and watches until the statue disappears once more into the shadows of the temple.

When the statue has been returned to the shrine the people begin to leave the courtyard. As it clears, you are left alone, and once again you notice the sacred pool in the centre. Walk over to it. The moon is reflected in its depths. Here, you kneel for a while and scry in the water. A message may be given to you.

Allow a few moments for scrying in the pool.

The charge-reader says:

> *We will go forth from this place,*
> *To the world we know.*
> *Bast, great goddess, send your blessing through us*
> *Unto all the world,*
> *That once more we may turn our faces to the gods*
> *And greet them by name.*

Everyone repeats after the charge-reader:

> *So let it be spoken.*
> *So let it be done.*

The visualizer brings the visualization to a conclusion:

Now you leave the temple and return to the boats which will take you back down the Nile to your cone of power.

Moonlight makes silver on the water, and your travelling companions are singing softly. In your heart, you still speak to Bast, thanking her for the feeling of peace that will be with you in the days and weeks to come. You feel enlivened and strengthened by your meeting with her.

When you see your cone on the shore, the boat lands again at the little jetty, and you step from it. Walk back up the bank of the Nile to where your cone stands waiting and step back inside.

Return and dismantle the cone as usual.

After this ritual we usually continue feasting and drinking and often spend the rest of the evening dancing, singing and talking. The festival of Bast should be celebrated with a party of some kind. She is, after all, a goddess of pleasure.

15

A Meeting with the Goddess Sekhmet

Delightful eyes, you burn with mystic rays
Like candles in broad day; red suns may blaze,
But cannot quench their still, fantastic light.
From 'The Living torch' by Charles Baudelaire

Anyone who has had dealings with this mighty goddess will tell you the same thing: she is not a lady to be messed with. In our group we find it impossible to imagine her as a nurturing mother goddess, simply because, in our view, she is not and never has been. If we approach her temple, it is because we need her help with a very

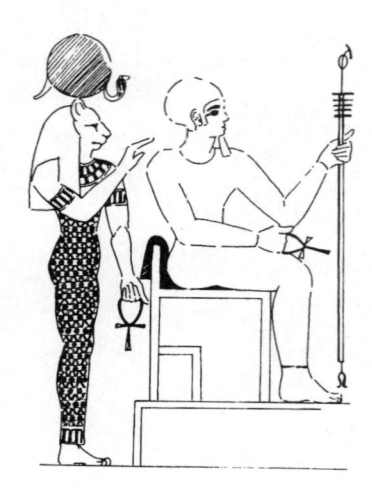

serious problem. As we have said, Sekhmet does have a healing aspect and can be approached for requests concerning ill health, but is best to remain aware that her power is a purging fire, and if not correctly requested, the cure might be worse than the illness itself.

We approach Sekhmet with the utmost respect and temerity. We have performed rituals to her for ourselves and people we knew who were in trouble and needed help. Sekhmet has helped us in matters to do with the law, personal protection and self-empowerment when a boost to inner strength and confidence was sorely needed. We have also invoked her to protect a child in danger and to shield someone from the malign intentions of an enemy,.

Preparations

Obviously, before performing rituals to her, you should experience Sekhmet's presence and character. As with Bast, a visit to her temple is required, but this is a time when the heart beats fast and you wonder what might manifest from the shadows.

Sekhmet is not malign in herself, but she is fierce and powerful. The only time we visit her other than to request her help is on her festival day. This is when we bring her a feast and thank her for her help throughout the year. On this occasion, she feels more mellow to us. However, most of our group have had very enlightening and comforting visits to Sekhmet, whatever the time of year. In some instances, she has appeared almost playful to them, as if aware, and forgiving, of their inexperience. The relationship you develop with this goddess is really dictated by how you feel about her attributes and their presence, or absence, within yourself. She can impart great inner strength and make us more than we currently are. Her fire can burn fear from us, and give us clarity of sight.

The music we play for Sekhmet visualizations is always more passionate, if not darker, than we use for Bast. To appreciate her fully, you need to invoke the right mood in yourself for the visit.

For the ritual bath, add some herbs or oil of a spicy, fiery nature to the water. As you lie in your aromatic bath water, you should imagine yourself as a powerful yet languid lioness, a child of the goddess. You should feel the sleek, confident vigour of the lioness within you, whether you are male or female. By the time you enter your ritual room, you should feel as if you move with Sekhmet's deadly grace, as if nothing can harm you. These feelings are obviously easier to invoke after you have visited Sekhmet's temple for the first time, but try to feel them as much as you can beforehand.

Prepare your altar with a representation of the goddess, flanked by red candles. Light some fiery incense and have ready a small candle of your own colour ray.

The rite

Light your colour ray candle and place it before your representation of the goddess. After your breathing exercises and the construction of a travelling cone, see yourself emerge in ancient Khem, at the city of Memphis. The red desert surrounds you and the air is hot and dry. Ahead of you is an oasis pool. Lionesses laze around the edge of the water under the shade of tall palms. Here, as at the temple of Bast, the lionesses seem as though they are the guardians of the place and you bow to them as you pass by. There is a vast temple ahead of you that is dedicated to the god Ptah. He is the husband of Sekhmet and she resides in the heart of his temple.

Walk towards the temple. As you draw closer, you see that it is constructed of sandstone and comprises many colossal columns that are covered in bas-relief hierogylphs. An avenue of sphinx statues leads up to the entrance. Walk along it and through the immense gateway at the end.

The inside of the temple consists of a labyrinth of columns with no apparent altar. This is because Ptah has no visible altar. There is only a statue of the god. To enter the shrine to Sekhmet we must declare our intent to the presence of Ptah her husband and ask him to reveal it to us. Approach the statue of Ptah and ask his permission to pass by him to the fiery depths of Sekhmet's inner sanctum.

When you have done this, you hear a loud rumble and a doorway opens up in the floor behind the statue of Ptah. You can see a steep sandstone ramp leading down into the depths below. Begin to walk down the ramp. As you descend, an orange-red glow lights your way. You can see that fiery torches are alight upon colossal smooth stone walls.

When you reach the bottom you find yourself in an enormous circular amphitheatre. It is completely lit by fire and there is a large pit in the centre where fire from deep within the earth roars upwards and into the shrine. Opposite you, in an alcove in the far wall, stands a statue of the goddess Sekhmet. It is about twice life size and made of smooth black granite. Around the foot of the statue sit proud and attentive lionesses. There are no priests or priestesses present because this is the sanctuary of fire, storm, dread, war, death, yet also of life.

Stand before the statue and stare up into the goddess's face. In your mind, ask her to awaken to your presence. Tell her you wish, in the future, to work in her name, for the good of those who need her power. Ask her to acknowledge you.

See the statue open its eyes. The gaze of the powerful goddess stares expectantly down upon you. Her open eyes are pure red orbs of light. A red glow is beginning to form around her as she comes alive. It becomes stronger until it is radiating out of all parts of the mighty statue. Upon her head a large orange solar disc burns brightly with raging fire. In her hand she holds a radiant gold *ankh* that shines with a solar, life-giving light. It is almost too bright to look upon.

You see the statue begin to move, slowly yet sinuously. Her footsteps shake the floor of the shrine. She towers over you, moving inexorably towards you, intensely black, yet shining with red light. She growls softly beneath her breath, like the rumble of a sleeping volcano.

Now cast your inner eye back to the statue on your altar at home and see it begin to glow with a red light. It too is coming alive. Sekhmet's presence is in the room with you now as well as in the temple.

Concentrate for a while on the candle of your colour and see a shaft of light of the same colour stretch out of the candle and flow towards the glowing statue of Sekhmet. Before you ask anything of her, she must see you for who you really are. She will only see you by the true colour of your spirit light.

As your coloured rays hit her statue she absorbs your very essence and at once knows who stands before her, for she can see into your soul, mind and heart with her gaze, and knows your every will and intention. Keep visualizing your colour ray flowing from the candle to the statue. Clear your mind of everything else. Let Sekhmet know you and your intention.

Now return again in your mind to the inside of the shrine where you stand before the goddess. This is the time when she might have knowledge to impart to you, or offer a symbolic gift of some kind. She may even ask you to do something for her.

Spend some minutes communing with the goddess. This is the time to talk with her so that she may know you. Perhaps you could tell her about your magical work and ask for her help.

When you feel that the audience has come to an end, thank Sekhmet for her presence. Bow your head to her and then see her begin to retreat into her shrine. Again feel the floor shake as she walks.

When she reaches her alcove, she turns back once more into a sleeping statue. Her eyes are no longer orange flame but shining black stone.

Turn to leave, paying your respects to the lionesses that protect the shrine. Pass back across the amphitheatre and climb back up to Ptah's temple. When you reach the top, the opening in the floor rumbles closed again behind you, sealing the secret shrine. Thank Ptah for allowing you access and walk back out of the temple towards your cone of power. As you pass the oasis, bid farewell to the lionesses there.

Once you are back inside the cone visualize yourself returning through time to the present and when you are ready dismantle the cone.

After this working you may like to make a note of your experience in your diary while it is fresh in your mind.

16

A Sekhmet Self-empowerment Ritual

Then, too, she has that vagrant
And subtle air of danger that makes fragrant
Her body, lithe and brown.

From 'The Cat' by Charles Baudelaire

Sekhmet personifies female strength and power. She is courageous, assertive and sometimes fierce. She is also protective, wise, healing and just. Nowadays, she is the natural choice when we turn to a goddess for inner strength. In a time when women are fighting for equality, choice and respect, Sekhmet's frequency has real relevance for us.

Sekhmet teaches us to be strong and decisive and not to accept second best. When members of our own group have interacted with her during rituals her message has always been clear: she encourages strength and assertiveness and sees no reason why we should be fearful or indecisive. Sometimes she lends us some of her power and we come out of those rituals feeling tall and proud. It is to capture this feeling that we devised the following rite. The main charge within it was adapted from a longer prayer, translated by E. A. St George, from *Under Regulus*.

Everyone feels bewildered and confused at some time in their life. There are times when we do not have the courage to make difficult decisions or to face our problems head on; at others we may just be feeling a little run down or depressed. This ritual is for those times. It will lend you a little of Sekhmet's strength. Often, some encouragement from her is all we need to find the right way of dealing with things.

As ever, Sekhmet should only be approached when you have a genuine need. In our experience, if she knows that you already have the answers you seek, she can manifest as impatient and irritable. Sometimes her response is simply 'Grow up and sort yourself out.' If you genuinely need her aid, then she will help you; if not, she will tell you so in no uncertain terms!

For this ritual you will need:

- a Sekhmet statue
- red candles
- Sekhmet incense
- a small piece of red paper and a pen
- a small feast of spicy foods
- a chalice of red wine

The Ritual

Set up your altar with the statue, light the red altar candles and the incense, and lay your feast ready before it. Begin with some breathing exercises and when you feel relaxed, construct a travelling cone of power and visualize the journey to ancient Khem.

The visualizer says:

When the cone comes to a halt get up and step outside. You find yourself in the desert near a rocky outcrop at the head of a wadi. The sand beneath your feet is red and littered with rough stone. You can feel the heat of the midday sun on your skin. The sky is bright and clear and the sun a burning orb above you. You are standing just above a narrow trickling stream of rusty-coloured water. The land around you is rough and barren.

There is no temple in this empty place, but ahead of you, in the distance, you can see a cluster of strangely shaped trees around the mouth of the wadi. Walk down along the edge of the stream towards the trees.

The terrain is uneven and difficult to negotiate. Sharp stones dig into the soles of your feet as you walk. The heat is overwhelming. Your need is great, so you will bear these discomforts.

Suddenly you hear a low, grumbling growl and look up. On the cliff above you a huge golden lioness basks in the heat of the sun.

She looks down at you inscrutably. What are your feelings as you see this magnificent creature?

As you draw closer to the mouth of the wadi, the stream grows stronger until it widens out into a flowing river in the middle of the desert. You can see a group of lionesses sheltering in the shade of the trees. These are Sekhmet's daughters and you must now approach them, for they will lead you to her.

The lionesses lift their heads as you approach and appraise you lazily through slitted eyes. You must ask them to call forth Sekhmet for you. In your mind, talk to them now and tell them why you are there. Explain that you need Sekhmet's help and want to talk with her. Ask the lionesses to call forth their mother on your behalf.

As you stand waiting, the great lioness on the cliff above you stands up and stretches sleepily. You watch her begin to descend a rocky path towards you. She negotiates the rocks with graceful ease.

Nearing the bottom of the cliff she leaps onto a huge red boulder and lands crouched like a cat. As you watch, she rises up onto her hind legs and takes on the shape of a woman with the head of a lioness. She wears a long tunic dress of red linen and on her head is a head-dress which represents a solar disc. At her neck the golden fur of the lioness begins to fade into golden skin. Sekhmet has answered your call and stands before you.

The charge-reader says:

> *Oh, mighty Sekhmet,*
> *Whose name means 'powerful',*
> *Golden lady of flame,*
> *Daughter of Ra,*
> *Mistress of the two lands,*
> *Goddess of the mouth of the wadi,*
> *Awaken to our presence.*
> *Hear us, who come to your feet with humble worth.*
> *Awaken to our call, so that we may bask in the power of*
> *your presence.*

Now open your eyes and draw the hieroglyph of Sekhmet on the piece of red paper. This will be a talisman for you to carry with you. When you have finished lay the amulet on the altar in front of your candles and statue.

Bast and Sekhmet

The visualizer says:

Now spend a few minutes telling Sekhmet about your problems. Be clear and precise about what you want. Listen to any advice she has for you.

He or she leaves a pause for private meditation, then continues:

Now the goddess begins to emanate a bright red glow. It seems to shine out from her skin, her eyes, even her clothes. Visualize that the red light of Sekhmet shines brighter and brighter until you are enveloped by it. Breathe it in and fill your body with her light. This is her gift to you. She is filling you with her strengthening essence. See yourself as an empty vessel, a black void, being filled with red light. Imagine that the amulet on your altar at home is also bathed in the red energy of Sekhmet. This will empower it, and when you carry it with you over the days to come, you will be reminded of the goddess's strength.

As you are filled with the red radiance, so you feel yourself standing taller, feeling more in control and able to cope. When you feel that you have absorbed the energy that you need, all say together:

Behold, I am a child of Sekhmet.
I am with her, and she is within me.
My hair is the hair of the golden one.
My eyes are the eyes of the lioness,
And they shine with her fire.
My ears are the ears of the goddess.
My nose is the nose of her that can sniff out all evil.
My teeth are those that can devour darkness.
My body is as the powerful body of Sekhmet.
My feet are the clawed feet of the lion goddess.
There is no part of me that is not of the goddess.
I shine with her divine light and banish the darkness from my
*   path.*

It is time to make offerings to her now in thanks for her help. The charge-reader says:

Oh Sekhmet, at this time we have nothing but humble offerings
*   to give you,*
But with the grace of our hearts, we will give them with joy and
*   with humility.*

A Sekhmet Self-empowerment Ritual

We beseech you that you take pleasure from them, as we will,
And accept them as a symbol of our love and our gratitude.
We will never leave your side, oh Sekhmet.
We will praise and celebrate your majesty and your strength in
   our minds.

Now open your eyes and share the feast, leaving part of every-thing for the goddess. Let each person present offer a sprinkling of incense to her and make a toast to her with the red wine. The visu-alizer says:

Now return to your visualization and see Sekhmet standing before you. She is pleased with your offerings and has enjoyed them. As you stand before the goddess you can already feel the changes within you. You feel strong, confident and brimming with renewed energy. As you look down you see that your skin is covered with soft, golden fur that ruffles in the breeze. Your body has become the sleek body of a lioness. You have become as one of her daughters.

It is time now for you to return to the cone of power. Thank Sekhmet for her help and bid her farewell in your own words.

When this is done, see her begin to retreat again up the rocky path to the cliff top. As she walks, she turns back into a lioness. When she reaches the top of the cliff, she again lies down in the warm sun and goes back to sleep.

Thank the lionesses at the wadi, your sisters, for their help and begin to make your way back along the rocky path. This time the journey is easy as you can run with the strength and speed of a lion. You follow the river as it thins out again and becomes a stream trick-ling over the parched floor of the desert. The heat of the sun is no longer uncomfortable to you; instead you relish it as it warms your fur. Bask in the strength of this body. Feel the muscles move beneath the skin, the energy stored within them. This power is yours to keep. Even in mundane life.

Now you can see your cone of power shining on the red sand in the distance. As you draw close, you feel your body changing once again. The image of you as a lion gradually fades away, until you are an upright human being, walking towards the cone. But, in the days to come, whenever you feel uncertain or need help, you will be able to remember how it felt to have the strength of a lion. This knowl-edge is Sekhmet's gift to you.

Once you are back inside the cone visualize the return journey as usual. When this is finished dismantle the cone.

After this ritual keep your Sekhmet talisman with you, perhaps in a locket or a pouch that you can wear around your neck. Bury the remains of your feast in the garden.

17

A Sekhmet Ritual of Protection

Climb you from gulfs, or from the stars descend?
Fate, like a fawning hound, to heel you've brought;
You scatter joy and ruin without end,
Ruling all things, yet answering for naught.
From *'Hymn to Beauty'* by Charles Baudelaire

This ritual should be used only in dire need, but because sometimes in our lives we do feel threatened, afraid or even damaged because of others' actions, we should have recourse to a ritual that will help us. Never perform it on a whim, or because of a temporary fit of pique; it is very powerful, and if ill-used will rebound back upon whoever performs it. We always perform it at least a week after the event that inspires us to want to do it. Everyone

should have a cooling-off period and, in that time we might decide not to perform it after all. It is an accepted rule of magic that you should never do anything magically to harm another. This ritual does not set out to harm others, but if others are harming us, they will certainly feel the blaze of Sekhmet's fire. Therefore, think very carefully before performing it – we cannot stress this enough.

Because it is quite complicated, with a lot of switching between the visualizer and the charge-reader, if you cannot learn it off by heart beforehand you might prefer to have one person read the entire thing.

You will need:

- Sekhmet incense
- red altar candles
- a small mirror
- a photograph, if possible, of whoever or whatever is causing harm (if not, a sketched representation will suffice)
- candle of your personal colour

The Ritual

Construct a travelling cone of power and visualize a journey back to ancient Khem. The visualizer then says:

> When the cone has come to a halt, see the blackness outside begin to thin out and become a swirling, grey fog. The fog gradually diminishes and through it penetrates a brilliant solar light, which clears the last of the fog away. You can see a desert beyond the cone. The sky above is so blue its brilliance is astounding. The sand is an orange-pink colour, while the distant horizon seems impossibly far away.
>
> Stand up and step through the doorway in the cone of power. Step out into the desert landscape. Feel the heat of the sun immediately; overwhelming heat. Your feet are almost scorced by the hot sand. There is no breeze.
>
> In front of you, you see an oasis surrounded by palm trees. Lionesses loll in the shade of the trees, close to the pool. Beyond the oasis, you can see the pylons of a great temple, which you know contains the shrine of Ptah, and beneath it the secret shrine of his consort, Sekhmet.

A Sekhmet Ritual of Protection

Approach the lionesses and nod your head in respect as they grant you passage through their territory to reach the temple.

As you approach the temple, you see it is constructed of sandstone, comprising many colossal columns that are covered in bas-relief hieroglyphs. Walk through the pylons and enter the temple. To enter the shrine of Sekhmet, you must first declare your intent to Ptah, her husband. He will reveal to you her secret altar. But before you voice your intention, remember that Ptah is the constant companion of Maat, of truth and of justice. Remember this, and be aware that you cannot stand before him, or Sekhmet, unless you are pure of heart and intention.

At the rear of the temple stands an ancient golden statue of Ptah. He is represented as a man wearing a tight-fitting skullcap. He has a straight, pharaonic beard and is dressed in a long line tunic with a high collar, almost wrapped like a mummy. In his hands he holds the *was*, also known as the sceptre of dominion. This combines the *ankh* with the *djed* column, symbols that represent life and stability. Walk over and stand at the foot of the statue with your arms outstretched.

The charge reader says:

Oh Great god Ptah,
Who came into being in the earliest of times,
And spoke the world into life,
Father of fathers, power of powers,
Father of beginnings and creator of the eggs of the sun and
*   the moon,*
Lord of Maat, king of the two lands,
Golden god of the beautiful face,
Keeper of the laws of stone and construction,
Bringer of divine wisdom,
He who bestows the sacred knowledge of the starry firma-
*   ment,*
We beseech you that you grant us access
*   to the fiery depths of Sekhmet's most inner sanctum.*
We stand before you, pure in heart,
In need of Sekhmet's protection.
Gaze upon our hearts, great Ptah,
And once you have seen the truth within,
Show us the way to Sekhmet's presence.

Bast and Sekhmet

The visualizer continues:

Stand for a few moments, imagining that the eyes of Ptah can see into your soul. Show him your intention. If you falter now, you must walk from the temple and cease the ritual. The gods will not hold your honesty against you. But if you are true of intention, you will hear a rumble of stone. Ptah has heard you.

Behind him, the floor of the shrine opens up to reveal a ramp that leads into the depths below the temple floor. Walk down it. The last of the sun and heat fades away and all you can perceive is an orange-red glow, which lights your way.

As you move downwards, you see that fiery torches are alight upon colossal smooth stone walls. When you reach the end of the ramp, you find yourself within an enormous circular amphitheatre. For a few moments, stand and take in your surroundings.

The amphitheatre is lit completely by fire. There is a large pit in its centre where flames from deep within the earth roar upwards and into the shrine. Directly opposite, in an alcove in the far wall, stands a statue of the goddess, Sekhmet. It is about twice life size and made completely of black granite. Around the foot of the statue sit proud and attentive lionesses. There are no priests or priestesses present here, for this is the sanctuary of fire, of storm, of dread, of war, of death, but also of life.

Walk past the fiery pit and approach the statue of the goddess Sekhmet, for you must now awaken her and call her to your presence.

Raise your arms before the goddess.

The charge-reader says:

> Oh, mighty Sekhmet,
> Whose name means 'powerful'
> Lady of flame,
> Daughter of Ra,
> Greatly beloved of Ptah,
> Mistress of the two lands,
> Awaken to our presence,
> Hear us, who come to your feet with humble worth.
> Goddess of the mouth of the wadi,
> Awaken to our call, so that we may bask in the power of
>   your presence.

194

A Sekhmet Ritual of Protection

The visualizer resumes:

The mighty statue opens her eyes. It is the first glimmer of life. The gaze of the powerful goddess stares expectantly down upon you. Her open eyes are pure red orbs of light, of fire. A red glow is beginning to form around her as she comes alive to you. It becomes stronger and stronger, radiating out of all parts of her mighty statue. Upon her head, the large solar disc begins to burn brightly with a raging orange fire. That too is coming alive. It is the seat of her power, the radiance of her father, the sun. In her hands she holds a shining golden *ankh* which gleams with a solar, life-giving light. Do not gaze upon this, for it is too powerful for your spirit eyes to behold. Concentrate on Sekhmet's face. Look into her eyes.

Now the statue begins to move, slowly, sinuously. Sekhmet starts to move towards you. Her footsteps shake the floor of the shrine. The vibrations go right through your spirit body. She growls softly in her throat, and it is the sound of a sleeping volcano.

Now see the statue on your altar at home also begin to glow with the same red light. It too is coming alive. You have made the link. Sekhmet's presence is with you, at home, where your earthly body is.

Concentrate once more upon the visualization. The goddess is awake before you, gazing down with a fiery light. Her eyes shoot out rays of red light, which pierce you in your solar plexus. These are her eyes of fire. They purge from you all things that do not belong within you or your soul. She will cast out any alien spirit, force, energy or intent from you. Feel yourself beginning to glow with that red light, which moves through your whole body. The eyes of your statue at home are also gleaming red, the light radiating towards you. It is the same statue as in the mighty temple. Feel that red light purging straight through you.

The charge-reader says:

Sekhmet, we stand true before you.
Mighty goddess, lady of the bright red linen,
May your eyes of fire purge from us all our fear,
Our paranoia, our sadness, our melancholy, our insecurity
    [adapt as appropriate].
May you purge from us all darkness,
And leave in its wake nothing but light;

195

Bast and Sekhmet

A light that is strong, a light that is pure.
Through your eyes of fire, purge from us the darkness we have
    been under.
Give us that shriving. Give us that deliverance, oh Sekhmet.

The visualizer continues:

As the coloured ray hits you, it scourges you, purges you. Sekhmet also absorbs your very essence, and at once she knows who stands before her. For with her gaze, she can see into your soul, your mind, your heart, and as such she will know your every will and intention.

For now, clear your mind of everything else. Empty your mind, for she is partaking of all that you are, your worthiness.

Now return with the full focus of your inner eye to the shrine in ancient Khem, the temple of Ptah and its inner, fiery sanctum. You are before the feet of the majestic, mighty Sekhmet once more. Now you must tell her why you are there, and make known to her your boon.

The charge-reader says:

Sekhmet, lady of life,
She who opens the ways of the stormy rains,
Turn your face of mercy unto us, your servants.
We bring unto you at this time merely ourselves
And a meagre offering for your pleasure.
Through our own very essence of intent,
Which you taste and you know, and you sense and feel,
Which we bring to you with love, joy and humility, hear our
    plea.

Now the visualizer says:

Keep concentrating. You are before the goddess. Visualize everybody whom you know and love. You must make them known to her also.

The charge-reader continues:

Sekhmet, we are on a mighty web, the web of the soul.
All those who of the same intent, the same fate, the same
    destiny, are on this web.

A Sekhmet Ritual of Protection

We will give to you their names, so you may know them.
Let your power and strength protect them also.
We give to you the name of [insert a name and repeat this line
as many times as necessary for each person you wish
Sekhmet to protect].
We give to you all of these names, all of these people,
Who have felt the darkness around us.
Sekhmet, may all that they do be good and be true,
Sekhmet, through you, make it right.

Everyone opens their eyes and takes a sip of the wine, making a small libation to the goddess in a separate cup. Each person says, before they drink:

May all that they do be good and be true,
Sekhmet, through you, make it right.

The charge-reader resumes:

Sekhmet, lastly, we who stand before you,
Your daughters, your sisters, your priestesses, are also on the
web of the soul: [insert the names of group]
May the love that we share lend grace to our hearts.
Sekhmet, through you, make it right, make it true.
May all that in which we collude be in peace and in strength.
Sekhmet, through you, make it right, make it true.
May what we hold most sacred to our lives, the truth,
Sekhmet, through you, make it right, make it true.

Each member of the group again takes a sip of wine, makes a libation and says:

May all that we do be good and be true,
Sekhmet, through us, make it right.

The visualizer now says:

Close your eyes and return to the shrine. See yourself once more before the gargantuan presence of the glowing red, fiery goddess. She appears to be more awake and alive than before, for she has heard you.

Bast and Sekhmet

The charge-reader says:

Sekhmet, you who are the vengeful eye of Ra,
Mistress of war, smiter of the enemies of the sun's light of truth
*   and of justice,*
She who breathes fire against all those who dare to oppose the
*   will of the gods,*
Punisher and bringer of retribution,
Powerful lady of the bright red linen,
Hear our humble petition.
Grant us these boons that we ask, in return for our eternal
*   devotion,*
And the offerings we will give to you now and in the future.
Grant us, we beseech, your protection and your justice.
Goddess who brings life from the ashes of fire,
Goddess who is the personification of truth and of will and of
*   justice,*
Through the light of our spirits look upon the desires in our
*   hearts.*

The visualizer says:

Now show Sekhmet your problem, and how you wish it to be solved.
Send it to her as strongly and clearly as you can.

The charge-reader continues:

Sekhmet, beseech your sisters, Bast, Mut and Hathor
For their aid and constant protection
From [name the agency of harm]
May it/they be kept from doing harm to [recite names],
And all whom they love and whom they know.
May your protective fire be forever around our countenance.
From this point shall [name the agency of harm] have no power
*   to hurt us in spirit or in flesh.*
May your divine justice seek out the will of [name the agency of
*   harm],*
And cause them to pay all recompense for their actions
And for that which they are responsible.
Sekhmet, protect us from their ill intent,

A Sekhmet Ritual of Protection

So shall this be, for the rest of our lives and for the rest of the
*   life of [name the agency of harm].*
Sekhmet protect us and let it harm none.
Sekhmet defend us and let it harm none.
Sekhmet empower us and let it harm none.

Take up the small mirror and place it before the photograph and the statue of the goddess. The charge-reader resumes:

If [name the agency of harm] should attempt to do ill to any we
*   have named,*
May they see nothing but this mirror,
May this mirror be a shield to us and those we have named.
May this mirror represent your protection, oh Sekhmet.
All who dare to strike against your will may be struck
*   by the reflection of their own anger and violence.*
By the laws of the universe, may any who attempt to harm
*   those who are bound to you, hurt only themselves.*
And, mighty Sekhmet, may the strength of your will,
*   through the light of this candle, which is your fire,*
*   forever touch the spirit of [name those to be helped],*
so that they will never be in fear of the presence and intent of
*   [name the agency of harm]*
from this moment onwards.

The visualizer says:

Now you have given your boons to the goddess. She is fully aware of your intent and your plea to her.

The charge-reader continues:

Oh Sekhmet, at this time we have nothing but meagre offerings
*   to give you,*
But with the grace of our hearts, we will give them with joy and
*   with humility.*
When we go from your presence, we shall feast in your honour.
We beseech you that you take pleasure from it, as we will.
We will never leave your side, Sekhmet.
We will return to you,

We will praise and celebrate your majesty and your strength in our minds.

Now the visualizer says:

Now see the eyes of the goddess, the eyes of the fire, begin to dim, growing less strong. She will grant your boon, for what you do, you do in truth and in love. Her eyes are closing. She is going back into a sleeping state now. And after this rite, you will feast in her honour, for she will still be with you. Remember the crimson light of her eyes of fire fills your very soul. It will be in you, and when you partake of the offerings, she will taste them also. But for now she is going back, retreating into her niche. Feel her footsteps heading backwards, the red glow around her sinking back into the granite.

See the orange glow of her solar disc retreating back into the stone, the *ankh*'s light diminishing, until there is nothing before you but black granite.

It is time for you to leave this temple, for no one lingers here without purpose. Walk back around the fiery pit, back to the ramp that leads out, and without looking back, begin to climb it. Walk up into the light, up to the sun.

You have asked Sekhmet to lift a blight that has been upon your life. You are walking back into the sunlight. You reach the top of the ramp and the sun hits your head. Raise your face to the light. The warmth and the heat, which is Sekhmet's domain, is the land of the life-giving light. Feel it on your face. This is your future. This is where you belong, the land of life and of warmth and heat.

Walk back through the shrine of Ptah. Feel the inner sanctum closing up, shutting itself off until the next acolyte comes to ask a boon from Sekhmet. Walk back out of the temple, onto the sand, still feeling that nourishing light and heat. The fire of Sekhmet is still within your body, filling you up. You are taller, you are stronger, you are alive – alive in her land.

Walk back through the oasis, nodding farewell to the lionesses, acknowledging their presence. Thank them. They are Sekhmet's daughters and your sisters.

Go back toward the cone of power, which you can see on the desert's sandy floor – a blue cone, humming, ready to take you back. Step back within its light, and leave the desert imagery behind. When the cone of light closes up, no more can you see the desert land of Egypt. Black fog surrounds the cone once more, getting denser and denser. It is once again the abyss. Then you feel the movement going forward in time, away from that place, back to your earthly room, back through the millennia to this century.

Return to ritual room, take down the cone and partake of the feast.

18

The Festival of Sekhmet

Don't stint the fires with which you flare,
Warm up my dull heart to delight.
From 'Pagan Prayer' by Charles Baudelaire

The ritual that follows is our own group's festival rite. It has been updated this year to incorporate adaptations from some of the prayers translated by E.A. St George. Like the Festival of Bast, this is a celebratory ritual and we often invite people from outside our usual working group to attend.

Although there are several different theories as to the correct date for Sekhmet's festival, for reasons personal to ourselves we chose to incorporate it into our New Year's Eve celebrations. We

thought this was the perfect time to ask for luck and protection for the coming year. Recently, we have discovered that the Egyptians also celebrated a feast of Sekhmet on this date, so it is entirely appropriate. Another Sekhmet feast day is 17 October, while the Day of Sekhmet and the Purifying Flame is 20 November and the Day of Offerings to Sekhmet is 24 November (our thanks again to the Revd Christina Paul for these dates). Another significant time to celebrate a festival of Sekhmet is in August, when the star Regulus, of the constellation Leo, shines high in the sky. The words of the ritual below can be changed to suit whichever date you choose.

It is widely believed that New Year celebrations in ancient Egypt included the giving of Sekhmet amulets as gifts to loved ones. The Egyptians believed that receiving one of these magical charms would ensure good health, protection and luck throughout the coming year. The making and exchanging of Sekhmet amulets is therefore something that could be incorporated into this rite. Alternatively, it would be a good time to empower any appropriate jewellery you may already have, by visualizing them absorbing the red light of the goddess during your working.

You will need:

- Sekhmet or other solar/fire incense and scented oil
- spicy bread and spicy wheat-based food for the feast
- red wine or Sekhmet beer
- sistra
- red and gold altar candles
- votive candles of the appropriate colour

The Ritual

During this ritual we refer to our magical group or sisterhood. Mixed groups or solo practitioners should amend the wording as appropriate.

Anoint your coloured candle with spicy Sekhmet oil, all the time visualizing clearly what you want for the coming year. Set the candles aside for later.

Begin with some breathing exercises and then start to build a travelling cone of power.

The visualizer says:

Bast and Sekhmet

Visualize that the cone lands in Thebes, at the temple complex of Karnak. When you are ready, come out of the cone and find yourself in the ruins. It is dark outside, except for the light of the stars, for it is the hour before dawn on the last day of the old year, and you have come to pay your respects to Sekhmet on this her festival day. You will ask her for her protection in the coming year, and for her energy and light. Imagine that you have come bearing gifts; see yourself carrying baskets of food and flagons of wine and beer in your arms. The rest of your magical group is there with you. See yourselves walking together down the long avenue of sphinxes and into the ancient complex, all in ritual finery of the Pharoanic age, your faces made up in the ancient fashion.

You walk with eager, light steps, for you know that on this night, you shall lay all the spectres of the old year to rest and begin anew.

Keep walking through the temple until you have left the ruins behind you and are a short way into the desert itself. It is this way that you will approach the temple of Ptah, who is the consort of Sekhmet.

As you approach his temple you can see that it is constructed of sandstone, comprising many colossal columns that are covered in bas-relief hieroglyphs. Walk up the wide entrance path, through the pylons, and enter the temple. To enter the shrine of Sekhmet, you must first declare your intent to Ptah. He will reveal it to you.

At the rear of the temple stands a carved golden statue of Ptah. He would once have been shown as a man wearing a tight-fitting skullcap with a straight beard but the statue is ancient and is headless now. You can still make out that he is dressed in a long linen tunic with a high collar and in his hands he holds the *was*, also known as the sceptre of dominion. This combines the *ankh* with the *djed* column, which represent life and stability. Walk over and stand at the foot of the statue with your arms outstretched.

The charge-reader says:

Oh great god Ptah,
Who came into being in the earliest of times,
And spoke the world into life,
Father of fathers, power of powers,
Father of beginnings and creator of the eggs of the sun and the
*   moon,*
Lord of Maat, king of the two lands,

The Festival of Sekhmet

Golden god of the beautiful face,
Keeper of the laws of stone and construction,
Bringer of divine wisdom,
He who bestows the sacred knowledge of the starry firmament,
We beseech you that you grant us access
To the shrine of your consort Sekhmet

The visualizer resumes:

You feel that Ptah has granted you permission. Behind his statue you can see a dark doorway, and through this you pass into the shrine of Sekhmet.

The shrine is a long narrow room, unadorned and in darkness but for some dim lamps which are burning on the floor. At its far end you can see the statue of the goddess. It is carved from smooth, black granite and is very tall. She is standing erect, with a representation of the solar disc upon her head. In her left hand she carries a lotus staff, and in her right hand an *ankh*. Above her head is a hole in the ceiling of the shrine, and through this the first rays of the morning sun will strike the head of the goddess. But for now, she is asleep, waiting for the new dawn.

As you stand before her, contemplate for a few moments all the aspects of the past year, both good and bad. Perhaps you still have things to resolve, but there are also other things which you can let go of or forget.

The charge-reader says:

Oh great goddess Sekhmet, awaken to our presence.
Hear us who come to your feet with humble worth.
Stretch forth your hand to your priestesses,
Come to us in gentleness, lest your claws destroy us.
Speak in your quieter voice, oh Sekhmet.
Blast us not with your fury,
But instead shower upon us your blessings.
Daughter of Ra, life of the two lands,
Awaken to our call.
Let us rejoice in your light.
On this, the day of your festival.

The visualizer continues:

The lights in the shrine now appear to fade into darkness, but you see the eyes of the goddess open up, and within them is the light of the sun. It is not a harsh, glaring light, but is enough for you to perceive her glance and see the outline of her body, which emanates a faint, ruddy glow. She stares down upon you.

Now see the statue on your altar at home begin to glow with a red light. It too is coming alive. Her presence is in the room with you, here where your earthly bodies are. Now open your eyes, light your votive candle and set it before your statue at home.

Sekhmet absorbs your very essence and at once knows who stands before her, for she can see into your souls, minds and hearts with her gaze and will know your every will and intention.

Now return with your inner eyes to the inside of the shrine where you stand before the feet of the mighty Sekhmet once more.

The charge-reader says:

Accept our offerings, oh Sekhmet, for they are symbols of our love.
Accept our offering of incense, may it cause your nostrils to rejoice.
Accept our offering of wine, may it cause your mouth to rejoice.
Accept our offering of food, may it cause your heart to rejoice.
Behold, your people whom you have blessed forever glorify you.

Open your eyes and burn some of the incense, then eat the food and drink the wine. Leave small portions for the goddess on paper to wrap and place on the altar afterwards. When the feast is finished, close your eyes and return to the visualization. The visualizer resumes:

See yourself standing again before the gargantuan presence of the glowing goddess. She is much pleased with your feast, which has been offered and consumed in her honour. She appears to be more awake and alive than before and the red glow that surrounds her is brighter. Now move close to her and visualize that you are placing before her the offerings that you carried into the temple. Place the large platters of food, wine and beer at the feet of the statue. When this is done Sekhmet is ready to hear your petition.

The charge-reader now says:

The Festival of Sekhmet

Sekhmet, you who are the light of the sun,
The watchful eye of your father, Ra,
Powerful lady of the bright red linen,
Hear our humble petition and grant us our wishes.
Grant us your blessings and we shall rejoice before you.
Give us your protection throughout the coming year.
Stretch forth your hand and defend those who serve you.
Goddess, who brings life from the ashes of fire,
Who personifies light, truth and strength,
Through the light of our spirits, look upon the desires of our
hearts.

The visualizer continues:

Now visualize all your wishes for health, happiness, peace and contentment in the coming year. Do this not only for yourselves, but also for all your friends and loved ones. See yourself happy, strong, healthy and content. Visualise all that you desire in the way of successful work ventures. Imagine that all the opportunities that you require are accessible to you. Picture yourself gaining financial rewards for the work that is undertaken in the new year. See the security that results from your labour. Visualize yourself comfortable in a place that represents your ideal home. See those you love around you also healthy, happy and content. Spend a few moments on this. Show your hopes and desires in clear pictures and ask that any help Sekhmet gives you will be for the good of everyone concerned.

Leave some time for private meditation. Then the charge-reader says:

Sekhmet, mighty mother and giver of life,
May we speak now for ourselves, your daughters who stand
before you,
[Insert names].
Draw close the ties that bind our sisterhood.
Throughout the coming year, we shall work in your name,
With justice, compassion and strong will.
Strengthen our unity and our hearts,
That we may draw strength from one another,
And forever find happiness in each other's company.

Let nothing strike this bond asunder,
Let nothing weaken our resolve.

Spend a few moments now seeing all the members of your magical group happy, all together, in both social and magical gatherings. Then the charge-reader continues:

Mighty Sekhmet, we wish to give thanks
For all the gifts that you have bestowed upon us in the last
*   year.*
As it draws to a close we give praise to you for your divine pres-
*   ence,*
Which has touched all our lives.
We offer you our love and our gratitude,
For the protection of your fire that has surrounded us in times
*   of uncertainty.*
We beseech that your light may never leave us in the year to
*   come,*
May it nourish our spirits, lending strength and truth to all that
*   we do.*
May your light continue to unite us in sacred purpose.
And through this unity, oh divine lady Sekhmet,
May the love that is shared between all present here,
And all those others that are also a part of our lives,
Be forever strong, in grace, truth and virtue.

The visualizer now resumes:

Now see Sekhmet raising up her right hand, which holds the *ankh*, symbol of life. She stretches out her hand, holding the *ankh* towards you. As you gaze upon it, the rising sun of the New Year casts its first golden rays down through the hole in the ceiling of the shrine above your heads. You see the sunlight streaming down to shine onto the statue of the goddess.

Sekhmet absorbs this radiance until her whole form is glowing brightly with a golden light. It flows into the raised *ankh* in her hand, which transforms into an instrument of pure, life-giving energy. As you watch it grows brighter and brighter, until you can hardly bear to look upon it, and you have to close your eyes. Then, from the stem of the *ankh*, a golden ray of light shoots outwards to touch you.

You instinctively feel the ray of energy touching you and you raise your face up to the bright warmth. Even though your eyes are closed, you can feel the light enveloping you, as it would on a sunny summer's day. The light penetrates through your skin and spreads down throughout your body. Visualize yourself being filled up with the light, for this is the life-giving power of the sun that touches you. Let yourself be filled up with light for it is limitless and comes from the source of all creation.

Sekhmet is charging us with this light so that we may have strength, love and enlightenment for the coming year. Her light drives out darkness and doubt and fills us with energy and bright hope. We will go forward from her temple renewed.

Now, feel the change within you as you are filled with the divine light. You feel strong and positive and alive. You are brimming with energy.

The charge-reader says:

> *Sekhmet, we rejoice in your light,*
> *And thank you for your presence here.*
> *Your spirit is alive within the world,*
> *Ever gaining in strength and power.*
> *Your hands will brush away the sands of time,*
> *And reclaim all that has been lost.*
> *We pledge all that has been lost.*
> *We pledge ourselves to you, Sekhmet.*
> *For we remember the power of the old gods,*
> *And we will meet again, to call your name*
> *And celebrate the day of your festival.*
> *Until the next time we approach your divine feet,*
> *We give you our thanks and bid you farewell.*

The visualizer resumes:

Now see the shrine of Sekhmet around you again and see the light of the early morning sun flooding the chamber. As the sun moves overhead it slowly begins to fade from the statue of Sekhmet itself, even though the stone still glows faintly. You can see that the spirit of the goddess has retreated, leaving only a sleeping statue of stone in a sacred shrine, its walls still bathed in golden light.

Now it is time to leave so turn and walk back into the temple of Ptah. When you reach his statue say a few words of thanks for granting you access to the shrine of his consort. Then make your way back through the ruins until you can see your cone of power shining in the distance. Make your way towards the cone and go back inside. When you are ready visualize the journey home and dismantle the cone.

After this ritual wrap the remains of the feast and bury them in the garden. Leave the candles to burn down. As with any other rite, it is all the better if your group can make a donation of some kind to a relevant animal charity. Sekhmet appreciates those who show her their thanks in a practical way.

19

A Bes Ritual

Show us your memory's casket, and the glories
Streaming from gems made out of stars and rays!
From 'The Voyage' by Charles Baudelaire

Bes is best known for his role as the protector of women in childbirth together with his 'wife', the hippopotamus goddess Taweret. However, it was thought that Bes would also bring luck and prosperity. He was one of the most loved deities among the common people of Egypt, owing to his benevolent and accessible nature. Unlike many deities, he was most often worshipped in the home rather than with elaborate temple rituals.

The ritual we have given below is designed purely to ask for money. We have used this rite when finances have been dire and bills could not be paid. It is designed as an appeal to Bes in his role as a god of luck and prosperity. While we have always had positive results from this working, we would not advocate its use if your motive is purely one of greed. Bes will answer you happily if you need his help, but would no doubt be unimpressed if your request is not based on genuine need.

This is not our only rite to Bes. We would also call on him for help with any new project that was close to our hearts, as well as for help with children and women who are either pregnant or trying to conceive. We will hopefully give more rituals along these lines in a later book.

To get the best results from this working, it is advisable to keep the imagery you use as simple as possible. During the visualization, do not offer Bes images of things like getting a better job, just concentrate clearly and firmly on money and symbols of your wealth increasing. In your minds, use the strongest words and images. It is important to aim high and imagine the most wealth that you can. There are two reasons for this. The first is that the main thing that prevents us acquiring money is the guilt and anxiety we feel about wanting it. This ritual's purpose is to help us traverse the barrier in our minds. The second is simply that particular amounts of money probably mean little to a god-form, and by sending images of plentiful wealth your desire is made clearer and more immediate.

Note that the cone of power we give in this ritual is a slight variation on the usual travelling cone.

For this ritual, you will need:

- a Bes statue
- a candle of appropriate colour for each member of the group
- fresh fruit: bananas or oranges
- fruit juice or pina colada
- a pound coin for each participant
- Bes incense
- a tambourine
- tribal drum-based music to be played in the background from before the start – something with a definite beat to it

The ritual

The candles should be anointed and placed in a circle within the group, unlit. They should surround the statue of Bes. After the ritual, the coins should be kept in a secure place and never be spent.

Construct the cone of power.

Each member of the group should place a pound coin beneath his or her candle, after which the candles should be lit. The visualizer says:

Imagine that part of the wall of the cone of power is beginning to swirl around, to create a doorway. It gets bigger and bigger and you can see that it leads out onto a tunnel of light. Now see yourself rise up out of your body and walk down the tunnel.

As you emerge from the tunnel, you see that you are in a jungle clearing. Tall trees in many shades of vibrant green rise all around you. You can hear the song of exotic birds and see their jewel colours as they flit amongst the leaves. The air is full of the calls of monkeys and the cries of other jungle creatures. The air is very hot and feels damp and humid.

In the middle of the clearing there is a simple bamboo hut. It is constructed roughly and has an open front. The hut is a shrine to the dwarf god, Bes. You are now in Bes's realm, for he hails originally from the darkest reaches of the Congo. You can see, in the entrance to the shrine, a carved wooden statue of Bes. He is depicted as a grinning dwarf, who seems to have been caught by the artist in the pose of a wild dance. He wears a panther skin over his shoulder, and his face is almost leonine in appearance, but comical, like a caricature of a lion. He has a lion's mane and lion's ears, and his tongue protrudes from his mouth in a playful fashion. His face is bearded and this gives the impression of a lion's mane. He also has a lion's tail and short, bandy legs. His appearance is bizarre and grotesque, yet welcoming and friendly.

All around the statue are offerings left by those who have visited the shrine before you. There are gifts wrapped in large, shiny leaves, beautiful flowers, piles of ripe fruits and coconuts, all brimming with sweet juices. Bes's incense fills the air with a scent of coconut and fruit and the heady exotic perfume of strange flowers.

Now, stand before the shrine and call to Bes. Ask him to reveal himself to you.

The visualizer shakes the tambourine.

The charge-reader says:

Bast and Sekhmet

Oh Bes, dancing god,
Attendant of the birth-house,
Protector of the home,
Lord of luck and fortune,
Banisher of demons,
Consort of Tawaret,
We call to you
And ask that we might speak with you.

The visualizer resumes:

Now stand and listen for Bes's arrival. After a while you can hear a noise in the trees behind the shrine. You look and see that the trees are shaking. Someone is approaching, swinging his way through the branches.

Presently a small, squat figure leaps into the clearing and bounds around you. It is Bes. He looks just like the carving in the shrine. He wears a panther skin over his shoulder, the head fastened to the belt of his kilt at his belly, the tail dangling down his back. His lion's mane is thick and luxuriant and he swishes his tasselled tail proudly. On his head he wears a crown of tall feathers. His tongue sticks out and he grins at you. He carries a tambourine. He seems like a joker, yet you can sense his wisdom, his power and his role as protector.

While this is happening, cast your inner eye back to the room where your statue of the god stands within the ring of anointed candles. Imagine that the light of these candles shines into the statue, which is like an extension of the senses of Bes as he appears to you before his shrine. Through the light of these candles, Bes can see your soul, and recognizes you.

The visualizer shakes the tambourine.
The charge-reader says:

Oh, Bes, leader of the panther tribe,
Ancient lord of home and family,
We bring offerings to you
As symbols of our respect and to give you pleasure.
Please accept our offerings for they are given in love.
Through us, may you experience their delights.
As we eat this fruit, may you taste its perfumed flesh.

214

A Bes Ritual

As we drink this juice, may you savour its sweetness.
As we burn this incense may you savour its rich smoke.

Now share your offertory feast, remembering to leave a portion of everything for Bes. As you eat, imagine that Bes is eating the food as well. Your visualization does not end. Imagine that you are sharing your feast with Bes in the jungle clearing. Try to picture him enjoying it, and believe that it is making him happy.

The visualizer shakes the tambourine and the charge-reader continues:

Oh, Bes, companion of the lion,
Lord of luck and fortune,
We hope that our offerings have pleased you.
May we now ask of you our boon.

The visualizer resumes:

Concentrate again on the visualization. See yourself back in the clearing before the shrine. Bes is finishing off with enthusiasm the offerings you have brought for him. He is so pleased by them that he begins to dance around you, strangely graceful, despite his grotesque shape. He shakes his tambourine and leaps and jumps among you. He sees you as the coloured light of your votive candle.

Now it is time to send to Bes images of your desires using the clearest, strongest imagery possible. Remember that in this case this is purely to do with money. To give your magic potency, these desires must never be spoken, not even amongst your group. They are between only yourselves and the god. Speak now to Bes in your minds. Tell him in simple, strong words and clear pictures what you want from him. Tell him that it is one of the things that you need in your life in order to be fulfilled and to live and work comfortably. Free from care about money, you will be able to do more in the world around you. Remember to tell Bes that you do not want to gain money through unfortunate or undesirable means. Ask him that your request should harm no one.

As Bes receives your message, his dance becomes faster and wilder. He dances around you, creating a force, like a circle of power. The force weaves around you. As you send Bes your images, thoughts and requests, he winds his dancing around them, encapsulating them in his energy. You must give him your highest aims, the most you can imagine, for his energy creates more of it. As he dances, so your money increases. Now visualize images of your wealth increasing. Use clear, concise images and see Bes acknowledging each image and weaving it into his dance. Do this as if it has already happened to you. Believe that it has. Feel the weight of anxiety lifting from your body and your soul. Use all your will and know that your money problems have been solved in a harmless and beneficial way.

Bes's dance reaches a whirling climax. He jumps and whirls closer and bestows upon each of the group a large lotus flower. In your mind, visualize placing this flower beneath your personal candle in the circle. Once it is there, it becomes the coin you placed there earlier. The two objects become one. Bes has instilled his power into your coin through his symbol of the lotus. When you take the coins from beneath the candles, they will also be like dried, pressed flowers, a permanent keepsake of this ritual, carrying within them Bes's power and your intention.

The visualizer shakes the tambourine.
The charge-reader says:

> Bes, we thank you for this audience
> And vow that should there be anything in our power
> That we may do for you, we will do it gladly.
> If we can assume your role of protector
> For any innocent or vulnerable person in this world
> We will do so willingly.
> Whatever tasks you might have for us
> We will do them gladly and with thanks.

The visualizer continues:

See yourself bow to Bes to show your thanks and see him turn and begin to walk back into his jungle realm. You might want to follow him now as he heads back amongst the trees. He may show you images of a task he might have for you or have words of wisdom to impart. Perhaps some other aspect of the visualization might draw your attention, which you want to investigate. If so, this will be a message from Bes. Spend a few minutes wandering in your mind in Bes's realm. Go wherever you feel you should.

The visualizer leaves a few minutes here for meditation and then resumes:

> When you feel ready see yourself returning to the clearing and to your cone of power. Walk back up the tunnel of light and into the cone.

Return and dismantle the cone as usual.

The candles should be left burning and once they have burned down, the coins should be removed. The coins should then be kept in a safe place, and never be used by their owners. They have become amulets of power rather than simple coins. Coins that we have used for this ritual are left in our Bes shrine as a permanent offering.

20

Attuning to
Your Cat

*Our companion the cat is the warm, furry, whiskered and
purring reminder of a lost paradise.*

Leonor Fini
From *The Secret Life of Cats* by Robert De Laroche and
Jean Michel Labat

In ages past, witches and magicians were reputed to have familiars
– spirits in animal form that helped them with their work. The cat,
especially, was seen in this light. It may be that those who understood the ways of nature felt closer to the animals around them and
therefore enjoyed a relationship with them that transcended the
normal feline/human association of a cat by the hearth which did
not interact with the householders much beyond killing vermin. If
circumstances permit, those who are drawn to magic usually have
animals sharing their homes, with at least one cat. We shrink from
calling these companions 'pets', as that implies a sense of ownership, and we do not think that anyone can actually 'own' a cat. As
the saying goes. 'What can you own of a cat, but their skin?'

In this chapter we would like to discuss deepening your relationship with your own cat, with short, simple rites and rituals to Bast. We have performed these working ourselves, either to strengthen our bonds with our cats or when certain problems have arisen to do with feline health and well-being. We also give rites for the dedication and protection of a new cat and a funeral for when a beloved cat dies.

As we have said many magical practitioners find themselves naturally drawn to cats. This may have more than a little to do with the cat's ancient image as a creature of magic. Even if you do not currently live with cats, you might find that once you have begun interacting regularly with the feline goddesses, you will want to offer a cat a home. Alternatively, as has happened with the majority of our own group, stray cats might start turning up on your doorstep with astonishing frequency.

When you ask Bast for help with your cat, you can also make an offering by giving a donation to your local cat charity. This does not just have to be money. Many large pet stores have a bin where you can deposit tinned food and packets of cat biscuits for charity, and organizations such as the Cats' Protection League welcome donations of food for the animals in their care, no matter how big or small.

For some of the workings that follow, you will need some of your cat's shed claws. Cats shed their claws all the time, and they can usually be found where your cat sharpens them.

Responsibility for lost cats

In our Bast rituals we pledge to take care of any cats that cross our path and need our help. Bast seems to take this offer literally, so it is a serious pledge and we only say it if we mean it, and can stand by it. Once you start communing with Bast on a regular basis, you will find that cats seem to be attracted to you as if by magic. This has happened with almost every member of our group. Strays find their way to our doors, kittens in pet shop windows seem to call to us, people bring cats to us because they know we can help and adverts for unwanted cats at local charities catch our eye. This is something that any person in tune with Bast should be prepared for.

The pledge to care for Bast's children in this world does not mean you are obliged to fill your home with cats you cannot afford to keep, but it does mean that you should be prepared to find any cat that needs it a good home. Your local animal charities will no doubt have foster homes overflowing with homeless cats, so if your circumstances allow it, part of your magical work should ideally include offering one of these animals a home. When you speak the promise to Bast, you are taking on a responsibility which extends beyond opening your door to needy cats. For example, if we ever find someone being cruel to a cat, we feel it is our duty to step in, whether literally or by informing the RSPCA.

If you are not in a position to offer a cat a home, even temporarily, then we suggest that you reword your pledge in the rituals. Instead, you could promise to help an animal charity with a donation of some kind.

Cats and ritual

Our cats are always welcome to join us during rituals if they want to. Some are not interested at all, but others seem to love being with us as we perform our rites. If someone has accidentally shut the door, our visualizations are often interrupted by outraged scratching and howling. Through experience, we have learned to make sure the feast is out of the cat's reach. Our rituals have been disturbed many times by sounds of eating, as one of our cats does its best to consume the entire feast before we open our eyes from our visualization. In the same way, we make sure that any lit candles are safely away from inquisitive noses. Cats seem to have a dangerous fascination for fire that often results in singed tails or whiskers.

Although we all aspire to the romantic ideal that our cats will be like witches' familiars, glued to our side throughout every ritual and visualization, we have discovered that some cats are more attracted to magical rituals than others. We never force a cat to be in the room as we work. We simply leave the door ajar and the cats can please themselves. On one occasion, a member of our group nearly had a heart attack as she was invoking Bast – a cat chose that precise moment to leap with great force into her lap, all claws bared.

All of the rites given below were first thought up long before we began performing rituals to Bast on a regular basis or had delved into the mysteries of Egyptian magic. They are instinctive and derive from the time when the goddess was simply a presence in our hearts, to whom we turned in times of need that were directly connected with our cats. Although we have rewritten some of the words to comply with what we now know about Egyptian magic, they are still little more than simple spells. We have to thank the writer E.A. St George, whose work has helped us revamp these rites to evoke more of an Egyptian feel. These workings can be extended and changed to include whatever words and actions you feel are appropriate. In most respects, they are only a guideline.

Dedication of a new cat

When a new cat comes into our lives, we perform this rite to ask for Bast's protection and blessing. If you can possibly have the cat in the room with you when you do it, so much the better. But as cats can be rather contrary creatures, the chances are that if you try to confine them, they will be scratting and yowling at the door to be let out. Some cats, however, will curl contentedly in your lap for the entire working. Whatever their temperament, the cat has to be present once you are ready to offer the feast, as their consumption of the food is actually part of the ritual. As anyone who has lived with a cat will know, they can be fussy eaters, so be sure to include food that you know they will consume. If they refuse to go for something special like prawns or cream, then just put down a plate of their favourite cat food. If needs be – and sometimes you have to be as sneaky as the cat in these matters – perform the ritual just before their usual feeding time.

Equipment

You will need:

- a Bast statue
- a white candle
- protection oil
- a small pouch containing some fur and shed claws
- a photograph of the cat
- a length of white ribbon

- a small offertory feast that your cat will eat (perhaps including items like prawns or cream)

The rite

Arrange your altar, placing your statue in the middle with the candle before it. Place the pouch next to the candle. Make sure that all your other equipment is close at hand. Close your eyes and relax with some deep breathing.

When you feel ready, anoint your candle, all the time picturing your cat happy and safe. Set the candle in its holder and say:

> *Oh Bast, divine mother of all cats,*
> *Daughter of Ra,*
> *Hail unto you, lady of the east.*
> *Oh, Bast, come forth from your realm.*
> *Come forth, oh beautiful one.*
> *Hear my prayer*
> *And awaken to my presence.*
> *Bast, lady of Asheru,*
> *Great cat of the heavens,*
> *Abide here in gentleness,*
> *For I am true to you.*

Now light the white candle, pick up the pouch and say:

> *Oh Bast, mistress of magic and love,*
> *Lady of Ankhtawy, ruler of the divine field,*
> *I ask you to bless and watch over [insert the cat's name].*
> *As I light this candle, may you see him/her as I do.*
> *As I offer these symbols may you know him/her as I do.*
> *He/she is your child, oh Bast,*
> *May you be as a fierce mother cat*
> *As you protect him/her from those who would do him/her harm.*
> *May you walk at his/her side at all times.*
> *His/her cry is your name, oh Bast.*
> *May you light his/her path with your divine radiance.*
> *I ask this in your name, oh Bast,*
> *Lady of Ankhtawy,*
> *Ruler of the divine field,*
> *Ruler of Sekhet-Neter.*

Spend a few quiet moments showing Bast all that you ask. Visualize your cat healthy, happy and safe, and show her that image. Be very clear about what you want. When you feel ready open your eyes and say:

> *Bast, daughter of Ra,*
> *Divine mother of all cats,*
> *I offer warmth and love to the daughter/son of the great cat.*
> *I offer him/her happiness and safety.*
> *I offer him/her a place to live, and a place to die.*
> *Let your blessing be upon him/her.*
> *I offer this food unto the great goddess in her temple.*
> *I offer drink to the cat of the heavens.*
> *Through [insert the cat's name], may you experience its*
> *   pleasures.*
> *Accepting this offering, oh Bast,*
> *Grant to me my desire.*

Now offer the feast to your cat and wait while it eats it. Allow the candle to burn almost to the end, and when there is only an inch or two left, carefully pinch it out with your fingers or a snuffer. Put it into the pouch with the fur, shed claws and photographs. Wrap the pouch with the white ribbon and seal it tightly. Keep the pouch in a safe place. You can perhaps give it to your statue as an offering.

In addition to this ritual you can draw Bast's symbol onto a small piece of paper, which the cat can wear on its collar (if it has one) in an identification barrel, available from most pet shops. The barrel will then act as a protective amulet.

Strengthening your bond with your cat

This working is very simple and involves asking for Bast's blessing as you exchange a talisman with your cat. You both then wear a part of each other close to your heart in order to encourage your bond to grow. The ideal time to perform this working is during the new moon, since you are asking for the growth and strengthening of your relationship.

Equipment

You will need:

- a small silver locket, preferably heart-shaped, on a chain
- a silver-coloured identification barrel that can be attached to your cat's collar
- some clippings of your own hair and nails
- some clippings of your cat's fur and a few shed claws
- pen and paper

Gather together all your equipment and spend some time breathing deeply until you feel relaxed.

The rite

When you feel ready, begin to assemble the talismans. Into the silver barrel, place some of your hair and one of your fingernail clippings, together with your name written on a piece of paper. Into the locket place your cat's shed claws and fur clippings and either its name or a paw print on a piece of paper. You will have to fold the paper very tightly to make it fit, but it is possible. Once this is done hold the talismans and say:

> *Oh Bast, divine mother of all cats,*
> *Grant to us your blessing.*
> *As [insert the cat's name] and I wear these charms*
> *May our bond grow strong.*
> *Give us your love and protection.*
> *Save us from terror, save us from darkness.*
> *From evil defend us.*
> *May our eyes be your eyes, oh Bast.*
> *May our limbs be your limbs.*
> *Give us your grace and your strength.*
> *Give us unity, oh Bast.*
> *So let it be spoken.*
> *So let it be done.*

Then attach the barrel to your cat's collar and wear the locket around your neck. Your relationship with your cat should become stronger with each day.

Visualization to find a missing cat

Cats are notorious for disappearing mysteriously, and often reappearing again just as mysteriously. However, whether the cat is your own or someone else's, its unexplained absence is always a time of anxiety and sadness. This rite is designed to bring a straying cat home.

Equipment

You will need:

- a photograph of the missing cat if possible
- a Bast statue
- a white candle

The visualization

Arrange your equipment on a window sill where the candle can burn down safely.

Spend some time breathing deeply until you are relaxed. When you feel ready place the photograph in front of the statue. Now close your eyes and visualize that Bast looks out through the eyes of your statue. In your mind show her the picture (or else a visualized image of the cat). Tell her that the cat is missing and that you want her help so that it returns home safely.

Then light your white candle and visualize that Bast carries the candle outside and into the darkness and searches for the cat. Imagine that the light she holds will lead the cat home. Concentrate on this image for a while until you can picture it really clearly. Visualize locked doors opening, and all obstructions between the cat and its home vanishing. Visualize the cat seeing the light and following it home.

When you have finished, thank Bast for her help and allow the candle to burn away.

If the cat does not return straight away, simply light a fresh candle every evening, leave it burning in the window and imagine that the light will guide it home.

Obviously, it will sometimes be impossible for the cat to return. This is why it is important to visualize it as following a light home. If the cat is now a spirit, that light will lead it to Bast's realm.

However, we have found that after communing regularly with Bast, we instinctively know whether a cat is alive or not.

We have experienced a remarkable success rate with this rite, both for ourselves and for friends and family. Sometimes group members receive messages from Bast during the rite, occasionally naming the exact day the cat will return. This might sound incredible, but it has happened too many times for us to regard it as coincidental.

Other actions

As well as the full rite, there are a couple of other simple magical actions that can be performed when a cat strays away from home.

You can simply go outside into your garden or yard and call your cat's name. As you do so, visualize the sound of your voice travelling to wherever your cat is. Spend a few minutes willing your voice to carry as far as it needs to for your cat to hear it and come home.

Alternatively – and this method has proved just as effective as a full rite – you can speak to Bast in your mind during a time of relaxation, such as in the bath or just before you go to sleep. Visualize Bast in your mind. Ask for your cat to come home and promise to offer something to Bast in return. We generally say to her that we will happily undertake any task she gives us.

Helping a sick cat

As with missing cats, there are a number of ritual actions you can perform to help a cat which is sick. However, magic alone cannot always cure a cat. We never take the risk of attempting to treat our cats ourselves without professional advice. All of our healing rites are designed to be used in conjunction with veterinary treatment.

When your cat is ill, you can simply stroke it and visualize healing blue energy passing from your hands into its body. You can do as the Egyptians did and paint the hieroglyphs of Bast's name (in a non-toxic medium) onto the cat's food bowl and milk or water dish, so that as it eats or drinks, it absorbs the *heka* of the goddess.

As we saw in Chapter 4, Egyptian physician-priests would also inscribe hieroglyphs onto a piece of parchment or linen and give this to their patient to eat, so that they would absorb the healing *heka* of the gods. Even when a cat is healthy, it would be neither practical nor kind to force a piece of paper or cloth down its throat, but there is an alternative. A dish of milk can be imbued with Bast's healing energy. Place the dish before your statue of the goddess prior to feeding its contents to the cat. Visualize Bast's *heka* pouring into it.

Sometimes, when cats are really ill, they refuse to drink or eat. When this occurs, you have to keep them hydrated. Our vet taught us how to feed a cat liquid, such as milk or glucose and water, using a syringe (without a needle). This treatment has saved the lives of many of our cats when they have had serious illnesses. Sometimes the risk of dehydration is more dangerous than the illness itself.

To feed the cat, you fill the syringe with the fluid, and gently squirt it into its mouth. This method would be ideal for giving *heka*-filled milk to an ailing cat. However, if you have not attempted it before, do seek advice from your vet on how to do this. If it is done incorrectly, it will only increase the cat's distress, and may even be dangerous. Syringes can be acquired from any veterinary surgery.

The visualization

Our working for a sick cat can be performed before or after a trip to the vet's. It involves only a brief visualization.

Sit before your statue of Bast and regulate your breathing. Show Bast an image of your vet, or if you are about to visit a new vet an image of a person wearing a white coat with the words 'veterinary surgeon' written across it. See the vet in their surgery in front of the consultation table. Visualize Bast materializing tall and powerful behind the vet with her arms extended as if to embrace him or her. Visualize that Bast and the vet are one and that Bast's healing energy will be part of whatever treatment is decided upon. Imagine that energy streaming out of the vet's hands into the cat.

If you wanted to, you could expand this little working to include invocations and ritual actions such as the lighting of a candle.

A prayer for a sick cat

The following is an authentic Egyptian prayer, taken from an arte-fact called the Metternich Stele. While it is unlikely any of our cats will be stung by scorpions, we can still use the words if we now regard the scorpion as a metaphor for sickness in general. If you prefer, you could change the wording slightly to be more pertinent to a particular sickness. (Our thanks go to Tamara Siuda for the translation).

Hail Ra, come to your daughter!
A scorpion has stung her on a lonely road.
Her cry has penetrated the heights of heaven, and is heard
*   along the roads.*
The poison has entered into her body, and circulates through
*   her flesh.*
She has set her mouth against it; truly, the poison is in her
*   members.*
Come, then, with your strength, with your fierce attack, and
*   with your power like the Red [i.e., like Set], and force it to be*
*   hidden before you.*
Behold, the poison had entered all the members of this cat
*   which is under my fingers.*
Be not afraid, be not afraid, my daughter, my shining one, for I
*   have set myself behind you.*
I have overthrown the poison, which is in all the limbs of this cat.
O Cat, your head is the head of Ra, lord of the two lands,
*   smiter of the rebellious ones.*
Your fear is in all lands, O lord of the living, lord of eternity.
O you Cat, your two eyes are the Eye of the Lord of the
*   Shining Uraeus, who illumines the two lands with his eye,*
*   and illumines the [one who is] upon on the path of darkness.*
O Cat, your nose is the nose of Thoth, twice great, Lord of
*   Khmenu, chief of the two lands of Ra, who puts breath in*
*   the nostrils of every person.*
O Cat, your ears are the ears of the Lord to the Limit, who
*   listens to the voices of all persons when they appeal to him,*
*   and weighs words in the entire land.*
O Cat, your mouth is the mouth of Tem, Lord of Life, united of
*   creation, who causes the union of creation; he shall deliver*
*   you from every poison.*
O Cat, your neck is the neck of Neheb-ka, presider of the Great
*   House, who makes men and women to live by means of the*
*   utterance of his two arms.*
O Cat, your breast is the breast of Thoth, Lord or Truth, who
*   has given breath to that which is within it.*
O Cat, your heart is the heart of Ptah, who heals your heart of
*   the evil poison, which is in all your limbs.*

O Cat, your hands are the hands of the Great Ennead and the Lesser Ennead, and they shall deliver your hands from the poison of the mouth of every serpent.

O Cat, your belly is the belly of Osiris, Lord of Busiris, the poison shall not work its wishes in your belly.

O Cat, your thighs are the thighs of Montu, who shall make your thighs stand up, and bring the poison to the ground.

O Cat, your leg-bones are the leg-bones of Khonsu, who travels across the two lands by day and night, and shall lead the poison to the ground.

O Cat, your feet are the feet of Amen the Great, Horus Lord of Thebes, who establishes your feet on the earth and overthrows the poison.

O Cat, your haunch is the haunch of Horus, avenger of his father Osiris, and they shall place Set in the wrongdoing which he has made.

O Cat, the soles of your feet are the soles of Ra, who makes the poison return to earth.

O Cat, your bowel is the bowel of Mehet-weret, who overthrows and cuts to pieces the poison in your belly, and in all your members, and in all the members of the gods of heaven, and in all the members of the gods on earth, and shall overthrow every poison in you.

There is no part of you that is without the goddess who will overthrow and cut in pieces the poison of every male serpent, and every female serpent, and every scorpion, and every reptile, which may be in any member of this Cat which is under the knife.

Look, Isis and Nephthys spin against the poison.

This woven garment strengthens this being, who is perfect in words of power, through the speech of Ra-Horakthy, great god, President of the South and the North: 'O evil poison which is in any member of this cat which is under the knife, issue forth upon the earth!'

A funeral rite

When a beloved cat dies, whether from old age, illness or accident, it is always a traumatic experience. Sometimes it is easier to accept when we perform a funeral ritual to say our goodbyes and send our

cat's spirit on its way to Bast's realm in peace. The rite given below
is one that we use when one of our own cats passes on and we
have all found it to be a great comfort at a difficult time. It is
designed to be performed at the graveside. This rite has recently
been rewritten, and we have adapted some of the prayers of E.A.
St George to be included in it, because of their moving and powerful lines.

Equipment

You will need:

- a silver candle for each person
- a beautiful flower to place on the grave (preferably a white rose)
- a sistrum
- Bast incense

The ritual

All stand in a circle around the grave and light the candles and
incense. Shake the sistrum three times. Say:

> *Oh Bast, lady of Asheru, ruler of Sekhet-Neter,*
> *Lady of Ankhtawy, ruler of the divine field,*
> *Life of the two lands,*
> *We call to you.*
> *Hear our prayers*
> *And awaken to our presence.*
> *We gather this night to mark the passing of [insert cat's name],*
> *Our friend and your son/daughter,*
> *Into your eternal realm.*
>
> *Bast, you are the power of the sun,*
> *You are beauty, health and gentleness.*
> *You comfort those who are made mad by the moon,*
> *When you walk at their side in the shadow lands.*
> *You, oh lady, are of the gods who protect this world.*
> *Thunder and lightning strike the skies,*
> *But you return in glory with your father, the sun.*
> *You can blast and you can forgive.*
> *You can punish and you can reward.*

You can grant sunshine unto children.
You can grant moonshine unto lovers.
You have died and yet you live.
It is whispered that if one man or woman should believe in
    your power
You can harken to the prayers of all the world.
Hear us, oh Bast,
You can twist the skein and weave the thread of destiny.
You are sacred and beautiful, a lady of music.
You are lustrous and all-powerful,
And the world rides upon the arch of your back.
You are venerated and called the lady of the east.
Take your son/daughter, [insert cat's name], into your temple of
    silver
May she/he be reunited with those who have passed before
    him/her,
And dwell for ever between your sacred paws.

Shake the sistrum three times. Everyone should now place their lit candles in the ground around the grave. Then continue:

Bast the divine, ruler of the night,
Goddess of love, infinite, all-wise and all-knowing,
Great cat, who is the cat of the heavens,
We give you this candle light for [insert cat's name],
Who has passed over,
From this earth plane onto the other side.
We all remember her/him as she/he was in life
And we remember her/his life among us and our friends.
We give this light for [insert cat's name]
That she/he may be taken up
In your arms, oh Bast,
Divine mother of all cats.
May her/his soul come to rest in your shining temple.
May her/his spirit pass through the portal
Between this world and the next,
To find rest, peace and happiness.
May her/his time spent with you
Upon your golden stairs
Be in comfort.
May [insert cat's name] be at peace and rest,

Confident in the knowledge
That her/his family, friends and tribe of cats
On this earth plane
Are thinking of her/him,
And directing their love towards her/him.

Place the flower on the grave, and shake the sistrum three times. Then say:

Receive unto you, oh Bast
This, our symbol of our cat's body.
Peace be with you, [insert cat's name].

The beautiful cat that endures,
Lead [insert cat's name] to peace, oh Bast.
We wait for the sound of your footfall,
Grant her/him your sleep, oh Bast.
Most beautiful cat that endures,
Guide her/him through night, oh Bast.
We watch for your eyes in the dark,
Lead her/him to light, oh Bast.

Now visualize the cat ascending the golden steps of Bast's temple, with any other cats around it that it may have known who have also passed on, to be reunited with the goddess. See Bast take the cat in her arms. Say any final goodbyes.

When you feel that you are ready let each person present sprinkle some incense onto the charcoal and as the smoke rises imagine that it carries the soul of your cat with it into the realm of Bast.

When the rite is ended let the candles burn down. If you like you can then place a small statue of Bast on the grave.

21

The Bridge Across Time

We are all longing to go home to some place we have never been – a place, half-remembered and half-envisioned we can only catch glimpses of from time to time.
From Dreaming the Dark *by Starhawk*

Religions across the world rise and fall, much as political empires do. What was once a prevailing belief system might now have faded into the fringe area, grouped together in the spiritual storehouse and a host of other systems, with a sign on the door that simply says 'pagan'.

In its literal sense, 'pagan' means different things to different people. In the *Oxford English Dictionary* it is defined as: 'villager, rustic, civilian, non-militant, opp. to *milles* "soldier".' This derives from the Latin word *paganus*, which means literally villager. In Christian terms it means heathen, as opposed to Christian or Jewish. It is also defined as 'a person holding religious beliefs other than those of any of the main religions of the world; or a derogatory term for a follower of a polytheistic or pantheistic religion'.

So in one sense, adhering to a system based on ancient Egyptian beliefs *is* pagan, but in another it is not. An intrinsically modern interpretation of the word 'pagan' is anything pertaining to the belief system which has grown up around the Western tradition of magic. This alone is an umbrella term for many different systems, from Wicca to shamanism to high ceremonial magic.

Most practitioners of magic would regard themselves as part of the neo-pagan movement, which derives mainly from the teachings of individuals such as Gerald Gardner, who helped revive witchcraft in the West following the repeal of the witchcraft laws in the 1950s.

Practitioners of other systems, who follow different teachings and whose practices derive from high ceremonial magic groups such as the Golden Dawn, might also consider themselves to be pagan. It is just a term, but because we always give words particular associations, the word is sometimes important. Some of the people we have contacted in writing this chapter have made it clear that they do not wish to be labelled as pagan.

We feel it is really up to the individual. Although we ourselves have been members of pagan groups in the past, we do not see our current group as neo-pagan in the sense of closely following the Western tradition. However, it would be foolish of us to say that our past experiences do not, to some degree, influence our present work, so we also cannot claim our practices are purely Egyptian. In fact, we do not stick rigorously to performing Egyptian-influenced rituals. We also like to celebrate the eight seasonal festivals of the Celtic tradition, because we feel it is a way of connecting with the spirit of our native land. These occasions are also important in that they allow our group to get together, socialize and celebrate life without doing any 'heavy' magical work. Our festivals have been written by members of the group and are very different from any used by a traditional Wiccan group. And as well as these festivals, we might occasionally design a ritual around deities of a completely different belief system because it is pertinent to work we are involved in at the time.

We are not particularly religious, in the sense of blindly worshipping a deity, although do see ourselves as spiritual, and turn to the goddesses not only for help in a magical sense, but for strength, comfort and courage.

For a long time, the Egyptian system was effectively a dead one. If anyone did still practise it, they did so in secret, no doubt in fear of persecution from Christians and Muslims. Following the repeal of the anti-witchcraft laws in the 1950s, the rise of magical movements in the Western world meant that people could once again turn to alternative belief systems without fear of prosecution or revilement. Thousands of years had elapsed. The Egyptian system was not a living religion, like that of say Voodoo, which has survived as an oral tradition for centuries. The Egyptian system had to be virtually reinvented by modern practitioners, and there were no ancient Egyptians around to verify or criticize interpretations and translations of their sacred texts. Because so many people became involved in this revival, many different interpretations inevitably arose. Variety is not a bad thing, and even if some people have beliefs very different from our own, we feel they have to be respected. Otherwise, we are in danger of falling into the trap of religious intolerance and persecution which as magical practitioners we tend to scorn in members of organized religions.

In researching this book, we came across many differing practices among people who, in their own way, were passionate about what they believed in. In this chapter, we would like to show how different people interact with Bast and Sekhmet. We could write a book entirely about this subject, and there are certainly a host of practitioners, movements and temples with whom we have yet to establish contact. What we offer here is only a brief sample of different beliefs; it does not by any means present the full picture. Those of you who have access to the Internet and are interested in studying this subject further need only do a search on any of the goddesses' names to access an immense amount of sites to browse through.

The accounts given below come from a small selection of the people who have been kind enough to tell us about their beliefs. We have not commented on the content of each account, as we wanted to give people the opportunity to speak frankly. We hope they will offer a glimpse of the variety of guises under which Bast and Sekhmet now appear in our modern world.

E.A. St George

E.A. St George is a practising cabbalist who has a great affinity for cats and does much in a practical way to help them. She has written books about Bast and Sekhmet, including chapbooks of hymns and prayers, some of which we have mentioned and quoted from in this book. This is what she has to say about her beliefs and practices.

I have always been involved with the animal gods, even as a child. The cats chose me, I suspect. I talked to them and they talked to me and the bond grew stronger with the passing years. I have worked with other cat goddesses, and other animal gods and goddesses.

I started with the British Library and talked to several Egyptologists to get some idea of what Egyptian ritual was like. I

235

then started collecting prayers and writing my own rituals. I was fortunate in being able to travel to Egypt and other countries and meditate in sacred spots. Knowledge was there – I had only to listen.

I have a permanent working temple in my own house. It does not need a circle because it stays consecrated. If I were going off to work in a strange place, then I might draw a circle and would have to dig out a formula for such a ritual. My temple is an erstwhile bedroom, 14ft square, with a window facing east. I have a black and white flecked carpet on the floor. If I lived in the Middle East, I would be using black and white floor tiles. I recently painted the walls a very pale blue to symbolize the New Age, and the ceiling is painted white. I have bookshelves, which carry some of my occult books. Other shelves carry statuettes of gods from various countries and ages. A ceiling light casts a bright beam on to the altar surface. There used to be a hanging lamp but my eyesight is not what it was. There is a white, double-cubed altar in front of the window, along with a white side table. Silver curtains veil the window. I also keep a small tape recorder and various tapes with suitable music in my temple.

As for equipment, I have a rod, a sword (for Sekhmet), a dagger (Bast), a cup, a panticle, several offering bowls, candlesticks, an incense burner and relevant statuettes. The rod was consecrated by my teacher. The sword I won in ritual combat. The cup was given to me by one who loved me. I made the panticle myself. Silver offering bowls and candlesticks can be bought from jewellers. I got one incense burner from a church shop, another was left to me. Statuettes came from museum shops.

I did things the hard way. Most of these props would be available at many of the occult fairs and festivals. A novice would be very lucky to get them all at once, but most of them could be run to earth without too much trouble. A simple consecration is necessary. The Festival of Bast – as near as I can figure out – took place on 9–10–11 May. This festival included naming dead pets before the goddess and we observe it every year. 'That which was named can be written down. That which is written can be remembered before the gods. That which is read unto the gods can achieve immortality.' (Well, that is what the manuscript says!) The Festival of Sekhmet takes place in the first week in August when Regulus is high in the sky. A minor celebration occurs every year called the National Cat Show. It usually takes place at the start of December.

I have been to Egypt many times. Last year I was there for a performance of *Aida* at Luxor. I went to pay a visit to my favourite Sekhmet shrine but the temple guardian would not leave me alone for meditation. He spent the entire time begging for money for his children. I could not be left alone for ten seconds, let alone half an hour, in the empty shrine. I got the impression that the statue in that shrine is very peeved about the way her visitors are treated. She wanted to come home with me and I wanted the same thing. Unfortunately the Muslims have not come to terms with the fact that some people are neither Muslim nor Christian. I would love to open a pagan temple to the cat goddess in this country and do things properly.

I have some sympathy with people who feel that their work should remain esoteric but it rather depends on what the work is. It seems to me that it is crunch time for the big cats. The human race will wipe them off the planet unless we all get together and stop the poachers killing tigers and so on. Why keep prayers and rituals hidden? That is not going to help conservation of tigers. We are more likely to help by getting cash to fund anti-poaching patrols. A united front making enough noise will usually encourage officialdom to get off its hind end and *do* something. I once told a prospective MP that if he insisted he wanted to be my servant, this was how he could start. He looked usefully devastated. Public servants should regularly be reminded that they are there to serve the people – they forget sometimes. But that is by the way.

You are right about the cat goddesses adapting. I tried to make that point in my novel *Cat Star*, when yesterday's priestess becomes today's cat vet and tomorrow's diplomat. The gods have not ceased to exist. It is humans who have closed their eyes to the gods.

Stephanie Cass

Stephanie Cass comes from an entirely different tradition, that of Kemetic Orthodoxy, which is based in America. She explains in her own words what this means and entails.

Like a lot of people, I hit a religious quandary around the age of thirteen. To cut to the chase, I figured out I was not Christian pretty quick. It did not stir me, and I had never been too keen on the Bible anyway, so I dropped it like a hot brick and went looking for something new. At the same time I had read a book by Robert Graves discussing the Greek pantheon, to which I had much undue affection. While I do not agree with many of Graves' theories, I do agree with his analysis of the Olympians: they were petty, they were arrogant, and they did not really care about the mortals who served them.

Exit Greek theology, enter Egyptian. I was fourteen by this point, borderline pagan, and through an accident of research found out about Bast. I did not find out *much* about Bast except what you can find in an encyclopaedia, which is usually one line that consists of the following: 'Bast – Egyptian cat goddess, connected to fertility and joy. Associated with Sekhmet. Herodotus wrote of her in his . . .' And that was it. Book after book, the same line repeated over and over. It did not wash with me – I am not sure why. And neither, I was learning, did paganism.

I am a historian. I have half a degree in history and expect to complete it some day with the possible outlook of going for a masters in either the same subject or Egyptology. I am especially picky about truth in the past. It bothered me that I could not find anything on Bast, and it bothered me that I felt something about paganism did not work with me. I wanted to like it – it seemed to be the only thing that worked with what I was worshipping – but I could not do it.

So, at twenty-one, I was religionless but not without spirituality. I had settled on the belief that God was one big lump of divinity and that that divinity had chosen to express itself to me through Bast. She started showing up in my writing and passed through my life in various forms, speaking through friends, speaking through coincidences. My first Bast cats came from two of my best friends (who were my housemates at the time) and my fiancé. I stumbled over Kemetic Orthodoxy by accident. My workmate at the time – Revd Craig Schaefer – had an AOL profile for an Internet account of his that hinted at being a priest of not only Egyptian religion, but Bast as well. I ambushed him and, in a very long three-hour chat, ruthlessly pumped him for information about her. I left with a URL (Internet address) for the homesite of the House of Netjer – Netjer being the Kemetic (ancient Egyptian) word for God. He called the religion to which the House subscribed Kemetic Orthodoxy.

It was quite clear from the beginning as I read up on the House that their religion was closer to what I had been doing most of my life than anything else I had ever encountered. It was not a Western religion; the belief system was closer to Ifa or Hinduism than anything else. There was a belief in a general force in life called *ma'at*. *Ma'at* can be loosely translated as 'truth' and 'what is right'. *Ma'at*'s symbol is a feather since when *ma'at* is proper in your life, this is how your heart feels. When it is not, you know it.

There was a belief that the Egyptians were not polytheistic. Based on the landmark thesis of Erik Hornung in his *Conceptions of God in Ancient Egypt: The One and the Many*, the House was under the opinion that Egyptian religion was monolatrous; that is one God who can become many at will. Netjer, being so big, is inherently impossible to comprehend. Therefore it breaks itself into a multitude that are easier to deal with. And Bast was part of them.

There was a belief that the Egyptian religion was recoverable, and that they generally halted all research on it around the Twentieth Dynasty (when the region began to be overrun by outside forces who, by virtue of overrunning the government, also overran the religion with permutations of their own). There was a belief that the Egyptian religion was not to be mixed with other religions. Just as one would not carry Michael the Archangel over to Buddhism, so one should not try to drag the Morrigan into Egyptian religion. Concepts of God were created for certain theologies; it is through the looking glass of those theologies that we can most accurately view that god. This all hit the spot for me. Four days after scouring the Internet and their website, I went home to the House of Netjer.

I do not usually like to run things into the ground, but I will in this case. Kemetic Orthodoxy is not neo-paganism or Wicca. There is a general misinterpretation that, because I worship God in plural, I am by default pagan. This may be true by the Catholic definition – which states that anyone non-Catholic is a pagan – but it is not true by definition of the earth-based religions that have gained popularity in the United States and Europe. I am no more neo-pagan than a worshipper of Hinduism or Ifa is.

I am expected, as a worshipper, to spend thirty minutes a day in shrine. 'In shrine' refers to a freeform worship in which I basically set aside time to listen to God. I enter purified by a mixture of water and natron, light incense and a candle or lamp, and make offerings of water and/or other stuffs to Netjer. I recite a few lines I have memorized and then meditate for a time. As clergy, I also attend to a shrine image of Bast, to whom I am a priest (Hemt-Bast or servant of Bast). Once a week I also venerate – but do not worship – my ancestors. This is a time when I pour out for them an offering of water and speak some more lines, then remember them for a time that their *kas* (or spirits) might be fed. In my shrine I have a photograph of my grandfather, who passed away on 5 May when I was seventeen.

During certain festivals, I drive to Chicago and join members of the House for festivals conducted by the House's Nisut or leader, Revd Tamara Siuda. The rites are frequently expansions on the shrine prayers except with more recitation, more ceremony in the form of costume and various ritual tools, and larger offerings. As in Voodoo or Ifa, there may be a *saq* or ritual appearance of God through one of the ritual's attendants. Unlike in Voodoo, *saq* is strictly reserved for the clergy, who are trained to handle possession. This is not trance or channelling – this is a full possession that is heavily taxing on the body of the person involved. The priest becomes a 'living shrine' through which God, as one of the names of Netjer, speaks with us. To date, I have seen the *saq* of four names – Bast twice and Aset (or Isis), Sekhmet and Nit (or Neith) once. They are at once frightening and exhilarating – as, on the one hand, you are talking to God, and, on the other, you realize – *you are talking to God*.

Afterwards we celebrate with a meal shared by all who attended the ritual, and discuss what we saw, what we felt and what we learned. The main focus of ritual in Kemetic Orthodoxy is the worship of God and honouring the divine. *Saq* does not always occur, and in fact any time that Netjer chooses to honour us with its presence we feel exceptionally blessed, even if the priest who is the name's instrument later feels as if she or he had been run over by a Mac truck.

All the rites and practices of the House are as close as possible to what the Kemetic peoples practised. While there are some obvious exceptions – we don't live next to the Nile, we don't have huge stone temples dedicated to Netjer (yet), etc. – for the most part we have tried our best not to alter the religion. Through research and reconstruction, the House has proved that it is indeed possible to do as the ancients did, while sacrificing as little as possible to modern-day conventions.

From the age of thirteen I can recall seeing Artemis from time to time. I stopped seeing her when I first learned of Bast. It is of very little surprise to me that Artemis was associated with Bast by the Greeks. I have always belonged to Bast, even though I did not always know her name.

During the first week of my entry into the House, I opened my eyes during shrine and saw Bast standing over me. She was dressed somewhat casually and when she saw my surprised expression, her only comment was, 'What did you expect? A toga?'

I have found that during certain days of the calendar that are attributed to Bast I tend to exhibit behaviour associated with her, whether or not I know that day is associated with her. I will never forget the day I was suddenly seized with the desire to completely rewrite, reformat and reillustrate my web site on her – only to look up after it was all done to see that the day was the Feast of Ra of the Eye of Ra. Bast, being the Eye of Ra, was to be looked out for that day.

Most frequently the time when I 'see' her is in my dreams. She wanders in and out to warn me, congratulate me, or tell me to pay attention. Bast is frequently a 'content' Netjer – it is her nature to be happy, but only on her terms. Her anger can be furious – and devious, much like the nature of the cat, who tends to express her anger by leaving unpleasant surprises in one's sock drawer or shoes. Bast is the cat waiting in the dark for you to let your guard down. And once you do . . . it is all over.

Bast enjoys music. I have performed in my shrine in her honour, and at conventions I have privately dedicated performances to her. One song I perform – 'Velvet' by Tallis Kimberly – is what I consider my Bast song. When I sing it, I am singing it for her – and she likes it.

One final (and opinionated) note on 'working' with God: I do not 'work' with God. This is a term that has become popular recently in New Age circles. It implies, to me, that I can control God some-how. It also implies impermanence: 'I am working with Mut this week. Next week I think I'll work with Set.'

I cannot 'work' with Bast; Bast works through me. In the same way I cannot 'work' with the sky, the rain or the air I breathe; it works around me and, whether or not I live or die, it will continue working after my bones and my children's bones are dust. In the cast of Bast, however, she has the compassion and the desire to work with me, but it is not on my time; it is on hers. No matter how much I like it or not, the truth remains: if she chose to drop an anvil on me, she could. She does not, however. And that is one of the reasons why I love her.

When people speak of fear for God, this is why. God is God because he or she or it could choose at any time to throw the power switch and turn off the sun. God could crumple up the world and toss us into the celestial wastebasket. God could rid itself of us and continue on without a thought, because it is that powerful, and that awe-inspiring. But it does not, and has not, and hopefully will not. This is why respect for God exists, and why I choose not to use the phrase 'working with Bast' or 'working with Sekhmet'. I honour Bast, I am in awe of her, I am her servant – but I am not her equal.

Stephanie has a web site at http://www/dm.net/~steph and is happy to accept e-mail at RevSCass@kemet.org

Trisha West

Trisha West has only recently become involved in magical activities, although she has studied astrology for the last twenty years. She describes this as the starting point for her inward journey.

Although I was christened in a Catholic church, then later attended a Church of England school, 'normal' religion never really felt like part of my life: nor was I an atheist. I always felt that there was something that held the universe together, but it never really had a face for me and it certainly did not have a name.

What alienated me from Christianity was in part the apparent dichotomy between what the Church preached and what I saw when they opened their doors to me: the crucifixes, the icons, the pomp and ceremony – for a God who demanded no 'graven images'? I never did understand.

What really alienated me, however, was religious education in school; when you are force fed something, you tend to go off it. Consequently, as a teenager I never fully investigated my own spirituality.

I have to say that in principle, and bearing in mind my limited exposure to Christianity, I have nothing against the religion itself. It is the apparently autocratic organizations that have evolved from it that really disturb me.

What is more, if God is all around us, why do I have to go to church to worship or give thanks? When the world is full of uncertainty, how can anyone be so sure that theirs is the only true faith? In Christianity uncertainty seems to be seen as a bad thing; why else would they use the phrase 'a crisis of faith' for those who abandon it?

If we are really to connect with the divine, surely the face we put on it is irrelevant? Is it not what is behind that face that counts? What often seems to be overlooked is that religions institutions present us with a façade that is all man-made. To accept this without question is a dangerous thing indeed, or so it seems to me, and has often been the cause of many religious conflicts. As someone once said, belief divides. Is doubt not the real uniting force, the spark that ignites action as opposed to reaction?

Uncertainty and the need to find out for myself were what led me to investigate alternative belief systems. Through a (non-magical) hobby of mine, I came into contact with a group of people who had a particular interest in Bast and was invited to attend one of their ceremonies – this occurred the night immediately after I had a dream in which someone sent a cat to protect me. I was pleased to find the group had no hierarchy to divide them, doubt enough to unite them. This was the freedom I craved. Now that I am part of this group, I am free to decide for myself what is right for me. But of course this is not religion; this is magic.

In exploring Bast I am finding out about myself. Perhaps this is what magic is: a tool for obtaining self-knowledge. In my religious education, looking inward was often frowned upon and equated with self-indulgence. Instead the teachings seemed to be about looking outwards, invariably through the censoring mind of a priest or vicar. However, that is not where I felt the answers were – well, not the ones I needed anyway.

If God is within each of us, why do I need a priest to connect me with the divine? Why should I accept answers fed to me, perhaps even selectively, by a man who has never walked in my shoes? If the Bible says 'Thou shalt not judge', why should I seek absolution from a priest who is after all only human himself?

The rituals for Bast, which I have performed with friends, have introduced me to visualization. The use of this technique has shown me what my religious education could not: how to tap my inner self. I want to shape rather than be shaped, to know my talents and how to make better use of them – for the good of all, I hope.

Since these inward trips began, I have noticed several changes within me. The most startling is what visualization seems to trigger.

Several times now, in the days following a ritual, I have seen white light around certain people. I am told these are auras, although I am not entirely sure of this myself. Nor am I about to accept the apparent link between the two without further investigation – and investigate it I shall, whilst still maintaining a healthy level of doubt, of course.

The irony of all this is that I am currently involved in something that uses rituals and symbols, the very things I deliberately left behind. Strange as it may seem, I now have a greater respect for Christianity and the man-made façade that it has placed upon the divine.

If I have learned anything, it is not to place too high a value on these 'masks', whilst at the same time not dismissing them entirely either. As far as I can see, symbolism is important in the way it unblocks the human psyche. There are wonders beyond the reach of our normal senses, and where better to start looking than inside yourself?

Caroline Wise

Caroline Wise is co-administrator of the Fellowship of Isis, a world-wide network with 15,000 members that is open to anyone who recognizes the feminine aspect of divinity as well as the male aspect favoured by the major world religions. She has worked as an occult bookseller and publisher for fifteen years and been actively involved in the earth mysteries, paganism and psychic questing for over twenty years. Her first magical lion was Aslan, whom she encountered at age five in the Narnia books by C.S. Lewis. She was moved by Aslan's power and wisdom, but frustrated by his Christ-like acceptance of suffering. Caroline has given us two short pieces concerning Sekhmet and Bast.

Sekmet and London

Egyptian traders used to sail up the River Thames aeons ago, the boats proudly displaying the eye of Osiris to ward off peril at sea. Sekhmet is one Egyptian deity with a strong presence in London, but that does not come from those ancient times or from the Roman era when the cult of Isis and Serapis flourished by the Thames. The London Sekhmets came here in the Victorian age and its later Egyptmania. There is said to be a huge statue of Sekhmet lying at the bottom of the Thames, which evokes magical and mysterious feelings in me as I picture her lying there, silent, brooding and pulsating with power in this sacred River of Isis that I cross twice a day. The statue was apparently pushed from a bridge where it was displayed in Victorian times, near Waterloo. So many statues of Sekhmet were brought back from the plunder of Egypt that they were unappreciated and used for ballast, dumped in the sea along the route! They are, presumably, still lying there, in their underwater dreamtime. Thousands of mummified cats, sacred to Bast, were brought back to Britain and unceremoniously used as fertilizer for crops eaten by our ancestors. Sekhmet is in our capital city, and Bast is in our blood!

A head of Sekhmet graces the door of one of the famous auction houses in Bond Street. If you walk from the British Museum, in Bloomsbury, down to Charing Cross and along the Embankment, you will, coincidentally, see lion imagery all around – in keystones, statues, drinking fountains and decorative work on buildings. There are said to be over 300 lion images.

The most impressive and awe-inspiring statues of Sekhmet to be found in London are the black granite ones in the British Museum. In 1978–9 two of my friends were working on the ground-breaking magazine, *Strange Phenomena*. Rather than just reporting anecdotal stories of the paranormal and the 'unexplained', as other similar publications did, the editors researched the stories thoroughly themselves. One of the projects was to investigate 'ordinary' people from all over the country who claimed psychic abilities. The *Strange Phenomena* team conducted surveys and tests to see what these people had in common – and to see how good they really were! They took psychics to visit the British Museum, a treasure house of magical and religious artefacts from all over the ancient world. They wanted to see what, if anything, inspired the psychics or triggered psychic information. These people had not visited the British Museum before, and they had no knowledge of the occult, ancient Egypt or the gods and goddesses. Time and again, when the psychics were taken past the four majestic black granite statues of Sekhmet, they would go into visionary trances, see themselves in ancient Egypt (often standing before a statue of Sekhmet in a shrine). Some reported conversations that they were having with Sekhmet in their heads. Often they would pour out images and knowledge from ancient Egypt. Several reported tingling sensations when they touched the statues. All reported some degree of altered state of consciousness. I became especially interested in Sekhmet because of this, but was not expecting her to turn up at a seance ten years later!

In 1990, I was invited to a seance at the Atlantis Bookshop in Museum Street, Bloomsbury, 100 yards away from the statues mentioned above. This shop was founded as an occult shop in 1922. Present at the seance were the owner of the shop, Karl Duncan, the previous owner and myself (totally unaware that I would become a custodian of the shop in the future – the past, present and future of the place were represented that night). Through our contacts in spiritualism, we were lucky to have with us one of the country's leading mediums. As the evening progressed, the past owner identified various spirit communicators, and obscure bits of history of the shop were recognized and confirmed. Then the medium said, 'You're going to think that I've gone mad, this sounds so crazy, but I can see a lioness under the shop, with a human female body. She's standing upright and it's as if her batteries need topping up, so to speak. She's trying to get our attention. This is really what I'm seeing!'

'Oh that's Sekhmet,' said the previous owner. 'We always had a statue of her in here. It belonged to Michael Houghton, who founded the shop in 1922, and it stayed here when we came. You must get one. She wants to be back here.'

Incidentally, when this statue, which was made of plaster covered by a bronze skin, was broken once, a bone was found inside. One of Sekhmet's titles is 'Bonesetter', so I wonder if she had been made as a magical talisman to heal someone's broken bones.

Karl Duncan had a statue and two large paintings commissioned as a result of this seance, and went on to become a priest of Sekhmet in the Fellowship of Isis. I am now at Atlantis Bookshop, and we frequently get people dropping by on their pilgrimage to the British Museum to see the statues. Many report experiences similar to those noted by the *Strange Phenomena* team. Sekhmet's time has definitely come again.

Bast

In 1990, an apport (an object produced by occult means) appeared in our garden under very strange circumstances that I will not relate here. It was a huge piece of citrine quartz, its rock face and facets covered in mud as if it had just been pulled out of the earth. To put it very simply, it was connected to some magical environmental work we had just done to save some ancient London woodland local to us. A psychic friend visited and told us, amongst other things, that there would be four stones in all, three more to come. The next two appeared in equally bizarre circumstances: one in the same place, heralded by a shooting star, and the other in a friend's garden in Ireland, where we had done the original environmental magic. Our friend in Ireland has been a priestess of Bast for over twenty years. The fourth piece arrived in 1992. I was at a friend's house but had an overwhelming sensation that I must return home for something important. I left my husband and friend, and hurried home. When I got there, I went into the kitchen and made a cup of tea, and started to drink it, looking out of the window. Forty feet away, where the first two chunks of citrine had apported, a statue of Bast appeared. It just sort of flickered into existence. I could see it clearly. I 'knew' that it was Victorian. It was plaster, and the black paint was chipped, so I could see beneath the slight pink colour of old plaster. The statue had a double-stranded gold collar round its neck, knotted in the middle with the four strands hanging down about 5 inches. She was about 18 inches high. I could see that it was unstable and was starting to flicker in and out of reality. Then it disappeared. Putting down my tea, I walked up the path to the spot where she had been. I knew I would find something. And there was a large, rather ordinary-looking stone. When I turned it over, it was of course the fourth piece of citrine that our psychic friend had predicted.

I have always had an uneasy relationship with Bast – she is not one of 'my' goddesses. I find her scratchy and difficult on a psychic level, and I know several people who can mediate her much better than I can. I do not know why she appeared to alert me to the fourth apport, or how she is connected.

Many women tell me that they feel a particular affinity with Bast, Sekhmet or both and ask, 'How can we contact them?' With any deity, I would suggest first building a shrine. Find a picture of the goddess that you especially like – there are some beautiful ones around – and invest in a statue. Place an appropriate cloth, e.g. red, on a shelf or small table – even window sill – and light a candle and some incense. Flowers and seasonal items can be added. It can be as simple or elaborate as you wish. There is space for a shrine even in the smallest bedroom. Then meditate, ask for guidance and illumination – have conversations with her. Cool cats and proud lions may not think much of you if you abase yourself at the shrine! Keep the shrine dusted and change it according to the seasons, astrological dates, Sekhmet and Bast festivals, special healing requests etc. The best way one can work with the cat goddesses, though, is to combine the above with some practical work on this plane. You can raise money for your local cat protection charity, 'adopt' a lion or tiger through one of the wildlife charities, organize conferences and write to MPs about the appalling cruelty to cats that still goes on legally in the vivisection trade. This way you are earthing the goddesses' divine energy, manifesting them in this plane of our everyday existence. And judging by the huge increase of interest in the cat goddesses, it is on this plane at this time that they seek a voice.

As an interesting coda to this account, on the day this piece was being added to the manuscript, Caroline called Storm to tell her of an intriguing synchronicity. Caroline had been very ill and our receipt of her account was quite close to deadline as she had been unable to work for a while. What with the phone calls back and forth, and writing the piece, Sekhmet had been very much on Caroline's mind for the past few days. The day after she had posted her account to us, she was out shopping in London, looking for Christmas presents. She went to a shop that sold glass ornaments to look for a present for a particular friend. In amongst the showy displays of rather vulgar glass animals, her eye was caught by something very different, an object she would never have dreamed of seeing in that particular shop: a foot high black glass figurine of a lioness-headed woman, with a white solar disc on her head. The figure was stylized, with long arms, a slender body and a tiny waist, but it had to be Sekhmet. It was so beautiful and exquisite Caroline felt she had to have it, but the shop was renowned for being very expensive so she thought the cost would be prohibitive. She was stunned therefore to see a price tag of only £22 or so. She thought this must be a mistake. The figure was French, pure art and clearly worth a lot more. But no. A shop assistant confirmed the price. Caroline bought it at once, and now says she is afraid of handling it because it is so delicate. It will, however, be given pride of place on a high shelf in the Atlantis Bookshop, out of harm's way. The most unusual aspect of this acquisition was that when Caroline held the figure up to the light, she discovered it was not made of black glass at all, but of dark blood-coloured glass, Sekhmet's own colour. Even more coincidental is that one of our artists, Ruby, had just sent us a fabulous painting of a black Sekhmet (now displayed on our web site) – almost identical to the figure Caroline had purchased.

Karen Deeley

Some practitioners are brushed by Bast's or Sekhmet's frequency when they least expect it. Karen Deeley works with author Andrew Collins, and has this experience to relate concerning the group of four statues of Sekhmet in the British Museum, which leads on from what Caroline related in her account.

Having collected visas for our forthcoming – and my first ever – visit to Egypt, my partner, Andrew, and I went to acclimatize ourselves in the Egyptian Hall at the British Museum. Passing the Sekhmet statues, I felt compelled to stand before them.

I ran my hand over the smooth stone, absorbing their shape. Reaching out to touch the *ankh* held in the left hand of one of the statues, I felt my own hand rest just an inch above, hovering, feeling at that distance the coolness of the granite. I could not push down.

Breathing in their presence, something in the pit of my stomach leapt, my focus slipped, blankness, my body was no longer mine. . . .

I am placing lilies at the feet of the statue. As I bend down, I feel the heat of the midday sun on the back of my neck. Looking at my feet I notice sand, feeling it between my toes. A snake slithers away.

I look up, the sun disc on her head catching the rays of the sun and burning my cheeks to red. Her face, the she-lion, a powerful protectress, a formidable foe. The *ankh* glows gold. I reach out to touch and feel the imprint still as I remove my hand. . . .

I am led away, back to the British Museum, back to Andrew. Dizzy, my vision obscured by black fog, I have to sit down.

After Egypt, I revisited the British Museum, seeking sanctuary from the noise of London, and found myself once again before the statues of Sekhmet. I sat opposite to gaze, understanding now that the midday sun is an aspect of her influence, and the snake her dominion over *Ur-hekau*, 'the magic power'. At the end of the bench sat a man who introduced himself as Egyptian.

'Are you an artist?' he asked.

'No,' I replied. 'Why?'

'Because you look at Sekhmet with the eyes of your soul.'

Andrew Collins's web site is at:
   http://members.aol.com/edenelder/

Julia Phillips

Julia Phillips now lives in Australia, after moving there from London some years ago. She first encountered the gods and goddesses of ancient Egypt in primary school, and so began a life-long fascination with both the country and its history. She has always felt a special affinity for Sekhmet, and for several years edited a magazine called *Children of Sekhmet*. It ceased publication in 1990 and was replaced by *Web of Wyrd*, but her interest in Sekhmet and other feline deities has never diminished.

In 1985 I was lucky enough to make my first visit to Egypt and discover its mystery and magic at first hand. In preparation for the trip, my partner and I worked Egyptian ritual three times each day for a month, although I have to admit strong visualization skills were necessary when hailing Ra at midday in the gloom of a London October in Hyde Park!

By the time we arrived in Cairo, we felt thoroughly attuned to the Egyptian magical current, but I have to say the reality still came as quite a jolt. Nothing had prepared me for the sheer vibrant power of Egypt – the heat, the dry wind, the dust. Even in the most mundane settings, Egypt had a way of saying, 'Listen! Feel me! I am alive as no other place on earth is alive!'

We travelled by train down to Aswan, and then cruised back up the Nile, visiting each of the temples along the way. Although part of a small group, my partner and I were able to get time alone in each temple, and either quietly meditated to soak up the atmosphere of the place or performed a ritual to try and make contact with the beings which once filled the temples with their power. I have to say that I did not, and do not, have a feeling of worship for

250

these beings. I am full of awe for their power and majesty, but to me they are guardians and helpers to those who would seek the mystery.

Having a lifelong affinity with Sekhmet, it is not surprising that I found her to be vibrantly alive in her homeland. Back at Giza we hired horses to ride out into the desert, thinking we might ride to the stepped pyramids at Saqqara. As we left civilization behind us, the hot dry wind whispered her name, and every grain of sand like a miniature crystal seemed to hold and magnify her power.

Some days later, we joined a conga of tourists to explore the inner chamber of the great Cheops pyramid. I had not expected much from the experience with so many others around, but in fact it was profoundly moving. Strangely, as we reached the chamber (having climbed in a 'Groucho Marx' position for what seemed an age), there were very few people around, and it was quite possible to spend time quietly, drifting along. I had no visions of Sekhmet in the chamber, and I suspect the very strong smell of cat had a rather mundane origin, but it was an incredible experience to sit in the centre of the Great Pyramid and just absorb the atmosphere.

Christina Paul

Like Stephanie Cass, Christina Paul is a member of the clergy of Kemetic Orthodoxy. Christina, however, is a child of Sekhmet rather than a child of Bast.

About five or six years ago, I encountered a Sekhmet book that was published by a mainstream occult publisher. Something about it appealed to me – the cover mainly! Everything I had ever heard about Sekhmet indicated that she was not a name of Netjer to mess with. So I resisted the impulse to purchase the book. About six months later, I was having very intense dreams about lions and other large cats, such as black panthers. When I went back to the same store, I decided to buy the book on Sekhmet. Next to it was a book by the Revd Tamara Siuda, *The Netjeru of Kemet*, which literally fell onto my head and then my foot! I ended up buying both books. Interestingly, prior to finding the Revd Siuda's book, about three people had told me that I should write to her and get to know her. My initial reaction was lukewarm. I had met far too many Egypto-Wiccans, and I just wanted to get to the reality of what

Egyptian religious practices were about. Since I am allergic to cats, I do not think that I would consciously have chosen a feline name of Netjer such as Sekhmet. In fact, in my view, I never really 'chose' Sekhmet; looking back I know now it was she who chose me. Our relationship to Netjer, according to Kemetic Orthodox belief, is one where our 'parent' Netjer chooses us, not the other way around. When I try to explain that to people I find I get confused looks from those who are actually 'drawn' to Sekhmet or any other name.

Before finding Kemetic Orthodoxy, I was in Wicca for several years, within a formal neo-Alexandrian tradition, which was very disciplined. It is probably the best way for me to have practised my spirituality – with a degree of focus and discipline. I know that this, in the end, helped me in becoming a priest of Sekhmet within Kemetic Orthodoxy, and I bless my elder mentor for having taught me as he did. All the while I was in Wicca, however, I found myself asking to be led to the truth of Egypt's religion and magic. It was a long search that consisted of weeding through a lot of material and sects. Some claimed to be many things, none of which could be substantiated, and others were outright frauds. But, Netjer provide, I ended up here where we rely very heavily on verifiable ancient sources, rather than things that were made up at the turn of the century or 'channelled' from questionable sources.

I was raised with traditional American Indian (Anayunweya or Cherokee) spiritual views on my father's side of the family, while my mother's side was Episcopalian. I have a very understanding family who gave me a deep appreciation of the divine being evident in everything we see around us, especially in nature. For as long as I can remember, I was always searching to be where I am now, practising the religion that I am. Since becoming ordained in Kemetic Orthodoxy, I do not participate in the rituals of other faiths, mainly because our faith does not allow it. Even though my domestic partner is still a witch, she does her rites on her own and I do mine on my own. We do not work together magically or ritu-ally. Even though on one level this makes me rather sad, we have an understanding about it. She is interested in my religion, and I still speak to her about hers. I feel fortunate that we can be together and not have it be an issue.

I commune with Sekhmet through daily prayer and meditation in my permanent shrine space in my home, as well as in group temple rites with other House of Netjer members. All of what I do in my herbalism, energy healing (for lack of a better term) etc., is a reflection of my work for Sekhmet and for Netjer. Most of my work is prayer, healing etc. I enjoy this daily interaction and feel a bit off kilter if I do not at least meditate on Netjer in some small space of my day.

My shrine space is set up permanently in my bedroom. It was a nightstand of walnut, and has two double doors on the front. Inside, there is a white linen cloth on the floor and my two icons: one of Sekhmet, the other of Maat, whom Sekhmet protects. I have a shrine lamp, which is a glass-enclosed white candle, and an incense burner that has sand in it (very Ptolemaic-looking). The latter item is for more intense, longer rituals, as incense burned on charcoal takes a bit of time and commitment. Some everyday rites are much shorter, and for these I have another incense implement, an incense boat for stick incense that has the head of Mut with the double crown on one end of it. This incense boat is ceramic. I keep my other ritual implements inside the shrine: a small container of natron, a small lotus goblet for the washing of the mouth ritual, a small bowl that has 'feet' on it, where I put my dry offerings. Actually, this is a metaphor for the hieroglyph 'to bring'. I have a different bowl for 'wet' offerings. I am the only one who is allowed to open the shrine or to be before it when it is open. At all other times the doors are closed. The icons inside are not seen by anyone other than myself or another ordained priest of Netjer. The icons only see sunlight once a year and that is for the Kemetic New Year in August, when the icons are ritually shown to the sunlight (which is in keeping with ancient practices).

I do have visions of Netjer, but do not consciously try to direct them as much as other occult traditions do. In my view, intuition etc. is a part of one's relationship with Netjer and the world that we live in and interact with. It is a tool, rather than the end goal. The end goal, in my view, is to use all available tools and abilities to reflect our love of Netjer and service to Maat.

As for meditation, again I will go into my shrine and look at my icon statue of Sekhmet. There are times when I feel quite drawn into that statue and I get messages from her. I often meditate on what certain dreams mean. Often in my work Netjer will 'tell' me directly, whereas other times the *akhu* or ancestors assist in furnishing more clues so that I can find out what is going on. I find that such messages are always pertinent. It sounds rather a cliché, but there are times when I feel my entire life becomes a meditation. Everything we do is for Netjer and reflects Maat as closely as possible.

Our rituals follow the traditional Kemetic calendar events and coincide with other House members' rites etc. Each of us do *dua* (worship) on our own, but when we can be together and do full rites, this is intense. Sometimes they can be overwhelming to those in attendance, but never have we had a rite that is not somehow eventful.

The Kemetic calendar is extensive. Two of the significant days are the Day of the Executioners of Sekhmet on 10 June, and the Day of the Anger of the Eye of Heru-Ur on 27 August. There are also festivals of Saq-Sekhmet and quite a few others. Most of my celebrations are personal, when I make offerings to her and say prayers in my shrine that specifically focus on the Netjer Sekhmet.

I have many prayers. Here is one of my favourites, used on 7 April, when Het-Hert is said to have 'gone forth'.

> *I make petition, so that you might hear, o person of gold!*
> *I make supplication that your heart might be turned to me!*
> *Hail to you, lady of plague,*
> *Sekhmet the great, lady to the limit!*
> *Extolled one upon her father;*
> *Eldest one before her maker;*
> *Foremost of place in the bark of millions,*
> *Free-striding in the cabin!*
> *It is your arms which give light,*
> *Your rays which illumine the two lands.*
> *The two banks are under your counsel.*
> *The sunfolk are your flock!*
> *Hail to you, o gold!*
> *May you favour me!*
> *O gold at your time of listening,*
> *Your hour of hearing!*
> *You are green for my request to you!*
> *May you release for me fair speech!*
> *You are the one who shall fashion the standard with your limbs,*
> *Make me fortunate within you!*
> *It is your love which shall give me a good traversing of eternity!*

And this one is on my web page:

How strong she is! Without contender,
She honours her name as queen of the cities.
Sharp-sighted, keen as God's protector, right Eye of Ra,
disciple facing her lord, bright with the glory of God,
wise upon her high throne,
She is most holy of places, a mecca the world cannot parallel.
　　　　Leyden Hymn 10, Nineteenth Dynasty, Foster Translation

We do not do 'spells' in Kemetic Orthodoxy. Instead, we have *heka*, which is more accurately defined as 'authoritative utterances'. These are reserved for specific worship and/or healing purposes. There are always 'magical' things that we do in order to help us help ourselves, and we know that in the end Netjer and the *akhu* do lend assistance (or not if the answer is indeed 'No' or 'Not this time, I have something else in mind for you.') Always, in my view, it works out. We are active partners in our lives and we are not mollycoddled, nor do we 'bargain' with Netjer within Kemetic Orthodoxy. By that I mean, you do not go before Netjer and say, 'I will sacrifice X if you will give me Y.' In my experience, it never works like that.

Worship is done in a daily shrine ritual, before which we ritually bathe. Purity is always an issue in Kemetic Orthodoxy. I do not use ingredients in my incenses that are of an unsavoury nature (those containing any sort of animal waste etc.), nor do I ever use perfume, but rather opt for essential oils. A substance called urea is used in many perfumes, and is by definition impure for this purpose. It is important that we use pure essential oils or resins of the absolute best quality. Our minds separate what is for worship and what is for every day. Ritual implements are only used in the shrine rite and at no other time. It is also preferable that these items have never previously been used for anything else, and again, purification of all implements is essential.

In healing others or myself I will visualize Sekhmet's searing and healing fire. Visualizations are something I use while concentrating during ritual or *heka*.

Our rituals consist mainly of devotion and prayer. Unfortunately, this is not the 'Cecil B. DeMille special effects' answer many people search for within what they believe is Egyptian religion. I am constantly besieged by people who request 'Sekhmet rituals'. I usually send them a bibliography of scholarly resources and let them look through what is most appropriate for what they need, with the caveat as stated in the priestly instructions on the wall of the Temple of Horus at Edfu.

It could be said that I do not have a sense of humour, or that I am highly uncooperative with such requests. Actually, I am very supportive and co-operative. However, I feel that people have to have the correct approach and mindset to make the proper connection with Netjer. If such a connection means that much to them, they should not have a problem with doing a little preparatory work before the ritual. Research is work and some sort of effort on the part of the petitioner should be expected.

We human beings have incredible capabilities, but I think that as magic and the occult have become more accessible in the mainstream marketplace, respect has been lost for the mystery of those 'unknowable' things, beings and events that are larger than we are. I think it is arrogant to believe that human beings are the most important element in all of creation and can manipulate both the subtle and physical worlds around them without a thought, or sense of responsibility. We have so much awesome power, but what is so often missing is the *judicious* use of that power within the confines of Maat, to whose laws we are all subject. What a tragedy! When I say 'Netjer provide', I shall allow for my own personal *sekhem* or power, but know full well that a 'veto power' still exists which can negate even the best-laid plans. For myself, I can say that I do not consider myself to be a 'devotee' of Sekhmet. I am her servant, and as such, I am *owned* – and that ownership is quite literal. Sekhmet is 'she who owns my head'. This ownership is a common concept within African religions, and because Egypt is part of Africa, the roots of Kemetic Orthodoxy are indisputably of African religious origin.

Rationalizing of the names or regarding representations of the divine as being nothing more than archetypes (which is such a common explanation among New Age and Jungian enthusiasts), is at best an annoying assessment. Metaphorically, it is like comparing a ripe succulent mango to a piece of wax mango fruit. Though they may look the same, the two are vastly different. One has the smell and feel and taste and texture that cannot be adequately duplicated except in nature, whereas while the wax fruit may look delicious, it has none of these things that make experiencing real mango a wondrous delight. When you remove the divine nature from Netjer, you are left with an empty, lifeless shell. It may appear you are experiencing the real thing but in fact you have only consumed a facsimile. I am not interested in something that merely looks like Egyptian religion. I am here because I opted for the reality.

Christina's web site address is:
http://www.netins.net/showcase/ankh

Debbie Benstead

Debbie Benstead is a founder member of our own temple group. She is a gifted psychic with a wide experience of many kinds of magic and religion. She is co-author, with Storm Constantine, of the self-development book *The Inward Revolution* and is currently studying philosophy as a mature student at university. Through Debbie and her former working partner, Andrew Collins, we learned a completely new way to perform rituals. Previously, our workings had had a distinctly Western tradition format. Andrew and Debbie's revolutionary methods, coupled with our studies of Egyptian magic, formed the core of our group's practices, which we continually expand and evolve. Because of her importance in our work, we felt it only right that she should be included in this chapter. Debbie's views show yet another aspect of communing with Bast and Sekhmet.

I come from a background of psychic questing, and because of that have a very functional approach to deities. Questing involves an interactive communication with gods and spirits, not worship. For example, one month I might have been investigating and communing with Chenrese the Bodhisattva, the next it could have been the Aztec deity Quetzalcoatl. The questing group I used to be with never touched on Bast in particular, although we did investigate Egyptian material – mainly to do with Akhenaten and the Aten. So although I knew of Bast's existence, I had never thought about interacting with her. She had never come up psychically for me.

In the questing group, the ritual format we used was a very functional meditation, where we would go into a realm relevant to the deity with whom we were trying to communicate, such as a temple of some kind. Then we would visualize the archetype of that deity appearing to us so that we could commune with it. It was primarily a mental, visualized process, although we might incorporate minor ritual actions such as making small offerings or speaking invocations to aid the visualizing process.

I moved town and became involved with the group of women who eventually became the core group who inspired the book. When I met them, they had been working magically in their own way for some time. The first ritual we did to Bast together incorporated the techniques I had learned and developed with the questing group. A time came when some of us had severe difficulties in our lives. We knew we had to do something different to solve the problems. We believed in magic, we knew it worked, so there had to be something extremely powerful we could actually *do* – some positive, mental ritual.

We thought about this and discussed it. Most of the group had cats, and everyone had a strong affinity with them. We thought that the best way to awaken the positive mental energy within the group was to focus on something everyone felt passionate about, or had unity with. So we all agreed that Bast was the appropriate goddess in this situation. We investigated her and wrote a ritual.

From that first ritual, we got amazing results. All the conditions were right and we all felt very emotional about it. In the past, when I had performed this kind of ritual on a regular basis, I had always seen positive results. I am sure it comes from hitting the right frequency with the right passionate emotional affinity at the same time – it should be a two-way thing. But this ritual was more than just getting physical effects. For the first time in my career in the occult and the psychic realm, a void within me began to fill. It was as if something had been missing from my life. Whereas before, my magical work had been functional and changeable, I suddenly felt that a part of me was being filled: the feminine in my soul. I experienced a great unity with the other women involved that I had never known before.

The people I had worked with previously had not considered interacting with a goddess frequency that was purely to do with what womanhood was really all about. We had always done rituals to gain information and insight, or to achieve results, but not necessarily to experience the raw energy in its own right, as a spiritual thing. I had done rituals and meditations based around Isis, who was female and motherly, but the experience was not the same as the ritual to Bast. Everything I got back from Bast affirmed how I was as a woman and I am sure the other women felt the same. You did not have to be virginal, motherly or any other standard archetype of womanhood to link with that Bast energy.

After doing one ritual, I realized that the energy generated from Bast's frequency, which fed me and which I could also give back, was simply my own energy. It was a female energy that loves a good time. It was languid, sexual, erotic, but also benevolent and wise. It was love, warmth and joy, but without many of the other aspects that are traditionally associated with a goddess, such as those of the mother or the crone. Bast did not seem to fit into the triple goddess archetype. Previously, I had a preconceived idea that all female deities had to fit into that system and cycle of life, but Bast seemed to be outside of that. It was a really good feeling. It made me want to do more and explore that part of myself through doing Bast rituals, and that was very important for me.

I also felt a unity with my women friends that I would not have got through Isis or any other goddess. Obviously, our affinity with cats was a factor, but it got to the point where I felt that the fact that Bast was a cat did not matter, it was not important. The cat was just a symbol of her personality.

That is why Bast became important to me, because sometimes you do not realize you have been missing something until you have it. You just know you have been missing out – a part of you was not whole.

I do not do rituals for every problem in life. I feel that there is something wrong if you cannot deal with problems without appealing to a deity for help. I think if you rely too much on the deities, they will stop helping you because you are not helping yourself.

The reason why I perform rituals and visualizations with my women friends is usually to clarify some uncertainty, or to help someone outside the group with a conflict or trouble. Obviously, I would still do a ritual for myself if I felt there was no other way round a situation. For me, going into Bast's temple and standing before her in visualization means I am standing before an aspect of my own womanhood – it is a way of going into the self.

Sometimes, I go into Bast's temple knowing that I am facing a part of myself that I am occasionally in conflict with. Perhaps I see Bast as the strongest aspect of being a woman, which are positive and worthy but which in excess can be problematical. In Bast's presence, I might ask myself: Have I pushed the limits? Have I gone too far? Am I being too selfish and self-centred, too decadent? Going before Bast is excellent for that, not only for women, but for men too.

As for Sekhmet, to begin with I knew far more about her than I did about Bast, because I had touched upon her in my questing work. We began interacting with Sekhmet when some of the other women and I needed to do a ritual for which Bast's energy did not seem appropriate. Our energy was depleted and we needed empowerment and strength. Because Bast is a good-time girl, she instils an energy within people which they can then give out, so they generate more of it themselves, but they can deplete themselves too.

Sekhmet is more measured. I feel that I do not have to do as much. I go before Sekhmet when I feel physically or mentally depleted and need energy and strength, a red energy. I feel that when I perform a Sekhmet ritual, I do not have to give up or give out as much life essence as when I do a Bast ritual.

We have also visited Sekhmet during times of conflict, when some of us have felt we needed her strength and protection. To me, Sekhmet is definitely more of a protecting influence than Bast. She is a guardian who will smite anyone who dares to interfere with someone she has recognized as an energy form, who has come to her for help.

I have quite strong views concerning the question of worshipping deities. I think the only reason people feel subservient to, or lesser beings than, spiritual or incorporeal entities is not a question of reality, but of psychology and conditioning. I believe that some people go in on that level because their teachers and mentors have told them that is the way it is, or because they have read books that have said this. The belief that non-corporeal beings are so much greater than we are is a concept that has been passed down through the generations. Yet there is no actual proof of it. We cannot say it is definitely so; it is a question of faith.

I have always questioned this belief. Basically, I think it derives from fear. People feel they are less than something because it is unknown to them. It appears greater because they have no knowledge of it and can therefore be afraid of it. Also people feel that something incorporeal is more omniscient or omnipotent than they are. It has a greater energy level than they do as a living being. In all honesty, I do not think that makes a spiritual entity greater in terms of a hierarchy of existence.

For me, the spiritual/unconscious/psychic/religious relationship I have with Bast and Sekhmet has to be based on understanding and knowledge of what they are. I cannot get close to them, nor can they touch my life, unless some part of my mind is open to them. I do not want to be subservient to or overwhelmed by them. I want to understand what they are, why they affect me and why I need them to be important in my life.

I do not believe people have a good relationship with their parents if they are oppressed or feel subservient to them. They have little understanding of what makes their parents who they are; they just know that the parents are authority. There is a huge distance between them, which can never be breached. Any relationship based on fear and authority cannot be close. In many religions, deities are viewed in much the same way as oppressive parents. All a child's needs – warmth, comfort, food and love – come from the mother, and initially knowledge does too. Consequently, a young child is subservient to its mother because she knows better, she is more powerful. But as a child grows up and evolves as an individual, this relationship should mature into something a lot deeper – an understanding of who and what that parent really is. When we first commune with incorporeal beings such as Bast and Sekhmet, it is similar to a child's relationship with a parent. We need guidance and sustenance. But as an adult, I do not want to live in fear, and certainly not fear of the incorporeal, because I feel there are more important things to be scared of – people are more frightening than beings of energy.

So for me, it has always been important to have a relationship with the goddesses based on understanding. The more one understands and interacts with them, the deeper the spiritual relationship is and the more one gets out of it. I am not necessarily saying we are equal to them, just different. But our relationship with them should not involve subservience and fear. Certain aspects of this interaction might seem worshipful, such as making offerings or sacrifices, not of animals or blood but of emotion, spirit, relevant food and objects. We try to please the goddesses, but I do not think that should involve submission, because the act of giving is no more than you would do for a friend or someone you love. If our friends receive gifts from us – and not just physical gifts – they are more likely to do things for us in return.

I think that you can go into a relationship with deities in the same way. To me, Bast and Sekhmet are not some huge cat-women in the sky, or spectres from the past that just happen to loom into our future. They are a conglomeration of energy and life force that has its own consciousness, memories and intelligence, which is the sum total of all the human input of ideas, emotion, and beliefs. Energy can hold onto these things and store them as a computer stores programs.

For example, Bast is a goddess, an energy being existing in another dimension outside our own four (three of space and one of time). She is an energy that holds onto all the ideas people have programmed into her. If we encounter her, she wears the archetype of a cat-headed woman, purely because this is the mask we have given her, so we can interact with her frequency. The human mind finds it very difficult to visualize talking to a blob of formless energy. We need symbols and signs, and have done since humans existed, otherwise we would not have language. Having this idea makes it easier for me not to be subservient to Bast.

I have performed many rituals and meditations, when I've touched these frequencies of energy, whether they were spirits, guardians of ancient sites or gods and goddesses. I know the results I have achieved are just as effective as those experienced by anyone who approaches the gods from a position of worship. In some ways, I feel my results are more effective, because I have been part of the process rather than just as a submissive observer. I do not interact with Bast and Sekhmet just to get something back from them; I do so to gain a kind of richness, and to experience the reality of its effects.

Some traditional staunch Christians might believe that God is 'Dad' and he punishes and rewards and that is it. They go to church, they bow their heads, they say the prayers, they go home and have tea. Nothing spiritual will ever happen to them. They will never experience a vision of a saint or be touched by a shaft of light from the altar. They will never really feel God's presence or hear him speak to them. But there are Christians who go into it on a different level. If you like, they have a personal relationship with God. He speaks to them. They feel energies, they experience effects, things happen to them. The point is that this can happen with ancient deities too, who are far older than Christ or the Christian God. I do not feel that human evolution should be overlooked in the modern revival of paganism, or indeed any other system based on ancient deities. If it is, then the evolution of our society is overlooked. If people really want what is best for humanity, they should want it to change and evolve, to become more spiritual, more of a brotherhood. Going into a magical system to worship and be subservient will prevent that. The spiritual evolution will remain static, and she will be no better than any member of a rigid, organized religion. Religious attitudes of oppression, submission and obedience are part of what keeps society static. Pagans and magical practitioners should be wary of these things. Human evolution, particularly self-evolution, should be the highest point of any constitution they may have. It is the most important thing.

Simon Beal

Many people who become interested in Bast and/or Sekhmet have had experiences in other areas of magical or spiritual work. Simon Beal is now a member of our own temple group and relates how he became interested in magic, which ultimately led him to investigate Bast.

I was first introduced to the ways of magic by having my Tarot read by a friend. This prompted the 'Yeah, I'm going to get into Tarot' response, which I am sure most of us went through at some point – I suppose it is the kindergarten of the occult (but by no means worthless). Anyway, I ended up getting some runes (I wanted to be a bit different), which gave astonishing results.

This got me thinking, 'What if these predictions are not really predictions at all, but a psycho-semantic/subconscious way of shaping reality?' Then I thought, if it works, what does it matter? I suppose it is a bit like the old axiom: is there such a thing as free will, or do we all have our destiny laid out before us? To this I once said, 'As long as we have the illusion of free will, who cares?' I guess this will be argued until the end of time.

I started doing Tai Chi, which also involved Qigong and meditation. This was when I first discovered the existence of *chi* energy. As I became more proficient with the Tai Chi form, my awareness of this energy increased and through awareness came understanding – a beginner's guide to the universe, if you will.

'It was around this time that I also started exploring my shamanic aspects and I became interested in Native American beliefs, especially their respect for life and the Earth. I guess this also had something to do with the fact that I come from Totnes, the supposed hippy capital of Britain and often referred to as the spiritual twin of Glastonbury.

Shortly after this I also began looking into Celtic magic and although I do resonate with the basic principles – that of the physical, mental, and spiritual aspects of being – I never progressed beyond this. I knew that my path lay elsewhere.

I continued my own studies of the occult and progressed with my Tai Chi. A few years ago, I got to know Storm and Eloise's working group in a social context. We soon found out that we were interested in the same subjects, and eventually I was invited to participate in a Papa Legba ritual, which was led by the earth mysteries writer Andy Collins, who was visiting at the time. Although I knew Storm and Eloise's group concentrated mainly on Bast and Sekhmet material, they also celebrated the eight seasonal Celtic festivals, and sometimes performed rituals revolving around other systems to achieve specific results. Papa Legba is actually a Voodoo *loa*. This working was my first step into the world of ritual magic and since then I have become more involved with the group, initially by joining in with the eight festivals, but now by also participating in much of the Egyptian work with Bast and other feline deities.

By practising different systems I began to understand about frequencies of energy and the universal subconscious – that deities are just a way of labelling energy frequencies and if we took away their masks, we would all see the same thing. Of course this does not invalidate ritual workings. Symbolism is an important part of our psychological makeup, and performing magical workings without imagery would be like trying to imagine infinity – a daunting task by anyone's standards.

Whilst doing these rituals, I began to notice a familiar figure hiding in the shadows of my visualizations. I had had several disturbing dreams about her before. She was an Egyptian lady, but I could never see or focus on her face. She never seemed to do any harm until eventually her true nature was revealed – this is a long story and I will not go into detail, but suffice to say she was none too pleasant. I felt threatened, both psychologically and physically.

It was suggested that I should appeal to Bast to help solve the problem. Without my realizing it, this ritual was also to be my initiation to Bast. I had not previously performed a ritual specifically to benefit myself. I have to say that out of all the frequencies I had worked with so far, I felt a connection to Bast unlike anything else. I felt not only her motherly, caring aspect but also her strength and power. Bast gave me the strength and confidence to confront this dark entity. It was quite an intense experience, but it solved the problem and my unwanted visitor has not appeared to me again.

Since then I have always felt the presence of Bast around me and I know that when times are hard, I can always call upon her for her strength and wisdom.

Lynn Hall

Sometimes people turn to Bast at a specific time, when normally they would not perform regular rituals to her. Our next account comes from Lynn Hall, who is a pagan involved with the Pagan Federation.

I have always kept cats and my little companions are very dear to me. It has always been heartbreaking when I have lost a cat, either from old age or by accidental death on the road. But none was more heartbreaking than the loss of little Tammy back in 1990. She came to live with us at about the same time as another cat, Tigger, and they soon became great friends. Tammy was like a little mother to her male companion. One evening I noticed that she was not around and she did not come when she was called for dinner. For several days we searched for her and asked around, but we did not find her. We were told that two children had taken a kitten of her description up to the woods and drowned it. I found this impossible to believe; surely children would not do something so cruel. But I went to the woods, and sure enough, there was her poor little body in a pool that had been deliberately created for the exercise. You can imagine how heartbroken we all were, but none more so than Tigger, who cried for his friend for days.

We replaced Tammy with Max, and when our oldest cat, Twinkle, died aged fourteen years, we fetched Gismo to make up the number. We were amused to find that there was another cat close by also called Gismo and he became my little friend, always running to greet me whenever I passed his house. I was particularly fond of him because of his friendliness, but this quality in him also disturbed me because of what had happened to Tammy. Whenever I passed Gismo's house, I would ask that he be protected, as well as asking for protection for my own cats.

In February, I went to New Zealand for a month. On the day we returned, the latest issue of our local newspaper came out. Imagine my horror when I read the report on the front cover; 'Cat Poisoner Strikes Again. Little Gismo Latest Victim.' I felt sick. My little friend had been murdered and his brother shot in the back leg with an air rifle. Two weeks later the paper carried another report, bringing the total of cat deaths in our area to twelve.

I spoke to my friend Sally Fisher. She is more acquainted with the cat goddesses than me so I felt her advice was important. I chose Friday to do my ritual, which really was very simple, nothing grand. I went to a clear space at the back of my garden and took the statue of Bast that usually sits on a shelf in full view of anyone visiting my house. I placed the statue on the ground and lit candles, seven green ones to be precise. As I have said, I am not familiar with the Egyptian goddesses, but I do know the Celtic and Roman/Greek ones, so I used the same ritual that I would use for invoking Venus, she being a nature goddess and therefore having an interest in animals. I called upon Bast, and spoke of the heart-break that was being caused by the deaths of local cats, not to mention the suffering of the cats themselves. The poison that was being used caused immense suffering and it took a long time for them to die. We were told that the vet had to destroy each cat that was brought to him, as they could not be saved. I put into that ritual all the pain that I had felt for each cat lost over the years, for Tammy and for little Gismo. I do not know if I did it right, just that it was done from the heart. I was joined by one of my own cats, Tigger, and a huge slug that crawled amongst the candles. I left the candles to burn safely down.

We have heard no more about cat deaths since that time. May Bast be praised that she continues to protect the cats in our area, as well as those that are suffering elsewhere.

Lorye Keats Hopper

Lorye Keats Hopper is associated with the Isle of Avalon Foundation in Glastonbury, Somerset.

I was first conscious of my strong link with Sekhmet in the early 1970s, when I was working as a student nurse at Great Ormond Street, a large London teaching hospital dedicated to children. On my off-duty days, I frequently used to walk to the British Museum, drawn towards the Egyptian rooms where the large statues of

Sekhmet stood radiantly. Whilst gazing intently upon her feline face, I felt stirred by familiar and ancient memories.

Ever since my younger years cats and lions have always appealed to me. Astrologically, I have five planets in the sign of Leo in the 10th House, and I birthed a Leo child in the early 1980s, who grew up on tales of Aslan and Narnia! I am also in a long-term relationship with a man who has strong Ptah-like qualities, and works with building and design.

Throughout my life, I have naturally been drawn to Leonine pursuits. As well as nursing, aromatherapy and massage, I have studied drama and dance, the art of clowning, ancient wisdom and teachings, and healing ritual and ceremony. As well as invoking other universal deities, I started working actively with the energies of Sekhmet nine years ago, when I began my teaching and healing work as a creative arts therapist, helping women who have suffered from physical and sexual abuse. This work grew from my own personal healing journey. Sekhmet came through strongly as a protective deity, to help women honour themselves, to clear and transform the psychic and emotional residues of both childhood and female abuse and to help them take back their own creative power and self-respect.

I felt her presence in guiding me to work with young people, encouraging and empowering them to be catalysists for change and to speak up for their rights and their future on our beautiful planet Earth. This youth-work has taken me to global conferences for unity and peace and healing the environment.

May the lion-hearted lady goddess of the sacred solar flame awaken our hearts and the heart of humanity.

For details of healing and teaching work. Lorye can be contacted through the Isle of Avalon Foundation, whose address is in our index of suppliers.

Paul Weston

Our final account leads us into the strange territory of psychic questing. Paul Weston and his partner, Chandira, live in Glastonbury, perhaps the most magical of English towns. Paul has been involved with magic and questing for many years and is now a Reiki healing master. Sometimes the events that occur during questing can be astounding, and can sound incredible when written down. As the saying goes, 'You had to have been there.' However, no matter how bizarre what follows sounds, we know that it is par for the course in the questing world. This is how Bast, in one of her more mysterious guises, came into Paul's life. It is a small part of a large quest he became involved in, the Thames Quest. Paul has produced tapes of the lectures he gave concerning this quest, which we can recommend as riveting listening to anyone interested in the paranormal and magic. We have given a contact address for Paul in the index of suppliers, should anyone wish to purchase these tapes.

In spring 1990, I was told by a psychic friend that I had a cat elemental of some kind living in my aura. It was described as having a form that was half human and half cat, i.e. humanoid, but with a cat's face and six breasts. It apparently loved me and usually sat on my left shoulder. The rest of the time it floated about as a ball of light, like Tinkerbell, and lived in a piece of wooden furniture. I was encouraged to talk to it and found that often, on doing so, a typical poltergeist rap would sound from its furniture home.

Various surreal adventures followed, but the real mystery began over Christmas 1990, when my psychic friend heard a strange wailing noise coming from my bedroom, apparently connected with the cat creature. On going to investigate, she saw a part of the wall dissolve to reveal a visionary scene showing the Sakkara complex by night. A frenzied ceremony was occurring in the desert around it, lit by numerous bonfires. It was from this space that my cat being had come. At this point, Bast became more apparent for the first time. My friend said that Bast was manifesting beyond her normal associations, that she was manifesting as a stellar goddess, who had an obscure connection with the cult of Sa Re. It was suggested that there was a mystery for me personally waiting to unfold and I should make contact with Bast. Another friend had a small Bast figurine which had been brought back from Egypt, and gave it to me. I placed it on the floor where the 'gateway' was and put pictures of Bast on the wall. To complete the process, I got some Starchild Bast incense and an invocation to Bast, and settled down to daily practice around her.

Bast proved to be the guardian of the threshold of my Thames adventures. The reason why it was specifically her was never established, and she played no real role in the rest of the story. It seemed she served to connect me through past lives etc. to a particular vibration or magical current.

In later years, she made other brief mysterious appearances. In spring 1994, I had done second-degree Reiki, which enables one to send healing at a distance. One of the people I worked with in an office came in disturbed by the illness of her cat, which was staying overnight at a vet's. Although she was a fairly 'normal' person, I mentioned that I could send absent healing to it if she wanted. She readily agreed and showed me a photograph of the cat and pointed out of the window to show me the rough location of where the cat currently was. That night, as I started to think about sending healing to it, I realized that the date (23 March) was one I had been led to believe was a feast of Bast (in Durdin Robertson's book, *The Year of the Goddess*). Considering my previous connections, I felt it was odd that my first ever opportunity to be involved in animal healing concerned a cat and was timed for a Bast feast. I therefore got my Bast figurine and surrounded it with nightlights to provide a focus when I did send out the Reiki. The cat was fine the next day and able to go home. I felt that after the heavy-duty stuff of the Thames Quest, this little episode indicated a purifying of my karma in relation to that magical current, and also a touching sense of Bast remaining with me. However, something of the old strangeness still lingered.

In October 1994, a friend of mine, who has a strong Egyptian background and is fairly psychic, came to stay. She had had no involvement with the Thames Quest and had never visited me in that particular home. I had given no real attention to Egyptian magic (other than the healing episode above) for two years. The Bast figurine was on display, but I barely noticed it, as the room was full of images and artefacts of different traditions. The moment my friend set foot in the door, an entity emerged from the Bast figurine that was obviously the old cat being. Because my friend has cats and is into Bast, it seemed able to manifest with greater power than ever. It was human-sized and tried to overshadow my friend and speak to me. My friend was not at all happy about this and spent a disturbed, distressing night repeatedly fighting off the attempts of this being to possess her. Periodic sightings of the cat being have occurred ever since. I have now passed the Bast figurine on to someone else.

Chandira takes up the story. She is psychic and a Reiki healer.

One evening, I was round at Paul's, when I just *knew* there was a cat in his wardrobe. It sounds strange, but that is what I thought. I could 'see' a cat woman standing in front of the wardrobe door. I told Paul, and said that the cat in the wardrobe was sitting in the bottom right hand corner and wanted to come out. It dawned on him that I was exactly right. There *was* a cat in the bottom of his wardrobe. He said, 'I'd better give you this, then,' and pulled out a big poster he had bought some years before, of the Bast statue from the British Museum.

Three years ago, there was a psychic fair on at the Assembly Rooms, at which there were some small Bast statues for sale. I could not really justify buying one at £25, but did so anyway. I walked round the corner and the next stall was a psychic's, who was asking for help healing one of her cats. I felt I could not really refuse. I worked with the cat over a number of months, sending healing, doing rituals to honour Bast, asking for her help. Several times during the rituals I felt a strong peaceful female presence in the room. Unfortunately, the cat died, but it was a peaceful death. When he finally went, his owner, the psychic, sent me exactly £25, with a big thank-you for my help. I have since been asked to work with sick cats many times, and now always include some things to honour Bast.

22

Travelling the Unlit Road

All knowledge, past and present, is available to mental sympathy. Only the techniques change with time – the quest is always the same.

Andrew Collins

One of the most exciting aspects of our work together as a group is the visionary questing we perform in order to glean more information about the shadowy deities of the past.

This technique has been popularized over the last fifteen years or so by psychic questers, who were inspired mainly by authors Andrew Collins and Graham Phillips. They could be said to have initiated this movement in the UK with the publication of Graham's ground-breaking first book *The Green Stone*, which was quickly followed by Andrew's own account of the same events in *The Sword and the Stone*. Andy then followed up this book with his controversial *The Black Alchemist*, which became the questers' bible in this country. Many other books followed as both authors became more deeply involved in the subject. (To anyone interested in investigating this topic further, a selection of titles is given in the bibliography.)

Questing involves projecting the mind back into the past or out into the landscape in order to uncover artefacts or unravel historical mysteries. It involves meditating on a site of interest and subsequently investigating, in a practical way, any imagery that crops up. If names, dates or places are revealed, these can often be checked through historical records or books. Some people are naturally very psychic and have produced incredible results, but anyone can train themselves to a greater or lesser degree to be able to pick up verifiable imagery. The technique is not a modern phenomenon however. The Terma tradition in Tibet involved *Terton* monks discovering hidden artefacts in the landscape.

We have used this technique to explore the lesser-known feline deities. Although it is impossible for us to verify the imagery we have received as fact, we do feel that the information that has come to us helps in expanding our understanding of these deities, as well as contributing towards the design of rituals and visualization exercises.

Some people might argue that this type of information cannot be used in conjunction with known facts about the Egyptian gods. There are several schools of thought about how the modern practitioner should best interact with those deities. Some people can see no reason why the original rituals that survive from ancient times should be tampered with or added to. If we want to communicate with this frequency of universal energy, surely it is best to use techniques that were used by the Egyptian priests for thousands of years. This is a valid and sound argument, and we would certainly agree that changing a deity's aspects wholesale, such as has happened with Sekhmet recently, does nothing to improve our understanding. We also feel uncomfortable with the idea of trying to squeeze Egyptian gods and goddesses into a Western format or using Western neo-pagan rituals to honour them. However, we do feel that if we can remain faithful to what the original energy frequency represents, we can fill in the considerable gaps in our knowledge through the power of our own imaginations. We could also say that through visionary questing we can tap into the vast pool of the collective unconscious of our species and perhaps recover forgotten 'facts' from there.

Scant information about certain deities has survived through time. We know that in the distant past they had thriving temples and cults surrounding them, but all that remains of this majesty is a befuddling fog of historical scraps and fragments. If, through the direction of our own will, intention and imagination, we can penetrate this fog, even only partially, it can surely be no bad thing. We have to accept that the bulk of the material we receive is subjective, our own minds' attempt to create a coherent picture of the past. We therefore, feel it is important to know as much about Egyptian history as possible before embarking upon this kind of visionary work. We should be clear about how the Egyptians regarded their gods and interacted with them, as well as how their world functioned. There are many excellent books on this subject available, and some of them are listed in the bibliography at the back of the book.

Images received from visions should be examined carefully to see whether they really fit into the pattern of what already exists. For example, you might see imagery concerning the primal mound of creation, but then see a Norse god swimming around in the primeval ocean. Obviously, it would not be appropriate to add that god to a ritual involving, say, Tefnut. Because we are only human, and our brains are quicksilver creative organs, we will inevitably pick up all kinds of imagery when we are mediating. The skill is in knowing what to keep and add to our cannon of knowledge, and what to discard. It is important to sift the 'facts'.

A Tefnut visualization

We shall use the goddess Tefnut as our example in this chapter, a deity about whom our group has experienced wonderfully vivid visualization.

Before embarking upon any visionary questing, you first need to design the beginning of the working, i.e. where your cone is going to alight in ancient Egypt and what imagery you will see to start the visualization off.

To begin a question visualization, you employ all the techniques used for ordinary rituals and meditations. After breathing exercises, you construct a travelling cone and direct it back to where your visualization is going to start.

In the case of Tefnut, we decided that we should begin by visiting the First Time, when the world was very young, and the primal mound was still surrounded by water. Tefnut is a very ancient deity, and according to the Hermopolitan version of the creation myth, the first goddess of all.

What follows is a transcription of the tape we made of some of our group's first visit to Tefnut. Debbie Benstead, who was the visualizer on this occasion, designed the visualization. This is a fairly literal transcription, which has retained the visualizer's mode of speech. Debbie is very psychic, so she herself was visualizing as she created this scene. She did not learn it or write it down beforehand, so it includes a lot of phrases and terms that Debbie knew the rest of the group understood and were familiar with. It will give you an idea of how we conduct these workings.

The visualization

You emerge into a desert landscape and find you are standing between two immense pillars. Before you is a lake of silvery water. It is night time and the sky is studded with brilliant stars. You can make out by the light of the moon that there is a mound in the middle of the lake. It is similar in appearance to Silbury Hill, a primal mound of creation. It has come into being through the union of Tefnut and Shu, the most primal beings, an Egyptian Adam and Eve, who were created to bring life and flesh and blood to the earth. But first they had to create the earth. They had to create the sky, they had to create the water. This lake is the primal water, the primal ooze from which life will come forth. That is what it represents. And the pillars you stand between represent Tefnut and Shu, the twins; they are Joachim and Boaz, Adam and Eve, the pillars of life. I want you to see a boat by that lake, but before you go, touch the columns, one at a time, and as you do, you feel the vibration of life within them, energy, pure *heka*, pure power, creative power. Touch them one by one and commune with the columns and ask for passageway to the primal mound.

When you are ready, step into the boat. As if by magic, the boat begins to glide across the lake. When you look down into the mirror-like water, you can see flashes of light, ripples, movement, convulsions, as if life is roiling and boiling within its murky depths – all manner of strange creatures that have yet to evolve.

You can see the mound looming up closer and closer, becoming less dense and dark. You can now see a temple, some kind of building on the top. This is the beginning of Heliopolis, built by Shu and Tefnut. This is their house. It is the entrance to the underworld below from when they came as Elder gods. But we are not going there. We are just going into the house.

Step off the boat and climb the primal mound. You are walking around it in a spiral, as if you were walking up Silbury Hill. It is like a processional path.

When you reach the top, the temple might look quite Grecian, with four columns at the front and three steps going up to it, and one door, white stone. Or perhaps you will see a completely white, very narrow pyramid, almost like an elongated pyramid, with just a door at the front. This has also been seen in the past to do with Tefnut and Shu. If you feel an urge to go into the temple, go inside, otherwise just stay outside.

Now I want you to call upon the presence of Tefnut, the first female, the primal mother, the mother from the cosmos who gave birth to all earth mothers. In another aspect she is Ishtar, she is Eve, she is the Eye of Ra. All female goddesses have been given this Eye. Ask her to appear, through the power of the air, through the power of the water, the power of the stars, the power of the moon.

You will see her as you wish. Commune with her and let her show you visions of her life, and of her purpose and her worship. I want you to commune now.

Our group then spent about twenty minutes roaming this landscape in our minds, meeting the goddess, talking with her. After this time, Debbie called us back and we went back down the hill to our waiting boat. When we alighted upon the opposite shore, Debbie told us to see the two columns of lions sitting back to back. These were the Aker lions, the lions of yesterday and today. They also represent Tefnut and Shu.

The lion who faces the east, he is Shu. He welcomes the light of the sun and of life, the light of the dawn. See that sun rushing up into the sky, moving across the heavens, as if the day has speeded up, arcing across to meet the gaze of the other lion, who is Tefnut. She will stand watch and guard over the setting sun, which represents the land of the dead in the west, Armenti. As the sun sets, it is a bloody red and darkness fills the sky.

Now turn around and walk back into the cone of power, and say goodbye to this most primal land of Egypt.

We then concluded the visualization and returned to normal consciousness.

The discussion of the visualization

Afterwards, we all talked about what we had seen and experienced. It was a particularly successful night's work. What follows is everyone's description of what they had seen.

Storm: The mound was very much like Bocklin's painting of the Isle of the Dead, and had poplar trees growing upon it. I saw the pyramid and went into it. It was very bare inside and it seemed to be a big room that filled the interior. I called to Tefnut, lady of heaven, lady of the first waters, and a woman came out of a side door. The room was suddenly different, and it was as if I was in a chamber. There was a door to my right. The woman did not have a cat's head. She was wearing a beautiful crepy, silvery-grey, pleated chiffony robe. She wore silver adornments. Her hands and wrists were painted black. She wore a black wig and big Trojan-looking earrings. She came forward and seemed reticent at first. I told her why I was there and she took me into a corridor that went off down the left. We walked along a spiralling corridor, almost like a maze. If was as if the building was far bigger inside than it appeared from the outside. I went round the narrow corridor that led to an inner chamber, which was like the cone of power. It was full of light, blazing with it. The doorway was like a weird kind of technology. The doors were heavy stone, but slid to the side to open. In this place, Tefnut did something she described as 'putting on the cat'. In the room she became a cat woman. She said that I could do it as well, as I had done it before anyway, she knew I had. Then the floor opened up and we could go down into a chamber underneath. I cannot remember much detail of this room, but there was a round silver pool in there, reminiscent of her water aspect. She just started talking. I said, 'What are you?'

She said, 'I am the water in the sky. I am what clears away the dust, when there's dust in the air, and this is the dust in your own mind. When you have dust in your mind, I can cleanse it. I am the great cleanser. I am the healer. This is what you should use me for. Use me for cleansing, use me for healing. Use me for clarity. I will give you clarity. I am the cleansing waters.'

She kept repeating that. 'I am the cleansing waters.' She was babbling, trying to say all these things, trying to get it through to me as if I could not understand. She said, 'You must understand, I get rid of the dust', and so on, and also, 'You must come back.'

I said, 'Yes, we will, I promise we will.' I got an immense impressions of loneliness, of wanting to communicate and reawaken. I told her I would have to leave, because I heard Deb's voice, but that we would come back. She did not want me to leave. She had turned back into a woman by then. She saw me to the gates of the temple and came outside, where she hugged me. When I went back down to the boat and was drifting back across the lake, I looked back and she was still waving to me. I felt really sad.

Eloise: I saw a pyramid as soon as I got out of the cone. The Grecian temple did not work, so I went back to the imagery of a pyramid. In the water, I saw things that looked like fishes, but I could see only the bones not the skin. I went up the hill and into the pyramid. Before I entered, I asked for permission to do so, and knew that I could, even though there was no answer. I walked in, and there was one path that went straight to the middle. In the middle of the room was a pool. And over the pool, on a huge tripod, going up to the ceiling, was a flame, and the flame was Shu and Tefnut keeping their father alive in the place. Round the side of the pool was a ring of mist. Tefnut appeared to me and she said, 'What is in this room is what we are.' She said, 'Come to me.'

Two paths led off from the main path. The right-hand one led to Shu, but I did not follow it. I went down the left-hand path which led me to Tefnut, and she was enthroned, and it was like ritual, a classical image. She was wearing a jade dress that was also like chiffon. Round the edge was a rim of silver. She had a lioness's head, but she was not the right colour for a lion. She was brown, and the fur stopped at her shoulders and neck and started to become skin – really dark skin. She asked me what I was doing and I explained why I was there. She said, 'I have been forgotten and you should come back.' I had that straight away. She said, 'My water is the water that makes things grow.' She implied healing, but the healing was earth healing rather than physical body healing. She looked like a brown rather than gold lion. She had a head-dress which was a solar disc, which I was not really expecting. She said, 'This is my birthright, this is my father.' She had a uraeus. Her feet were painted with black henna, and the patterns on them looked like flames, but I knew that they were not – they were grass; they were pictures of grass and drops like teardrops. They were painted up her legs to the hem of her dress. I told her I had to leave and she said, 'You will be back?' I said we would because we need to do this more. We do not know enough and we will be back soon. I came out with the impression that we should do the meditation again very soon.

When I went back to the pillars, they seemed closer together, so that I could touch both at the same time. But I knew that if I did so, I would buzz, as if I had had an electric shock. It would be a bad thing.

I had a strong impression that Shu was silent and miserable and dark in his own corner.

Freda: I saw the hill as having a cleft in it. It was very female, very obviously symbolic. When you said a temple, I saw columns. Inside I saw it as very bare and pale grey in colour. I was in there on my own and the first thing that came in was a grey leopard. I did not feel it was actually Tefnut. Eventually three leopards came in. One was black, one was white and one was grey. They sat in a circle around me. I got down to their level to see what they were. I did not feel they were threatening. I asked them what they were. The white one said, 'I am snow', the grey one said, 'I am rain', and the black one said, 'I am night.' I could not see Tefnut at first, then she appeared. She was huge, completely black, with a solar disc, obsidian. She opened a cloak or robe she was wearing and inside it was bright blue. She came down to human size, but I could not get her to say anything to me. I was in the middle, with the three leopards, and she walked round and round the outside. She kept saying, 'I have nothing to say to you yet.' Eventually, Debbie began to call us back, and I said I had to go, but I felt it was not finished. She did not want me to leave.

I saw an eagle flying round the top of the temple, and at one stage Tefnut seemed to have a flail in her hand. I thought that was the lightning.

Karen: When I first got to the pillars, they were both within reach and I could touch them immediately. It was like something opening. I went onto the boat and crossed to the mound. When I got there, it was very mossy, very damp, squelching. The temple I saw as columned. Even before I stepped through the pillars by the boat, there had been a face before me and lots of veils, but I could not pick up much detail then. But once I was on the hill, Tefnut came out, a figure in lots of ribbony veils, green, yellow, gold, and on her hands she had eyes painted in black. Her eyes were really peculiar, mottled green with slitted pupils. She would not say a great deal. There were lots of tiny bells, like flowers, tied into her hair, round her ankles, round her wrists. Her mouth seemed bigger than a normal human mouth. I kept asking, 'Who are you? What are you?' and she kept trying to come closer, but she would then just end up dancing around. She was dancing all the time. She said, 'I am change, I am life, I am resurrection.' The last time, she said, 'I am this', and thrust her hand forward, and something rippled through me. I started moving away. When we came back, I could still see her and those strange eyes, even when I was back in the cone. I kept trying to push her away and she disappeared in a blaze of light.

Debbie: I saw the narrow pyramid. I went in, just as before [this refers to an earlier visualization]. There was a complete moat around it, a walkway that you walk across the water onto a plinth, and there she was and she was *huge*. The pyramid was bigger on the inside than it was on the outside and she filled the whole thing. She was a woman, without a cat's head. She had a cloak of feathers and had feathers upon her head in black and white, reminiscent of a vulture. Her belly was bare and had a huge yellow disc eye on it with a tiny black slit. It was round rather than eye-shaped. She looked down at me and I could not actually see her eyes for they were dark and hooded. I was just about to say to her, 'Who are you, what are you?' when things sprang out of the eye on her belly – a sable lioness, then a black panther – and she said, 'This is the trinity. I am the mother of all goddesses. I am the mother of these animals. I have created all animals that give birth to their young, and I am the creator of the animals that give birth to their young in multiples.' She said she was every woman. She is the mother of Bast, and the mother of Sekhmet. The black panther was Bast and the lion was Sekhmet. They jumped in the air and merged, and produced a tiger, dark brown with black stripes on it. It had yellow eyes, really big. I went towards it and it jumped inside me.

The next thing I knew I was in grass, stalking through it. It was the tiger. It was damp underfoot, like dew. I could hear voices, rustlings and whisperings, and the excited chatter of women. I was in a grove of trees, but there was long grass around the trees. I was just watching. I felt I had gone forward in time to a later period in Egypt. My quest was that I wanted to find out how they worshipped Tefnut, what they did. I could see all these women with baskets, and they were going up to the trees and collecting fruit. I was in an orchard. They looked like apples, but they were soft, squashy fruit. I stood up and joined the women and picked one of the fruit. The air was rustling through the trees. When I bit into the fruit, it all turned to water and went down my throat. I knew this fruit was important because it was the culmination of air and water. It is what fruit trees are and what they represent, and it was Tefnut's thing, this fruit. The water of the fruit was cleansing, but more than that. It was a nectar of the gods. It brought enlightenment and wisdom. Tefnut could bring these things. I followed the women, and the landscape changed to a hard, desert plain. Here, the women were collecting stuff from the ground, grains of an ambery stuff that wasn't sticky, although it resembled honeycomb. I did not know what it was. I asked the women what it was and they told me it was manna – manna from heaven, and this again was associated with Tefnut and was sacred to her.

I became aware that I needed to get back into the temple to question Tefnut, so I made myself see it again. This time, Tefnut was not huge. She was sitting on a throne and there were women around her. I could not see her face, it was completely veiled, but it was veiled with tiny strings filled with crystal beads or drops. It completely covered her face and kept tinkling. The women next to me were dressed in the same way and rainbow-coloured light was being refracted from the crystals they wore. I asked why Tefnut was veiled and they said it was because her breath could invoke storms, hail and rain and they had to refract it. They had to protect themselves, so that Tefnut could speak without invoking the elements. She was dressed in a silvery grey gown, I could see sheens of different colours in it. She definitely had a cloak of vulture feathers, and I had the impression that she was also known as a vulture as well as a lioness. If a woman gave birth to twins, or more children at one time, it was seen as sacred to Tefnut.

Interpreting the results of the visualization

As you can see, we all picked up rich imagery in this visualization. Everyone saw Tefnut as a goddess dark in colour. Her robes were chiffony, suggestive of mist. Mist and water, and corresponding images, were seen by everyone. Two people saw big cats in the temple, while two others picked up bird imagery. Tefnut did not appear to everyone in a solely lioness-headed form. Her aspects were those of healing, cleansing and giving insight.

Already, we had the beginnings of a formal ritual in Tefnut's honour. the slim white pyramid was favoured by everyone as the location we would use for our visualizations. (This particular building had been seen before by Debbie Benstead, when she was working with Andy Collins on material concerning a 'lion king' of Africa, connected with lost civilizations and the Elder race.) We had imagery to include in our ritual, and ideas about what kind of feast Tefnut might like. After discussion, we decided that, for us, Tefnut was a goddess whom we could visit in order to progress along our magical path. She was a source of enlightenment, of clear thought and purity. Also, we envisaged that we would one day approach her in healing rituals but, as Eloise's visualization suggested, perhaps in respect of the environment rather than individuals.

We could perhaps say that our original understanding of Tefnut was fairly abstract. What we did by performing this visualization was bring her alive for us in a personal way. We each went away from that temple with clear ideas in our minds of what Tefnut now meant to us.

Our investigation of Tefnut is still on-going, and we plan to publish the results and subsequent rituals of this work at a later date.

This type of visualization can also be performed to glean information about Bast and Sekhmet. Instead of doing a ritual, you can simply visualize visiting a particular area and then wander around your inner landscape. This does take practice. Our conscious minds are reluctant to let go of control when we are awake.

Knowledge through dreams

Once we embark upon magical work of this nature, we quite often begin to dream about it. The imagery can be very similar to what is picked up in visualization, but this time there is no conscious, nagging mind getting in the way, reminding us of mundane trivialities.

If you do have a dream of Egypt, or an Egyptian deity, make sure you write it down as soon as you can. It is surprising how quickly details of these dreams can fade from our minds. Dreams of this nature can often add to your work, as in the example given below.

Even from the beginning, our group used sistra as part of our rituals, but one night some time ago, Storm had a specific dream, which seemed to indicate that we were not using them enough.

I dreamed that Eloise, myself and some other women were in my bedroom about to enact a rite of Bast. We stood in a line before the mantelpiece, where some of my Bast statues are. The room was in utter darkness. Some of us were standing on the bed, some on the floor. The atmosphere felt very strange, unknown to me.

Eloise began to speak an invocation, or something about what we were going to do. Then she fell silent and I realized we were about to do something new and untried, a different form of invoking. I began to speak, to say that now we would invite the goddess to us, but then Lou made a strange sound, like uttering a word in a foreign tongue. I felt I couldn't say anything further.

Everyone but me began to shake sistra, and the noise of it grew in strength, until it seemed another instrument was playing with us, on a higher note. The others continued to shake the sistra and the noise of it rose and fell, becoming stronger. The whole room was filled with the sound. It was a great clashing, louder than it should have been.

Then the sistra fell to silence and I spoke again. It was a whole string of words, invocations, but I can't remember them now. Lou also said something else in a foreign tongue and I stopped speaking to let her continue. I stood with my arms held out slightly from my sides. I could feel that we were about to draw down a great power. It would enter into us, in a way completely different from anything we had experienced before. I was slightly afraid of this, yet also excited and awed. Something was coming to us in the dark, something huge and amazing. It was Bast, but somehow more than Bast, perhaps a premonition for rituals we would do later. I could feel its immanence pressing down on me.

At this point, I woke up, my heart racing. I felt a little strange and scared, and although I wished I could go back into the dream, part of me wanted to just sit up in bed and put the light on!

After this, we began to use the sistra more in our rituals, and our workings to Bast have taken a step up in intensity.

Dreams of this nature are useful, because they can give an indication of where a facet of our work needs to be modified, changed or explored. Because we use dream material a lot in constructing our rituals, they never remain static, but are constantly evolving. Once rituals do become static and repetitive, the element of excitement they inspire can diminish. As humans, we mostly thrive on variety and change, but some people find comfort and stability in what is familiar and routine. Again, this is an individual preference. Whenever we come across something that can be added to our work, whether it is a snippet of information about an ancient practice, a prayer written by a modern practitioner or ritual actions gleaned from a dream, we incorporate them into our system.

In our temple group, we concentrate upon self-evolution and the search for knowledge, and constantly push back the boundaries of what we know and what we feel familiar with. We do not live solely for our magical work, and sometimes several weeks might elapse between group workings or meditations, because of members' outside commitments. Then, a week later, we might find ourselves doing several workings on consecutive days. In between, individual members might meditate or communicate with the goddesses privately. We do not feel it is vital to perform rituals together twice a week, regular as clockwork. Nor do we feel it is essential for every member to be present at every working. Sometimes two or three members might get together to work on a particular visualization, following a trail that one person has picked up, either through dreams or meditation.

We feel that the most important aspect of magical work is that each individual should do what he or she feels most comfortable doing. We hope that readers of this book will be inspired by our work, but then evolve it to suit themselves. Although we have obviously expressed our personal opinions in these pages, our aim is not to preach or set down a strict set of rules for interacting with the Egyptian feline deities. Our opinions, after all, are simply our own. The gods are out there, immense, formless, shining with ancient power. We have only to turn our psychic antennae towards them in order to establish a relationship.

A visionary working

When Julia Phillips, one of the contributors to the previous chapter, sent us her account, she described one of her own visionary workings, which we found was similar to the kind of visualization we performed ourselves. We decided to include part of her account in this chapter as her experience adds to the information we have given above on conducting visionary quests.

After we returned to Britain from our trip to Egypt, my partner and I continued working within the Hermetic system of magic in which we were trained. Hermetics operates on a system of guided visualization, with one person describing a journey, which others follow. It has many levels, but in its simplest form can be seen as a kind of pathworking.

The following excerpt from my magical dairy of 9 February 1986 is a visualization given by my partner, and shows just how profoundly I was affected by my first trip to Egypt.

1. Make your way to your astral temple, purify yourself with the four elements, and then enter the inner sanctum and temple of Stones.
2. Using the stones, create a spiral, which you use to ascend from your temple.
3. You see ahead of you great golden gates flanked by two guardians.
4. Open the gates, and pass through to find your guardian waiting for you. The guardian holds two eggs and indicates that you should follow.
5. Ahead of you is a temple unlike that which you have ever seen before. In the centre is a double-cubed altar; you and your guardian stand on either side of the altar, and then the guardian takes one of the eggs and smashes it.
6. A mist spreads around you, and you find it hard to see. Suddenly there is a great clanging and crashing all around you. As this dies away, you can see through the mist that there are metal doors all around the temple. Which door are you facing?
7. Look at the second egg and see if it has changed in any way.
8. Thank your guardian and if you wish, you can ask a question.
9. Make your way back to your astral temple, then return to your Earth body.

Here is my vision: 'Beginning in my astral temple, I use the power of the seven stones which are in the inner sanctum to create a spiral of energy, which then becomes a pathway. I am clothed in a golden robe, which is so light it feels like spun cobwebs. My feet are bare and I wear no ornaments.

I approach two great golden gates, and see two lion-headed figures standing before them. It is difficult to sense whether these are male or female, and at any rate such human distinctions are probably irrelevant in this place. As I get nearer, they open the gates so that I can enter.

I pass through the gates and find myself in a courtyard paved with honey-coloured stone with fig trees growing around a pool of water. Around the courtyard are pillars of the same honey-coloured stone, and I know that beyond lie temples of purification and magic.

It is hot, with a dry wind, though I cannot see any particular source for the heat, nor is it logical for such a wind in an enclosed place. It feels like the wind of the Egyptian desert – hot and dry, powerfully alive and imbued with the energy of the land and sun.

A figure is waiting for me by the side of the pool, tall and powerful, another lion-headed being, but this one is so much more vibrant than the guardians at the gateway. I can believe this is of a different order of being entirely.

The name of Sekhmet vibrates in my head, though she is golden coloured, not black like her statues. She holds a gold egg in one hand, and a silver egg in the other. She is naked above the waist, wearing only a white wrap-around skirt. Her feet are bare.

As I approach her, she turns and walks away, a voice in my head telling me I should follow. We make our way through two of the pillars, and enter a square room, which has a shallow circular pit in its centre. It seems very large, and has a highly polished, reflective surface. Like everything else, it has a golden glow about it. At first I do not notice an altar at the centre, but gradually my vision focuses, and a double-cubed altar seems to grow out of the floor. I am sure it was always there, but I could not see it till I allowed my vision to clear.

Now I notice there are steps leading to the floor of the pit, and watch Sekhmet as she descends, and walks to stand in front of the altar. I feel I should join her, though I am not aware of any words being spoken. I make my way to the altar to stand opposite Sekhmet.

She raises her arm, and without warning, smashes the silver egg upon the altar. A mist begins to fill the temple, and all of a sudden I cannot see anything beyond the altar and Sekhmet. A great cacophony of sound erupts all around us. I cover my ears trying to deaden it, but it makes no difference. It is as if the sound is inside my head, and only seems to be coming from outside.

When I feel I can bear no more, just as suddenly as it started, it stops. As if on cue, the mist begins to clear. Throughout all this, Sekhmet remained quite still, watching me. I have the feeling she was testing me, interested in what my reaction would be.

As the mist clears, I am able to see that the chamber has changed and is now circular, and that seven doors have appeared, evenly spaced around the perimeter. I know that the doors are made of metal, one each of copper, lead, tin, silver, mercury, iron, and bronze. I wonder whether they were connected in any way to the seven stones of my astral temple.

I glance back at the altar and see that Sekhmet has placed the golden egg in the centre, and that it now has a snake coiled around it. Although the egg is balanced on its narrow end, I know it will not tumble because it is the focus of a spiral of energy generated by the seven doors.

I ask Sekhmet how she knew to be in the temple courtyard, waiting for me, and she replies. 'You bring me with you.'

I hear a sound, and looking round, see that the copper door has opened. Sekhmet indicates that I should pass through the doorway, and hands me the golden egg with the serpent to carry with me. As I stand before the door, I turn to say farewell to Sekhmet, and notice that the mist has returned. I can just see her at the centre by the altar, but in the fading light, she is no longer golden but obsidian black. Even her skirt is black.

I pass through the doorway, and see a spiral pathway, which I begin to follow. I become aware that it is returning me to my earth body and gradually sense a heaviness in my limbs, and hear sounds from the mundane world once more.

I focus my awareness back into my earth body in the usual way, and then open my eyes.

Ritual design

We hope that by now you will be familiar enough with the components of rituals to design your own, incorporating material personal to you. As a recap, the basic formula is:

1. selection of a setting and a deity for the ritual
2. cone construction and a visualized journey to the setting of the ritual
3. invocation of the deity
4. offering of a feast
5. petitioning for boons or other magical task (i.e. the point of the ritual)
6. some time spent freely visualizing (which is optional)
7. thanks to the deity
8. return to real time and dismantling of the cone

We do feel it is important that anyone interested in this subject should conduct their own research into it. In designing your own rituals, you can look through translations of ancient works like the *Coffin Texts* and the *Pyramid Texts*, not just to get a feel of the way the Egyptians addressed their gods, but also in order to use or adapt certain phrases or whole prayers yourself. Even though Budge's work is now seen as rather outdated, his *Gods of the Egyptians* is still very useful for learning the various names and titles of the gods.

Initiation

No book on magic is complete without at least some mention of initiation. The majority of occult systems advocate a period of training for neophytes, when they will learn about the various magical techniques and the history of the subject, which may include the different belief systems around the world. In Wiccan circles, for example, this period is traditionally a year and a day. After this training is complete, the neophyte undergoes a ceremony of initiation to become a fully fledged member of the group or order, and may then be known as a priest or priestess. The initiation ritual is generally the same for every new member. It is seen as a rite of passage, and many systems incorporate a degree of fear or humiliation, so that by the end of the experience the newly initiated feels as if they are 'reborn' or have learned something new and enlightening. Some systems have a tier of initiation ceremonies, with group members progressing through various advanced stages of knowledge and experience.

We have not included a ritual for initiation in this book. The reason for this is that we see magical initiation as an intensely personal experience. To us, it is the 'signing on the dotted line', the point of no return, the pledging of one's life to the good of the universe, even if that might place one in difficult positions at times. We feel we cannot tell people when they are ready for that or what they should do when the moment occurs. If magical work revolves around the search for self-knowledge, then each individual will instinctively know when he or she is ready to take that ultimate step and what it should entail. It's like signing a contract with the cosmos.

Our group members design their own individual initiations and decide who they want to be present (if anyone) and what those participants should do in the ritual. Like many other groups, we feel that part of the rite should include facing your greatest fear, and this cannot be the same for any two people. By the time you undertake this task, you should have enough self-awareness to prevent the experience being totally debilitating or damaging. At this time you enter 'Chapel Perilous', experience the dark night of the soul, so that when you emerge from it, you feel you have been changed in some subtle way. An effective initiation involves the participant receiving what we refer to as an 'information update' concerning the universe itself. After this, you move to the next level of being.

Initiation can take many forms. It might incorporate spending a night alone somewhere, or performing a certain ritual and significant actions. It might be a visualized journey or a shattering dream, or could occur unexpectedly during the mundane activities of the day without involving a daunting ceremony at all. You might feel as if a shaft of life suddenly penetrates your body and a great sense of oneness with creation floods through you. Whatever form this takes for you, all we can say is do not be too eager to rush in and perform an initiation ritual for yourself after only a short time. Experience and knowledge should come first, otherwise the initiation will be worthless.

A final word

Now, as you finish this book, look towards your own cat, if you have one. Return its unblinking stare and see within its depthless eyes the starlight of vanished aeons. It is the sacred cat, mistress of mysteries, son or daughter of Bast. Where best to initiate acquaintance with the goddess than through her sacred animal's unwavering gaze?

Appendix I:
Pleasures of the
Gods

I will cause to be brought into thee fine oils and choice perfumes, and the incense of the temples, whereby every god is gladdened.

From an ancient Egyptian papyrus, 2000 BC

In our group, Eloise is responsible for making our oils and incenses, as well as any feast dishes that require cooking. The subject of this appendix is entirely her domain, and rather than incur the wrath of a fiery Italian chef, her co-author respectfully stays on the threshold!

Magical intention

The great benefit of making your own incenses or oils is that you can infuse them with your intention as you create them. Shop-bought products are fine but nothing is as personally rewarding as something that you have created yourself. The smoke of home-made incense will carry your hopes and desires within it. It will add to the power of your rite.

Let us imagine that you have decided to perform a ritual to Bast in which you want to ask for her help at a job interview. As part of this ritual you want to burn incense. How can you fill your incense with intent so that the act of burning it helps you in your endeavours?

Once you have decided on a recipe and gathered your ingredients together, ensure that you have a little time when you will not be disturbed. Wash your hands in running water and imagine that any negative feelings are being washed away. Then simply begin to make the mixture, all the while focusing clearly on what you want to achieve. See your result clearly in pictures. Imagining yourself shaking hands with the interviewer and seeing her or him handing you a piece of paper marked 'contract' would be ideal in this case. The most important thing is to keep it simple. As each ingredient is added imagine that the incense is becoming more and more imbued with your intention.

When everything has been added pick up the mixture, let it fall through your fingers, hold it in your hands. Try to imagine that your energy or intention is tangible. See it coming through your hands and into your incense. Perhaps you will see it as blue or white light. If you find it difficult to 'see', imagine it as heat instead. Feel the warmth spreading from your hands and into the mixture. Spend a few minutes doing this until you are satisfied that you have really saturated the incense.

Once you have finished, store your mixture in a clean jar until you need it.

When making oils, simply mix them in a bowl and stir them with your fingers as you add each ingredient. You can visualize your energy being transferred from the tips of your fingers into the oil.

If you are working with shop-bought incense or oil you can transfer it to a bowl and use the same technique. You can even just lay your hand over the jar and see the energy entering the incense or oil from your palms.

Incense

For thousands of years, incense and other types of perfume have played an important role in spiritual rituals. They have been used since the beginning of recorded history both as a tool to aid communication with the gods and for purification. Resins such as frankincense were once valued more highly than gold by some societies, including that of ancient Egypt where deities were said to live on perfume. In Egyptian religion it was widely believed that the smell of incense in the temple would attract the gods down into the sacred space to commune with the priests. Incense smoke was also used before each rite to fumigate the space and purify the priest in much the same way that practitioners of Native American magic use smudge sticks. Egyptian priests were also anointed with perfumed oils during purification rites.

Incense and scented oils are used in many of the rituals in this book. It is possible to buy good-quality incense ready made from any specialist shops but nothing is quite as rewarding as making your own and infusing it with your magical intention.

Below are some of the recipes for incenses that we use ourselves. I have also briefly explained the reasoning behind the choice of ingredients. Incense-making should not be a rigid process. If gum arabic is called for in a recipe and you have none handy then simply find a substitution with similar attributes or correspondences. In the case of arabic, another resin like frankincense or gum mastic would be a good choice. You would probably get a great deal of use from a general book on herbalism and incense-making. I find that *Cunningham's Encyclopaedia of Magical Herbs* is useful because it has very detailed tables of correspondences at the back that come in handy when devising your own recipes or finding suitable substitutes.

When making incense you will need a good-quality pestle and mortar with which to grind your ingredients. This should be fairly large or you will find yourself losing half your ingredients on the floor every time you try to add something new to your mixture. Pestles and mortars can be found in good kitchen supply shops and department stores and are usually quite reasonably priced. Most suppliers of incenses also stock more unusual ones but these can often be expensive.

The basic method for making incense is to add the ingredients one by one and grind each as it is added to the mixture. Always start with the resins and add other herbs before putting the essential oils and mixing well. Once mixed, an incense stored in a clean jar will last for a good few months.

When devising your own recipes it is important to include a good proportion of resin in each mixture. This slows the burning time of incenses and prevents the clouds of acrid smoke that a herb-only mixture would create. Obviously you will need a selection of clean jars in which to store your ingredients and some sticky labels to make identification easier.

Ingredients

There are a few staple ingredients that you will need to start off your incense-making. The essentials include:

- **Frankincense.** This is probably the most commonly used resin in the world. It is associated with Ra and is therefore perfect for use with his daughters. It is ruled by fire and the sun and widely used in rituals of protection.
- **Copal.** This is a masculine fire incense which is ruled by the sun yet is often used in incenses for matters of the heart.
- **Benzoin.** This resin is also ruled by the sun but unlike its counterparts it is associated with the element of air. It is essential for creating incenses for rituals involving the god Shu.
- **Myrrh.** The classic lunar resin, this is associated with the element of water. It is classically used for purification. We tend to use it to attune to the lunar aspect of Bast and with the god Nefertum.
- **Cinnamon and cloves.** Both are spicy and evocative of heat. Cinnamon was used in Egypt during mummification rites. Cloves are used for protection and are said to attract money, which makes them ideal for use with the leonine dwarf god Bes.
- **Red sandalwood and dragon's blood.** These two are both good for sun and fire incenses, because of both their colour and their pungent smoke. Beware of using too much dragon's blood in any compound, however, because the smoke can be very acrid. A little goes a long way.
- **Rose.** Rose petals are associated with water and the feminine and are most often used in matters of the heart. They are perfect for use with Bast because of her role as a goddess of love and pleasure and because of her affinity with beautiful perfumes. They could also be used with Tefnut because of her association with moisture.
- **Catnip.** This speaks for itself. Also known as cat mint, it is widely available as a plant which you can grow yourself in the garden. Cats love it and it is an important addition to any Bast incense since it personifies many of her characteristics. It is associated with water and the planet Venus and is used for love and happiness.
- **Rosemary.** This is a herb of the sun and fire and can sometimes be used for any psychic quest work that you may be undertaking.
- **Lavender.** This is associated with the element of air and is used for healing and love. We use it as a feminine herb but in fact its association is with the masculine.
- **Juniper.** This is ruled by the sun and is widely used for protection.

- **Orris root.** This derives from the iris, which is associated with Bast. It can be found growing in the damp ground on the banks of the Nile, and its association with moisture also makes it ideal for Tefnut incense. Historically orris is also associated with Isis.

Recipes

Bast incense. With this incense I decided to incorporate both solar and lunar influences to reflect Bast's dual attributes as both a sun and moon goddess. I was influenced also by her love of perfume and her various magical focuses such as love, happiness and fertility.

3 parts frankincense	1 part sandalwood (red or white)
2 parts gum arabic	½ part lavender
1 part myrrh	½ part orris root
1 part catnip	2 drops each of ylang ylang
1 part patchouli leaf	and carnation oil
1 part rose petal	

Sekhmet incense. This is a rich incense that smells spicy and immediately conjures up an impression of heat and fiery sunlight. It is a pungent smell that echoes the strength and power of Sekhmet.

3 parts frankincense	1 part benzoin
1½ parts dragon's blood	1 part sandalwood
1 copal	¾ part cloves
1 part juniper	a few drops each of frankincense
1 part cinnamon	and orange oil

Bes incense. As Bes is a god of African origins, I wanted to create an incense with an exotic, almost fruity scent that would reflect his links with fire and the sun.

2 parts frankincense	½ part gum arabic
1 part benzoin	½ part red sandalwood
1 part copal	½ part allspice
¾ part cinnamon	½ part rosemary
¾ part cloves	a few drops each of orange
¾ part heliotropin crystal	oil and lemon oil

Tefnut incense. This incense needed to have a real scent of moisture. I wanted it to smell like dew on the ground. I used some ingredients with air connotations but the majority are associated with water.

2 parts myrrh	½ part lavender
2 parts benzoin	½ part jasmine
1 part gum mastic	½ part camomile
1 part orris root	½ part rose petal
1 part catnip	

Protection incense

2 parts frankincense	1 part crushed juniper berries
1 part rosemary	

Prosperity incense

2 parts benzoin	½ part cinnamon
½ part nutmeg	a few drops of orange oil

Healing incense

3 parts myrrh	1 part sandalwood
1 part bay	

Temple incense. This is an all-purpose incense for use when you are not performing a specific rite. It is suitable for meditational exercises and burning as an offering in your temple room. This recipe and the one which follows are both taken from Scott Cunninghams *The Complete Book of Incense, Oils and Brews*.

3 parts frankincense	a few drops each of lavender
2 parts myrrh	oil and sandalwood oil

Kyphi. This is a traditional Egyptian incense, for which there are a variety of recipes that derive from ancient inscriptions.

3 parts frankincense	½ part cinnamon
2 parts benzoin	½ part cedar
2 parts myrrh	2 drops each of wine and honey
1 part juniper berries	a few raisins
½ part galangal	

Anointing Oils

In many of the rituals described later in this book, oil is used for anointing votive candles in order to imbue them with intention. For these you will need a good base oil such as jojoba or almond. I use a plain massage oil as my base oil and it always keeps well. As well as the base, you will need to collect some essential oils. These can be very expensive so only buy what you know you will use regularly and shop around for the best price – cost varies quite considerably from shop to shop. I would never advocate the use of synthetic oils unless the essential oil is unavailable or prohibitively expensive.

In order to make up a small amount of oil I use about four table-spoons of base oil, to which I add a few drops of each of the required essential oils and mix well. Smell you mixture as you go along and add the amount that feels right for you. Stored in a jar or bottle, any left-over oil can be used again for a good few weeks. The ones that I use the most of are:

- **orange and lemon;** orange has sun associations while lemon is lunar
- **rose;** for love, beauty and peace
- **lavender**
- **coconut** (synthetic oil is the only option here since essential oil of coconut is not produced – The Body Shop does a really good one); we use this when working with deities with a strong African influence such as Bes
- **frankincense**
- **myrrh**
- **sandalwood**
- **rosemary**

The uses for lavender, frankincense, myrrh, sandalwood and rose-mary oils are the same as for the incenses.

Recipes

- **Bast oil**. A few drops each of frankincense, myrrh and rose oil
- **Sekhmet oil**. A few drops each of frankincense, orange, sandal-wood and rosemary oils

- **Bes oil**. A few drops each of orange, coconut and frankincense oils
- **Tefnut oil**. A few drops each of myrrh, lemon and camomile oils
- **Healing oil**. A few drops each of rosemary, myrrh and carnation oils.
- **Protection oil**. A few drops each of myrrh and rosemary oils
- **Prosperity oil**. A few drops each of patchouli and pine oils.

Food and Drink

Feasting is a part of most of our rituals. We like our feasts to incorporate ingredients that we associate with the particular gods or goddesses we are honouring. In our group, everyone brings a donation towards the feast, which helps to cut the cost. Feasts are usually consumed during the ritual itself in keeping with the practices of the Egyptians who offered food to their gods as a ritual act. We dedicate our feast to the deity we are working with and ask that as we taste the food so might she. We then given a small portion of everything we eat to the goddess as an offering. Once a feast has been consumed we are left with a bowl of offerings which we will feed to our own cats, scatter in the garden for birds or bury depending on the type of food involved. Cats love a share of the cream cakes or prawns but are none too keen on chilli salsa! Use your own judgement on the best way to dispose of a feast but do not just throw it away. If you have no animal to help eat it then bury it outside, symbolically returning it to the earth as an act of thanks.

During Bast rituals we will eat foods that we associate with cats, such as cream or fish. We always include something that our own cats like and share the feast with them. As a result we have things like prawns, cheese and cream cakes. Bast is a goddess who appreciates lovely food and wine. When the feast is in honour of fiery Sekhmet we eat foods which are hot and spicy. Salsa dip, tortilla chips and ginger cake are all Sekhmet foots. With Bes, we feast on a platter of exotic fruits like coconut, banana or mango.

Recipes

Feasts can be made up of anything that you feel is appropriate, but there are a few recipes that we use again and again.

Chilli and coriander salsa. This is suitable for rituals to any fiery deity, but we use it for Sekhmet in particular.

6 firm tomatoes
1 red onion, roughly
    chopped
1 fresh green chilli,
    deseeded and sliced
1 small packet fresh
    coriander, stalks removed

4 sundried tomatoes, roughly
    chopped
a squeeze of lemon juice
a pinch each of salt and sugar
    and some freshly ground black
    pepper

First make a small slit in the skin of each tomato and sit them in boiling water for a minute to loosen their skins. When they are cool enough to handle peel and discard the skin. Then slice each tomato in half. Scoop our and discard the seeds.

Place the onion, chilli, sundried tomatoes and coriander in a food processor and process until the mixture is finely chopped. Then add all the other ingredients and process again until the tomatoes are well chopped but not pureed.

Set a sieve over a bowl or pan and tip the salsa into it. Leave it for ten minutes until the water from the tomatoes has drained out and you are left with a mixture of a firm consistency.

Arrange the salsa in a bowl and refrigerate it until needed.

Traditional spice cake. This is good for any ritual, as the ingredients are a mix of solar and lunar ingredients.

75 g (3 oz) runny honey
225 g (8 oz) plain flour
¼ teaspoon nutmeg
1 teaspoon ground ginger
¼ teaspoon allspice
1 teaspoon ground cinnamon
½ teaspoon ground cloves
75 g (3 oz) caster sugar
finely grated zest of 1 orange
For the icing:
175 g (6 oz) sifted icing sugar
1 tablespoon fresh orange juice

finely grated zest of 1 lemon
110 g (4 oz) soft butter
2 medium sized eggs, beaten
1 large teaspoon bicarbonate
    of soda, dissolved in 3
    tablespoons of cold water
75 g (3 oz) finely chopped
    mixed peel

1 tablespoon lemon juice

Preheat the oven to 325°F/165°C/gas mark 3.

Butter one 18 cm square tin or 20 cm round tin. Place a cup on the scales and weigh the honey into it. Then place the cup into a shallow saucepan of simmering water to warm gently.

Sift the flower, spices and sugar into a large mixing bowl and add the zest. Add the butter in small pieces, rubbing in with your fingers until the mixture resembles breadcrumbs. Next lightly mix in the egg and the warm honey using a large fork. Add the bicarbonate of soda mixed with water and beat until the mixture is smooth. Stir in the mixed peel and transfer the mixture to the prepared tin.

Bake for about fifty minutes and leave to cook on a wire tray.

Mix the icing ingredients together well, using a little water if necessary, to get a thin consistency. When the cake is cold coat the top with the icing and let the excess dribble down the sides.

Marie-Rose prawn dressing. We use this recipe during Bast rituals. It makes enough for about 200 g of prawns.

4 large tablespoons mayonnaise	dash of Worcestershire sauce
1 small tablespoon tomato sauce	dash of brandy
1 large tablespoon double cream	dash of tobasco sauce
1 teaspoon lemon juice	salt and pepper to taste

Gently blend all the ingredients together with a wooden spoon and chill until needed.

Festival of Sekhmet spiced wine. This makes about six large glasses.

1 bottle red wine	2 cinnamon sticks
½ pint lemonade	1 heaped tablespoon sugar
1 orange, not peeled	
whole cloves, enough to stud one half of an orange	

In a large pan mix the wine, lemonade and sugar. Add the cinnamon. Halve the orange. Stud one half with the cloves and roughly slice the other. Add these to the mixture and begin to warm it through gently. Adjust with more sugar or a sprinkle of ground cinnamon according to your own taste. It is important that the mixture does not boil or you will lose the alcohol, but it should be served as hot as possible.

Star and moon cookies. You will need some cookie cutters in the shape of stars and moons. These can be purchased cheaply from most cookware shops. If these are unavailable any others would do.

110 g (4 oz) softened butter	squeeze of fresh orange juice
50 g (2 oz) caster sugar	extra sugar for dusting
175 g (6 oz) plain flour, sifted	
pinch each of ground	
ginger and cinnamon	

Preheat the oven to 300°F/150°C/gas mark 2. Grease a baking tray with butter.

Beat the sugar into the butter with a wooden spoon and then beat in the sifted flour. And the spices. Next add the juice – not too much as you want a firm mixture. Bring the mixture together with your hands until it forms a ball.

Dust a surface with the extra sugar and on this roll out your dough until it is about 4 mm (approx ¼ inch) thick. Cut out the biscuits and arrange them on the baking tray. Bake for twenty-five minutes.

Turn them out onto a wire tray to cool and then dust them with a little sugar.

Smoked mackerel pate. This is ideal for rituals to Bast, or even Tefnut, for obvious reasons! The recipe will serve six.

4 smoked mackerel fillets	1 tablespoon finely chopped
50 g (2 oz) softened butter	parsley
75 g (3 oz) good-quality	freshly ground black pepper
cream cheese	

First peel the skin from the fillets and break the flesh up into the bowl of a food processor. Blend for a few moments until the fish is finely chopped. Then add all the other ingredients and blend until everything is well mixed and resembles a smooth paste. Turn the mixture out into an attractive bowl and chill. Remove from the refrigerator at least ten minutes before serving. Serve with toast or crackers.

Cheese and chive dip. This is a creamy, mild dip that we use in rituals to Bast. It will serve six.

1 tub mascarpone cheese	1 small clove fresh garlic
4 tablespoons good-quality mayonnaise	1 packet fresh chives
2 tablespoons double cream	salt and freshly ground black pepper to taste

First mix together the cheese, mayonnaise and cream with a fork until smooth. Then finely chop the chives, crush the garlic and add to the cheese mixture. Season to taste and then chill until required. Serve with crisps, chopped vegetables or pitta bread.

Sekhmet beer. In the famous Sekhmet myth we are told that in order to stop her bloodlust Ra and his priests disguised 7,000 jars of beer with red ochre to trick Sekhmet into thinking it was blood. When she drank it she became so drunk that she abandoned her killing spree, thereby saving mankind. Sometimes we colour beer with red food colouring in honour of this myth and drink it during our rituals to Sekhmet.

Avocado dip. One Egyptian belief was that once the sun set, a huge battle went on in the underworld between the sun god and his arch-enemy, the serpent Apep. The story tells of a fight that took place by a persea tree, which was regarded as sacred. Here, the sun god in cat form leapt upon a spotted serpent and hacked off its head with a knife. (During solar eclipses, people would actually shake sistra and knives in an attempt to frighten the serpent, so that the sun god would win the battle and rise again.) The Egyptians regarded two trees as sacred, the persea and the acacia. The persea has two varieties, one of which grows in Egypt, while the other grows in other parts of the world and is known by the common name of avocado. We discovered this some time after we had habitually included avocado as part of our ritual feast to Bast.

2 ripe avocados	squeeze of lemon juice
1 tablespoon cream cheese	small dash of tabasco sauce
1 tablespoon mayonnaise	salt and pepper to taste

Remove the skin and stones from the avocado and mash with a fork until smooth. Then blend in all the other ingredients. Serve immediately, since avocado has a tendency to discolour quickly.

Appendix II:
Useful Addresses

Suppliers

The addresses below will supply the equipment you need to start your own temple group. Everything can be obtained by mail order. We have bought items from all of these suppliers ourselves and can attest to their quality, but it is only a small sample of the suppliers available, and many more can be found on the Internet.

The Atlantis Bookshop
49A Museum Street
London
WC1A 1LY
020 7405 2120

A long-established occult bookstore, with an extremely wide range of titles, including many on Egyptian magic, religion, etc.

British Museum
Great Russell Street
London
WC1B 3DG
020 7636 1555

The British Museum gift shop sells copies of the Gayer Anderson cat, which are beautiful, virtually identical to the original, but very expensive. The cheapest is around £450, while the bronze representation is around £2,000. However, they also produce smaller statues of sacred cats, which are not so expensive. The bookshop in the museum has a huge range of titles on Egyptology.

Caduceus Jewellers
624 Leabridge Road
Leyton
London
E10 6AP
020 8539 3569

They offer an extensive range of Egyptian pendants, rings, earrings, etc., including a superb, reasonably priced silver pendant of Bast as a cat-headed woman. As far as we know, Caduceus is the only company in the UK which makes Bast pendants like this. They have a mail-order catalogue.

The Goddess Gallery
3535 SE Hawthorne Boulevard
Portland
OR 97214
USA
00 1 503 239 7458
Web site: http://www.goddess-gallery.com/feline.html

The gallery produces expensive but extremely beautiful hand-painted marble and gold-leafed statuettes of Bast and Sekhmet (as well as many other Egyptian deities). These pieces are certainly worth the price if you can afford it. Also available are less expensive statues of sacred cats (including a selection of very nice blue-glazed ones) and a seated Sekhmet. The Goddess Gallery does not have a catalogue, but their full stock can be viewed on their web site. You can order via credit card and e-mail or phone.

The Goddess and the Green Man
2 High Street
Glastonbury
Somerset
BA6 9DU
01458 834697

This store supplies one of the best Sekhmet figures we have ever seen, copies of the seated Sekhmet statue in the British Museum. The figure is available in a variety of colours. In 1998, it cost £58, but is well worth the price. The Goddess and the Green Man also produce beautiful statues of Isis, Hathor and Bast, and sell a wide range of books, incense and jewellery connected with different magical traditions. A mail-order catalogue is available.

Horus
Unit 7–8
1st Floor
Coliseum Shopping Centre
Manchester
M4 1PL
0161 907 3208

Run by an Egyptian, Horus supplies a vast range of imported statuettes and authentic beads and jewellery. They will also take commissions for statues to your own specifications, which will be created by Egyptian artists. The feline deity figures start from only £2, and include several different representations of Sekhmet, sacred cats, a male lion-headed god (which we have used to represent Mahes) and a male cat-headed god. We recommend the beautiful Bast candlesticks, but they are not always in stock, so call first to place an order. We have also purchased inexpensive Egyptian tablecloths from here that make excellent altar cloths.

The House of Netjer
Box 11188
Chicago
IL 60611-0188
USA
Web site: http://www/kemet.org
E-mail: hetnetjer@kemet.org

For information on Kemetic Orthodoxy.

The Isle of Avalon Foundation
(Lorye Keats Hopper)
2–4 High Street
Glastonbury
Somerset
BA6 9DU

Holds workshops on healing and associated subjects, and an annual Goddess Conference in August each year.

Pandora
17B High Street
Glastonbury
Somerset
BA6 9DP
01458 834975

Pandora supplies a wide variety of well-crafted and very reasonably priced Egyptian statues, including Bast, Sekhmet and Bes. They also sell scarabs, amulets and a comprehensive stock of artefacts copied from those found in the tomb of Tutankhamen, including an ornate looped sistrum in a presentation box. As far as we know, Pandora is the only supplier of authentic sistra in this country. A fair proportion of their stock can be purchased by mail order, but the weight of certain items makes this prohibitive. A web site is in preparation.

Past Times
Witney
Oxford
OX8 6BH
01993 770440

A well-known high-street store, Past Times produces excellent sacred cat statues in a range of sizes. Their largest, complete with pierced ears, costs around £35 and stands 14½ inches/36 cm high. It makes a wonderful altar centrepiece. They supply mail order and a catalogue is available. The above address and phone number are for their mail-order centre.

Sacred Moon
New Age Centre
27 Wyle Cop
Shrewsbury
Shropshire
SY1 1XB
01743 352829

Suppliers of a vast range of equipment and paraphernalia, including incense burners, incense, jewellery, statues, oils, candles, Sekhmet pendants, etc. A mail-order catalogue is available.

Sacred Source/JBL
PO Box 163
Crozet
VA 22932
USA 00 1 804 823 1515
Web site: http://www.jblstatue.com/

They supply a vast range of mystical statues, including a comprehensive stock of Egyptian deities. They make several versions of Bast, her sacred cat and Sekhmet. They also supply other magical equipment, such as chalices, candle-holders, incense burners, etc. Prices are extremely reasonable, although if you live outside the USA, bear shipping costs in mind. In 1998, we purchased 6-inch Bast and 8-inch Sekhmet statues for $18 (around £11 each). Visit their web site to view their range, but it is really worth sending off for their full colour catalogue. You can order via credit card and e-mail or phone.

Spook Enterprises
38 Woodfield Avenue
London
W5 1PA

They publish E.A. St George's booklets *Under Regulus* and *Ancient and Modern Cat Worship* which we recommend highly. They also make high-quality Bast and Sekhmet incenses and oils. A full list of their oils, incenses and publications is given in all of their booklets.

Star Child
The Courtyard
2–4 High Street
Glastonbury
Somerset
NA6 9DU
01458 832920

Suppliers of incenses, oils, magical candles, pestles and mortars, including a huge range of raw ingredients to make your own incense. They produce a very good Bast incense as well as excellent Kyphi and other Egyptian deity incenses. A mail-order catalogue is available.

Paul Weston
8 Old Market Court
George Street
Glastonbury
Somerset
BA6 9LS

Supplies lecture tapes on psychic questing and associated subjects.
A list is available.

Wicked Wax Co
High Street
Glastonbury
Somerset
BA6 9DU

Supplies a wide range of candles in all colours and sizes, from the
minute to the massive. We always purchase our small votive candles
from them; they are really good value at 60p a pair.

For general ritual music, we recommend the Egyptian albums of
musician, Phil Thornton:

Pharoah
Eternal Egypt (with Hossam Ramzy)
Immortal Egypt (with Hossam Ramzy)

All of these albums are released through New World Music.

Artists

The artists whose work has appeared in this book are available for
commission. Their addresses are as follows:

Rob Kesterton
c/o Visionary Tongue
6 St Leonards Avenue
Stafford
ST17 4LT

Ellisa Mitchell
PO Box 47
Woodlawn
TX 75694
USA

Graham Stewart (photographer)
41 Wolverhampton Road
Stafford
ST17 4DA
01785 604055
E-mail: graham.stewart6@virgin.net

Ruby
8 Jordans
Hillfields
Welwyn Garden City
Herts
AL7 2HD

Kirsty Wood
c/o Visionary Tongue
6 St Leonards Avenue
Stafford
ST17 4LT

Charities

Born Free Foundation
UK Head Office
3 Grove House
Foundry Lane
Horsham
Sussex
RH13 5PL
01403 240170
Web site: http://www.bornfree.org.uk

Devoted to animal welfare and founded by *Born Free* stars Virginia McKenna and her late husband Bill Travers. Among many other projects, they have an 'adopt a lion' scheme.

Care for the Wild
1 Ashfolds
Horsham Road
Rusper
Sussex
RH12 4QX
01293 871596
Web site: http://www.careforthewild.org.uk

Work for endangered species worldwide, and have an 'adopt a tiger' campaign.

Cats' Protection League
17 Kings Road
Horsham
Sussex
RH13 5PN
01403 221900
Web site: http://www.cats.org.uk/

Has membership packages for both adults and children.

The Dogs' Home, Battersea
4 Battersea Park Road
London
SW8 4AA
020 7622 3626

Although primarily a charity devoted to homeless dogs, the home also takes in and rehomes abandoned and mistreated cats. Donations are always welcome, as well as offers of homes for animals.

People's Dispensary for Sick Animals
Public Relations Department
Whitechapel Way
Priorslee
Telford
TF2 9PQ
01952 290999

Donations can be sent, and the charity also has many shops to which you can donate goods.

Royal Society for the Prevention of Cruelty to Animals
Enquiries Services
Causeway
Horsham
Sussex
RH12 1HG
01403 264181
Web site: http://www.rspca.org.uk/

Always in need of donations and homes for abandoned and mistreated animals.

World Wild Fund for Nature
Freepost
Panda House
Godalming
Surrey
GU7 1BR
01483 426444
Web site UK: http://www.wwf-uk.org/
Web site USA: http://www.worldwildlife.org

The WWF does much to help endangered species worldwide, including many felines. To 'adopt a tiger', which costs approximately £2 per month, contact them at the above address.

Glossary

Abydos	An important site in northern Upper Egypt, which was a big religious centre in ancient times, famous for its Osirion (temple of Osiris – q.v.)
Adze	A tool used for working with wood that also had a ritualistic use. It had a curved metal blade and wooden handle. When used for ceremonial purposes it was made from 'metal of Heaven' which was meteoritic iron
Aker	An ancient lion deity, who was both an earth god and a guardian of the gates of the dawn, through which the sun god emerged each morning
Akeru	The lions of yesterday and today, equated with Shu and Tefnut (qq.v.)
Akhu	The Magical power, or a spirit of the dead after it has passed through various transformations in the underworld
Amarna	A city in Middle Egypt, founded by the 'heretic' pharaoh Akhenaten
Am-Khent	A nome (q.v.) of Egypt, of which Bubastis (q.v.) was capital
Amun-Ra	Creator/solar god of Thebes, husband of Mut (q.v.)
Anhur	A warrior and hunting god, known also as Onuris, credited with bringing home 'the distant one', the lioness goddess Mekhit (q.v.), who became his consort
Ankh	The symbol of life
Ankhtawy	A burial region at Sakkara associated with Bast (q.v.). Literally means 'life of the two lands'. An epithet of various goddesses, but mainly Bast

Anubis	A jackal-headed god of mummification and cemeteries
Apedemak	A lion-headed warrior god of the culture of Meroe (q.v.)
Apep	The serpent fiend of the underworld, who nightly battles with the sun god
Arensnuphis	A Meroitic god
Ari-hes-nefer	A lion god, perhaps another name for Mahes (q.v.)
Arrows of Sekhmet	Seven manifestations of Sekhmet (q.v.), said to bring plague
Asheru	Precinct in the temple of Mut (q.v.), also associated with Bast (q.v.)
Asthartet	A lioness goddess of the battlefield
Atet	A goddess who may have been a female counterpart of Ra, and also slew the serpent Apep (q.v.) in the form of a cat
Atum	A sun and creator god of Heliopolis (q.v.), father of Shu and Tefnut (q.v.)
Ba	Spirit of a deity, plural *bau*
Bast	A goddess associated with dancing, love, domestic matters and perfume. Can be depicted as a woman with either a lioness's or a cat's head.
Bastet	Sometimes seen as a permutation of Bast's name. Literally means 'she of the city of Bast'
Beni Hasan	A site in Middle Egypt, famous for its Speos Artemidos, a temple to Pakhet (q.v.) built by the female pharaoh Hatshepsut
Bes	A dwarf lion god of luck, the home, dancing and fertility
Beset	The female counterpart of Bes
Book of the Dead	Funerary texts, written on papyrus, giving instructions for the newly deceased on how to negotiate the underworld
Bubasteion	A temple to Bast (q.v.) in Bubastis (q.v.), constructed by Osorkon II
Bubastis	A city in Lower Egypt (the Delta), sacred to Bast (q.v.)
Cone of power	A visualized cone of energy in which to undertake visualized journeys into the past, or else to perform a magical ritual
Coptic	An Egyptian form of Christianity, but also the name of the last written form of the Egyptian

	language, comprising Greek and demotic (q.v.) symbols
Criosphinx	A ram-headed sphinx
Dehenet Imentet	The mountain, known as 'peak of the west', said to be the home of the goddess Meretseger (q.v.)
Deir-el-Medina	An ancient workman's village near Thebes, where artisans who worked on the royal tombs lived
Delta, the	The area in the north of Egypt known as Lower Egypt, where the Nile flows into the Mediterranean Sea
Demotic	A written form of the Egyptian language, later than hieroglyphics and hieratic (qq.v.)
Dendera	A site in northern Upper Egypt, famous for its temple of Hathor (q.v.)
Duat	The Egyptian Underworld
Edfu	A site in southern Upper Egypt, known for its temple of Horus (q.v.)
Ennead	In the Heliopolitan creation myth, a family of nine gods, comprising Atum, who created Shu and Refnut, who were the parents of Geb and Nut, who were the parents of Osiris, Isis, Nephthys and Set (qq.v.)
Epagomenal days	The five extra days in the Egyptian calendar, during which the children of Nut (q.v.) were said to have been born
Eye of Ra	A name given to several lioness goddesses, symbolizing the vengeful power of the sun god
Gayer Anderson cat	Perhaps the most famous of all Egyptian statues of seated sacred cats, now on display in the British Museum
Geb	The earth god in the Heliopolitan tradition, son of Shu and Tefnut (qq.v.)
Great Tom Cat, The	A form that the sun god Ra (q.v.) can assume, generally during his nightly battles with the serpent fiend, Apep (q.v.)
Harsomtus	The son of Hathor and Horus (qq.v.)
Hathor	A goddess worshipped widely throughout Egypt, who is strongly associated with Sekhmet (q.v.). Her sacred animal was primarily the cow, but she could take a leonine form
Hebi	A lion god
Heka	The energy of the gods, the force with which

312

	the gods created the world; also a god of magical power
Hekau	A term used to denote anyone who practised magic
Hekenth	A lioness goddess of the seventh hour of the night
Heliopolis	Known also as Iunu, an important site in Lower Egypt, now virtually a suburb of Cairo
Henutet	A term for a woman who worked in an Egyptian temple
Henuty	A term for a man who worked in an Egyptian temple
Hermetica	A set of magical texts, supposedly written by the god Thoth (q.v.)
Hermopolis	Also known in ancient Egyptian as Khmun, a city in Middle Egypt which was a cult centre for Thoth (q.v.)
Hert-ketit-s	A lioness goddess of the eleventh hour of the night
Heru-neb-mesen	A lion god
Hieracosphinx	A hawk-headed sphinx
Hieratic	A form of Egyptian script that was like a shorthand version of the more elaborate hieroglyphs
Hieroglyphics	The pictogram script used for the carvings of monuments and tombs
Horus	A hawk-headed god, son of Osiris (q.v.)
Huntheth	A lioness goddess of the tenth hour of the night
Inundation	The yearly flooding phenomenon whereby the Nile valley has remained consistently fertile
Isis	The wife of Osiris (q.v.), perhaps the best-known of all Egyptian goddesses, credited with great magical power
Iunu	The ancient name for Heliopolis, but also the first mound of creation that rose from the waters of the Nun (q.v.)
Karnak	Known in ancient Egypt as Ipet-Isut, now part of Thebes. Famous for its magnificent temple remains, including a shrine to Sekhmet (q.v.)
Ketuit-ken-ba	A cat-headed god of the second hour of the night
Khem	An ancient name for Egypt
Khonsu	A moon god, son of Sekhmet and sometimes of Bast (qq.v.)
Kush	An African kingdom south of Egypt

Leontopolis — A city in the northern Delta, sacred to Mahes (q.v.). Now known as Tell-el-Muqdam, in ancient times called Tameru

Luxor — Modern-day Thebes, home of the Karnak complex, renowned for its magnificent temples and monuments

Maat — Both a goddess and an abstract concept, Maat is truth, 'rightness' and justice, cosmic order

Mafdet — A lynx goddess

Mahes — Son of Bast (q.v.), a lion god whose main centre was at Leontopolis (q.v.)

Mau — A word meaning 'cat', which was sometimes used as a name of Ra (q.v.)

Mekhit — The consort of the god Anhur (q.v.), a lioness goddess whose associated myths strongly resemble those of Tefnut (q.v.)

Memphis — An important city of Lower Egypt, south of Giza, one of the greatest centres of Egyptian culture and home to many dynasties of kings

Menat — A lioness goddess of Heliopolis (q.v.)

Menkert — A lioness goddess of the tenth hour of the night

Meretseger — A goddess associated with Deir el-Medina (q.v.), whose main aspect is that of a serpent. She does, however, also have a leonine form.

Meroe — An ancient culture of Nubia (q.v.)

Miuty — A cat-headed deity, usually associated with guarding a gate of the underworld

Mut — A Theban goddess, wife of Amun-Ra, mother of Khonsu (qq.v.), strongly associated with the cat and the vulture. Her role was that of mother goddess to the pharaoh

Naga — The site in Meroe (q.v.) where the great temple to Apedemak (q.v.) was built

Nefertum — A god of the lotus blossom, a son of Sekhmet and Ptah (qq.v.). Sometimes referred to as a son of Bast (q.v.)

Neith — A goddess with a lioness aspect, having both male and female elements, principally worshipped at Sais (known in ancient times as Zau) (q.v.) in Lower Egypt

Nekhbet — A vulture goddess, known as the lady of the south. With Bast (east), Sekhmet (west) and Wadjet (north) (qq.v.), she is one of the goddesses of the four directions

314

Nephthys	The sister of Isis (q.v.), a funerary goddess, wife of Set (q.v.)
Netjer	The word for 'God' in ancient Egypt. All gods and goddesses were seen as 'names' or different aspects of this great force
Nome	An administrative division in ancient Egypt, similar to a county or a state. Each nome had its own capital city.
Nubia	The land south of Egypt
Nun	In the Heliopolitan tradition, the primal waters from which the first land, or sacred mound, arose
Nut	A sky and star goddess, daughter of Shu and Tefnut (qq.v.). With her brother Geb (q.v.), parent of Osiris, Isis, Nepthys and Set (qq.v.)
Ogdoad	In the Hermopolitan tradition, the set of eight gods who created the world
Osiris	Son of Nut and Geb (qq.v.). Like his sister/wife Isis (q.v.), he is perhaps one of the best known Egyptian deities. His domain was the *duat* (q.v.)
Pakhet	A lioness goddess who had a shrine at Beni Hasan (q.v.) and worshipped by the female pharaoh Hatshepsut
Pasht	Another name for Bast or Pakhet (qq.v.), now thought to be a mistranslation
Persea	A sacred tree of ancient Egypt, related to the avocado
Pibeseth	A biblical name for Bubastis (q.v.)
Psychic questing	A form of meditation or visualization in which practitioners attempt to project their minds into the past or out into the landscape to solve historical enigmas
Ptah	A creator god of Memphis (q.v.), consort of Sekhmet and father of Nefertum (qq.v.)
Ptolemaic	The period of history associated with the Greek rule of Egypt, 304–30 BC
Pylon	The entrance to a temple, a huge gateway
Ra	The sun god
Rat	An aspect of Bast (q.v.) as female form of the sun god.
Regulus	The brightest star of the constellation of Leo, high in the western sky in August, strongly associated with Sekhmet (q.v.)

315

Rekhet	A term for a woman. Means 'knowing one'. A wise woman or seeress
Renenet	A goddess with leonine associations, connected with suckling
Sais	A city in Lower Egypt known in ancient times as Zau
Sak	A mythical female beast comprising parts of a lion, a hawk and a horse
Sau	A secular worker of magic, of either sex
Sebqet	A lioness-goddess
Sef	One of the Akeru (q.v.) lions, the lion of yesterday
Sefer	A winged mythical beast similar to a griffin, being part lion, part eagle
Sekhet-Neter	The divine field, i.e. Egypt. An epithet of various deities is 'ruler of Sekhet-Neter'
Sekhmet	A lioness-headed goddess, known as an Eye of Ra. She has warlike destructive aspects, but is conversely also strongly associated with healing
Sekhmet-Bast-Ra	A deity comprising the aspects of the three deities of its name
Sekhmet-Min	A masculine form of Sekhmet (q.v.)
Sesenet-khu	A lioness goddess of the second hour of the night
Set	A god of chaos, brother of Osiris (q.v.), and consort of Bephthys (q.v.)
Setcha	A mythical beast with the body of a leopard and the head and neck of a serpent
Seven Hathors	A seven-fold form of Hathor (q.v.), who were said to pronounce a person's fate at birth
Shemayet	A female dancer of an Egyptian temple
Sheshesht	An ancient term for the sistrum or sacred rattle
Shesmetet	A lioness goddess, probably a form of Sekhmet (q.v.)
Shetat	A name of Bast (q.v.) which means 'hidden one'
Shu	Son of Atum (q.v.), brother/husband of Tefnut (q.v.), associated with the air
Sistrum	A sacred rattle
Slaughterers of Sekhmet	A malevolent seven-fold aspect of Sekhmet (q.v.), said to be active during the period prior to the inundation when disease is rife
Sobhek	A crocodile god, sometimes seen as a son of Neith (q.v.)
Sothis	The Egyptian name for the star Sirius, part of

	the constellation Canis Major. One of the hunting dogs of Orion. Regarded with great importance by the Egyptian priesthood
Sphinx	A mythical beast comprising the head of a man with the body of a lion. Pharaohs often had themselves portrayed in this form
Stela	An upright pillar or slab carved with inscriptions
Tuau	One of the Akeru (q.v.) lions, the lion of today
Tawaret	A hippopotamus/lioness goddess associated with childbirth
Tefnut	The daughter of Atum (q.v.), goddess of moisture, consort of her brother Shu (q.v.)
Tell Basta	The modern-day name for Bubastis (q.v.)
Tem	A creator god, another name for Atum (q.v.)
Temt	Bast (q.v.) in a feminine form of Tem (q.v.)
Thoth	An ibis-headed god of wisdom, magic and scribes
Tutu	A lion god
Two lands, the	A name for Egypt
Udjat Eye	The eye of Horus (q.v.)
Uraeus	The cobra on the crown of kings and the heads of certain deities
Urt Hekau	A goddess of magic, also known as Weret Hekau
Usit	A lioness goddess of the tenth hour of the night
Wadjet	A goddess usually portrayed in a serpent form, who also had a leonine aspect
Weret Khener	A title for the woman in charge of the temple musicians

Bibliography

There are very many books available on Egypt and magic. The ones listed below are just some of those we consulted in writing this book which could be of most help to someone new to the subject. We have also listed a few on psychic questing for those who wish to take this further and want to know about the subject's history.

Baines, John and Malek, Jaromir, *Atlas of Ancient Egypt* (Equinox, 1989)

Benstead, Deborah and Constantine, Storm, *The Inward Revolution* (Little Brown, 1998)

Budge, E.A. Wallis (trans.), *The Ancient Egyptian Book of the Dead* (Penguin, 1989)

—, *The Gods of the Egyptians Vols 1 and 2* (Dover Press, 1969)

Carmelo Betro, Maria, *Hieroglyphics* (Abbeville Press, 1996)

Collins, Andrew, *The Black Alchemist* (ABC Books, 1988)

—, *The Second Coming,* (Century, 1993)

—, *The Seventh Sword* (Arrow, 1992)

Cunningham, Scott, *The Complete Book of Incense, Oils and Brews* (Llewellyn, 1989)

—, *Cunningham's Encyclopedia of Magical Herbs* (Llewellyn, 1985)

De Laroche, R. and Labat, Jean Michel, *The Secret Life of Cats* (Aurum Press, 1993)

Farrar, Janet and Stewart, *The Witches' God* (Robert Hale, 1989)

—, *The Witches' Goddess,* (Robert Hale, 1987)

Faulker, R.O. (trans.), *The Ancient Egyptian Coffin Texts* (Warminster, 1973)

—, *The Ancient Egyptian Pyramid Texts* (Oxford University Press, 1969)

Hart, George, *A Dictionary of Egyptian Gods and Goddesses* (Routledge and Kegan Paul, 1986)

Bibliography

Hope, Murry, *Practical Egyptian Magic* (Aquarian Press, 1984)

Oldfield Howey, M., *The Cat in Magic* (Bracken, 1993)

Kingston, Karen, *Creating Sacred Space with Feng Shui* (Piatkus, 1996)

Malek, Jaromir, *The Cat in Ancient Egypt* (British Museum Press, 1993)

Phillips, Graham, *Act of God* (Macmillan, 1998)

—, *The Green Stone* (Grafton, 1981)

—, *The Eye of Fire* (Grafton, 1983)

Pinch, Geraldine, *Magic in Ancient Egypt* (British Museum Press, 1994)

Quirke, Stephen, *Ancient Egyptian Religion* (British Museum Press, 1992)

Regula, DeTraci, *The Mysteries of Isis* (Llewellyn, 1995)

Robins, Gay, *Women in Ancient Egypt* (British Museum Press, 1993)

St George, E.A., *Ancient and Modern Cat Worship* (Spook Enterprises, 1996)

—, *Under Regulus* (Spook Enterprises, 1995)

Spence, Lewis, *Egypt: Myths and Legends* (Senate, 1994)

Starhawk, *Dreaming the Dark* (Beacon Press, 1982)

—, *The Spiral Dance* (Harper & Row, 1989)

Tildesley, Joyce, *Hatshepsut* (Viking, 1996)

Watterson, Barbara, *Gods of Ancient Egypt* (Sutton, 1996)

—, *The House of Horus at Edfu: Ritual in an Ancient Egyptian Temple* (Tempus, 1998)

Author's Note

We would like to hear from anyone who reads this book, experiments with the rituals and meditations in it and is willing to tell us of their experiences and results. Our study into this subject is on-going and we intend to write a further book on it in the future. We can be contacted via our web site (http://www/members.aol.com/MahesBast), through Storm's official web site (http://members.aol.com/malaktawus/Storm.htm) or by mail via Storm's information service:

Inception
c/o Vikki Lee France and Steve Jeffery
44 White Way
Kidlington
Oxon
OX5 2XA
England
Please enclose a stamped addressed envelope.
E-mail Peverel@aol.com